CARTOON COLLECTIBLES

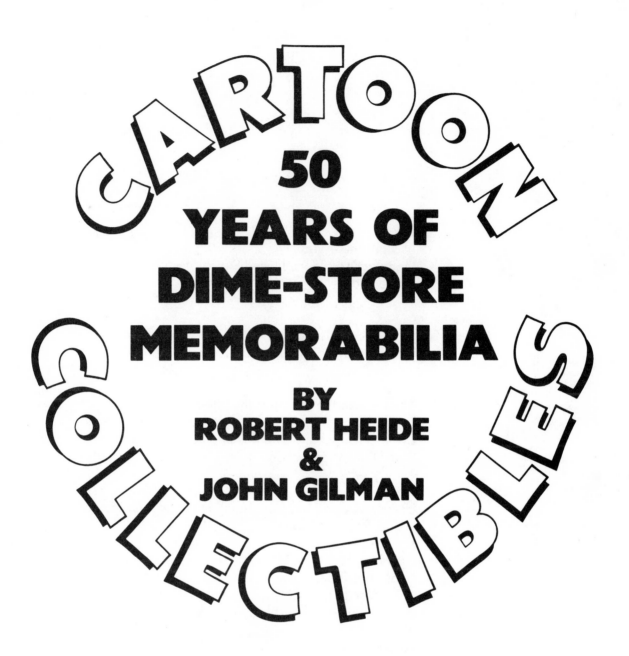

CARTOON COLLECTIBLES

50 YEARS OF DIME-STORE MEMORABILIA

BY ROBERT HEIDE & JOHN GILMAN

PHOTOGRAPHY BY TIMOTHY BISSELL

A DOLPHIN BOOK
DOUBLEDAY & COMPANY, INC.
GARDEN CITY, NEW YORK
1983

Designed by Tim Metevier
Produced by Lois de la Haba & James Charlton

Library of Congress Cataloging in Publication Data
Heide, Robert, 1939–
  Cartoon Collectibles
  "A Dolphin Book."
  Includes index.
    1. Cartoons—Collectibles. 2. Walt Disney
Productions—Collectibles. I. Gilman, John,
II. Title.
NK808.H34 1983   741.5'09749'93   83–9084
ISBN 0–385–19113–8

Library of Congress Catalog Card Number 83–9084

This book is dedicated to the
millions of Mickey Mouse fans
all over the world.

*Mickey Mouse target game, came in a cardboard box with a
metal gun, suction darts, and a three-leg stand. Made by Marks
Brothers of Boston, 1934.*

CONTENTS

Sharing the Dream   **9**
Road to Revival   13
Fifty Years of Pop Culture   15
Birth of Mickey Mouse Memorabilia   17
Auctions in the Eighties   41
Mickey Mouse Facts and Figures   45

Mickey, the Movie Star Mouse   **49**
A Complete List of Cartoons Starring Mickey Mouse   55
First Mickey Mouse Club   59
Sullivan's Travels to Mickey Mouse   61
William Faulkner and Mickey Mouse   62

An Obstreperous Duck   **63**
A Complete List of Cartoons Starring Donald Duck   66

Storybook Mickey   **73**

Mickey Mouse in Magazineland   **89**

Comic Book Mickey   **93**

Million Dollar Mouse at the 5 & 10 Cent Store   **97**
Disney Visits New York in the Great Depression   98
Mickey Mouse—First Dolls, Toys and Figurines   99
Mouse Merchant   113

Mickey Mouse Memories   **119**
Baby's First Mickey   121
Back to School with Mickey Mouse   124
Early Mickey Wearables   125
Mickey Back-to-School Practical Necessities   128
Tricky Mickey on Halloween   133
A Mickey Mouse Christmas   135
Mickey at Play in Winter   157
A Mickey Mouse Watch on Graduation Day   159
Mickey's Summer Fun   167
Mickey Mouse at Home in the Depression   173
Mickey Mouse Music   181

The Three Little Pigs (& a Big Bad Depression)   **191**
Other 'Silly' Characters   197
A Complete List of Silly Symphony Films   200

Snow White and the Seven Dwarfs   **203**

Pinocchio   **209**

Mickey Mouse Goes to War   **215**

The Forties Feature Films   **219**

The Television 1950s—Mickey, Davy & Zorro   **229**

That's Not All, Folks!   **237**

About the Authors   **247**

Bibliography   **249**

Index   **251**

SHARING THE DREAM

Collectors of Mickey Mouse memorabilia all share a common and persistent dream. It seems they travel mysteriously backward through a time tunnel into a downtown 1930s dime store—a Woolworth's, McCrory's, J. J. Newberry's, S. S. Kresge's, S. H. Kress or H. L. Green. Once inside and standing in front of the glittering toy-counter display, as children again, they carefully choose either a Mickey Mouse wind-up, a Silly Symphony Big Little Book, or a Donald Duck penny bank, which they purchase from the attractive, gum-chewing salesgirl, who, smiling through Tangee-red lips as she adjusts her marcelled peroxide-blonde hair, rings up the one-dime sale. Of course, many collectors would in fantasy like to buy out the entire stock or a warehouse supply in order to corner the market. The reality today is that some of these early Walt Disney toys from the Depression era, if available, are worth hundreds, even thousands of dollars. Some are still to be found, reasonably priced, in antique shops, at flea markets, in mail-order catalogues, at comic conventions, and at special collectibles auctions and paper memorabilia and toy and doll shows and events. Collecting Pop-culture artifacts or comic-character collectibles such as Mickey Mouse turned into a serious form of collecting somewhere in the mid-sixties, with the awareness

Mickey Mouse Sails for Treasure Island, a *Big Little Book* published in 1933 by Whitman Publishing Company.

brought about by Pop artists Andy Warhol, Roy Lichtenstein, Claes Oldenburg, Ray Johnson, and others, who liked to paint Mickey Mouse, Donald Duck, Popeye, Nancy and Sluggo, or other Pop-culture heroes. At about the same time, Pop-culture enthusiast-collectors began to dig about at country and city flea markets and garage or yard sales, like archeologists searching for lost treasures, but this time they were looking for things out of the recent past (the last fifty years) that they remembered from their childhoods, such as a Mickey Mouse bisque toothbrush holder that once stood on the bathroom sink, or a Lionel Mickey Mouse handcar they remembered running up and down on tracks under the family's Depression Christmas tree. If they were really lucky boys and girls, that Christmas evergreen would also have been decorated with Mickey Mouse Noma lights, sought-after collectibles today.

Some collectors who began to specialize in Mickey Mouse memorabilia became so obsessed with finding toys, books, games, figurines, dolls, watches, pencil boxes, cups, spoons, cookie jars, and other related mouse paraphernalia that they soon began to refer to themselves as "mouse junkies." Finding a collectible not previously seen before became an ecstatic experience for those hooked on the mouse-hunt. More sophisticated collectors of earlier Disney memorabilia after a time began to look only for items of more quality: original artwork from the Disney studios, early movie posters or lobby cards, art animation cels or some of the rarer toys manufactured in Germany, Spain, France, or England. Because Mickey Mouse was an important movie-star mouse, he seems always to have been regarded by collectors and dealers of Pop-culture collectibles as top-of-the-line. His popularity today among nostalgia collectible items far exceeds that of Betty Boop, Little Orphan Annie, Popeye, or Dick Tracy, who were also mass-marketed on a variety of merchandise. Although each of these certainly has its own special following, Mickey Mouse memorabilia, which include Mickey's family of friends, Minnie Mouse, Donald Duck, Pluto the Pup, Horace Horsecollar, Clarabelle Cow, and the others, have clearly taken the lead in the collectibles marketplace.

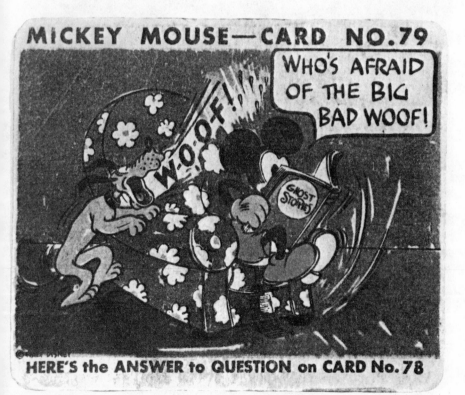

MICKEY MOUSE—CARD NO. 79

WHO'S AFRAID OF THE BIG BAD WOOF!

W-O-O-F!

GHOST STORIES

HERE'S the ANSWER to QUESTION on CARD No. 78

Mickey Mouse gum card #79, showing our hero safe at home in a typical overstuffed Mickey Mouse cartoon chair but still afraid of "the Big Bad Woof" just like a great many Americans in the 1930s.

In the *New York Post*, in March 1972, Willie Woo, son of Kya-Tang Woo, head of the Hong Kong Trade Commission in New York and a well-known jewelry and graphic arts designer, revealed to syndicated columnist Eugenia Sheppard that he identified, in private life, with Mickey Mouse. Miss Sheppard explained that Mr. Woo was a serious collector of all kinds of Mickey Mouse memorabilia, including china, glass, knives, forks, and silver spoons, which all feature Mickey on them. He slept on Mickey Mouse sheets and pillowcases and had come to believe that he actually was Mickey Mouse himself in another life.

It is indeed a fact that there have always been bona fide enthusiastic Mickey Mouse collectors, right from Disney's beginning. Museums such as the Metropolitan Museum of Art in New York exhibited Disney art in the 1930s, just as mom and pop collectors were carefully storing their children's toys and favorite books in the attic, cellar, or basement for future generations.

A lyric from the Depression song "When My Ship Comes In," sung by Eddie Cantor in the 1934 film *Kid Millions*, goes:

I'll have a golden castle grand
    and tall,
With eighteen butlers standing
    in the hall,
And Walter Disney paintings on
    the wall,
When my ship comes in,

indicating the fantasy aspirations of those on relief who longed to live in an imaginary Disney-land castle.

Today, warehouses and old stores just going out of business contain supplies of Disneyana that, although not endless, are plentiful enough to satisfy collectors. Many of these collectibles were made at a time when mass production goods were of higher quality than those of today—a plus even for beginning Mickey Mousers. Some collectors began the habit as precocious tots and continue to this day adding more and more mice and ducks to their crowded shelves. Collectors also invest in duplicates for trading and selling, and let go of certain other pieces they may grow tired of. And, of course, every so often a collector or a collector's heir will offer up that rare opportunity—an entire estate of Disney memorabilia. Collector sales and trading situations specializing in antique toys and Disney items, such as the yearly toy event held in the fall at Kennedy International Airport, attract collector-dealers from all over the world. Because collectors become involved in wheeling and dealing or mouse-trading, many become dealers. Also, a collector who takes a dealer table at a show has the jump on other collectors, since he has the opportunity of viewing dealer merchandise first. So fierce is the competition between Disney collectors who still like to pretend that it is all still just for fun, that many will check into a motel the night before a show opening, in order to get to see what the dealers have brought and to have the edge on other collectors. Collectors and dealers regularly place "I want to buy Mickey" ads in all the antique-toy and collectibles magazines in an attempt to ferret out the better items owned by the public.

Set of six new collectible Mickey story picture cards, printed in Italy by Edizioni Panini, 1978.

Painted, cast-iron Mickey Mouse bank, marked "Walt Disney Productions," 1970s.

Disney prewar items are usually the ones most sought after by knowledgeable collectors, and prices are always higher than for pieces from the forties and fifties. Mickey Mouse memorabiliacs prefer the early Disney period, from 1928 to 1940, feeling that this was the most creative period at the studios and in the areas of merchandising and quality design concept. Mickey Mouse as an impish white-faced rodent with red shorts and bulbous yellow shoes is preferable to the later pink-faced, more humanoid Mickey sometimes found wearing a zoot-suit, straw hat—and minus a tail. Today, the early Mickey is having a revival, so it is well to remember that there are many reproductions of this image on the market. Prewar items manufactured in the United States are marked "Walt E. Disney," "Walter Disney," or "Walt Disney Enterprises," while in the 1940s, 1950s and even to-

day, it is "Walt Disney Productions." Sometimes an import from Japan, Spain, France, England, Germany or Canada may have no mark whatsoever. World War II scrap and metal drives, which were sometimes conducted under the banner of Mickey Mouse, Donald Duck, Orphan Annie, or Kate Smith, helped to get rid of vast amounts of these desirable mass-marketed toys, games, and comic books, and consequently, artifacts from this time became scarce.

As the Mickey Mouse of the 1930s brightened up the despairing masses who were out of jobs or on the dole, so he seems to be repeating this role in the 1980s. Today many new collectors are investing in the limited-edition "instant" Disney collectibles that emerged in the 1960s and 1970s—special yearly plates, Christmas ornaments, bisque figurines, banks, pinback buttons, and dolls. Many of these are extremely attractive and will increase in value as collectibles for the future. The Disney Collection, a service of Grolier Enterprises Inc., 120 Brighton Road, Clifton, N.J. 07012, offers imported porcelain figurines of Snow White, Bambi, Mickey, Cinderella, Pinocchio, and others in limited editions of 15,000. Other "new" and "old-time" Mickey Mouse collectors go directly into the five-and-dime store, or toy shop, or to Disneyland or Walt Disney World to buy new merchandise, some of which has a limited run and can also become an instant collectible. In just a few years, the way the collectibles marketplace is raging, a Disney item purchased today at the dime store may become a future hard-to-find collectible.

ROAD TO REVIVAL

Since his creation in 1928 Mickey Mouse has never taken a day off. He has always been involved in one activity or another as an actor, salesman, corporate spokesman, and chiefly as a symbol of happiness, fun, and good cheer for millions of people all over the world. The critic Gilbert Seldes said in 1932, "His popularity has some of the elements of a fad, where it joins the Kewpie and the Teddy bear." This somewhat cynical quote was countered in 1934 by novelist E. M. Forster, who found Mickey "energetic without being elevated . . . he is never sentimental, indeed there is a scandalous element in him which I find most restful."

Mickey Mouse's cartoons achieved phenomenal success at the movies, and attendance fell off greatly at theaters that did not advertise Disney shorts. In 1930 Mickey was seen in a comic strip for King Features, the first Mickey book was published, and Mickey Mouse toys were flooding the United States and European markets. In 1931 Mickey Mouse was displayed at Madame Tussaud's Waxworks Museum in London, and there were a million members in the first Mickey Mouse fan clubs. The year 1933 saw the first Mickey Mouse watch, which was produced by Ingersoll. By 1934 Mickey Mouse was an established international movie star and the leader of a bunch of happy-go-lucky cartoon characters that included Minnie Mouse, Donald Duck, Clarabelle the Cow, Horace Horsecollar, and Pluto. That same year he was also the leader of Macy's Thanksgiving Day Parade, and

Pinback button featuring the old Mickey Mouse, 1970s.

Pinback button, 1970s.

his name was included in the *Encyclopedia Britannica*. Whatever happened, Mickey never rested on his accomplishments. In 1935 he saved Lionel Trains from bankruptcy, and by 1936 more and more fan clubs were springing up all over the world. In 1938 and 1939 an exhibition of original Mickey Mouse and Walt Disney art toured the United States and was seen by 4,770,000 Americans.

In the early 1930s Mickey had become a legend as well as being acknowledged by critics as a first-rate work of art. During World War II, Mickey did his part, being featured on military insignia and painted on planes and ships. His name was used as the password for the D-Day invasion. Even the enemy sometimes used the mouse image on their weapons and bombs. But somehow, by the end of the war Mickey's personality and image had changed. Looking more like a natty Frank Sinatra, the little-boy mouse seemed to have grown up. Stephen Jay Gould, a professor of science at Harvard University, believed the opposite—that Mickey Mouse actually reverted to an infantile state over the years, eventually looking more like one of his nephews, Morty or Ferdy. In an article entitled "Mickey Mouse Meets Konrad Lorenz" in *Natural History* magazine, (May 1979), Gould claimed that Disney artists, acting on an unconscious discovery of Konrad Lorenz's belief that the facial features of juvenility trigger "innate releasing mechanisms" eliciting powerful emotional responses from adults (and children), transformed Mickey. They lowered his pants line, covering his spindly legs with baggier pants. He got a larger head, with more youthful, infantile features, his snout was thickened, and he was given a rounded, rather than sloping, forehead. With the progression of this new look, he apparently appealed more to the unconscious of his fans. During the war, Donald Duck had actually outstripped Mickey in popularity; but the indomitable Mickey jumped, without a backward glance, from a starring role in his last film, *The Simple Things*, in 1953, right into television as the star of the *Disneyland Show*, and as master of ceremonies for the *Mouseketeers* TV Show. Mickey, over the years, has undergone drastic anthropomorphic changes; but perhaps it was inevitable for a mouse who had to perform as the congenial host of a TV series not to appear to be too rambunctious, as he had been in the early Disney days, when he enjoyed playing havoc with the barnyard creatures. Mickey's ultimate rise to urban respectability (he became the "official" host for Disneyland in Anaheim, California, in July 1955 and likewise for Disney World in Florida in October 1971) and his senior status as the figurehead of the Walt Disney empire made him the perfect symbol for the conservative business interests of the banks and boardrooms that had become the principal movers and backers of the theme parks and film ventures of the postwar years. Walt Disney died on December 15, 1966, but the down-and-out Mickey, featured on the cover of *Paris-Match* crying his heart out, vowed to carry on for his beloved creator.

FIFTY YEARS OF POP CULTURE

In 1978 America and other countries as well had fiftieth anniversary Disney commemorative celebrations led by and honoring the illustrious goodwill ambassador. The little mouse hit his midcentury mark more popular than ever.

During the 1960s, the decade of psychedelic, Pop, and Op art, a youthful, under-thirty counterculture took hold. It was a visual decade, in which LSD, marijuana, and other drugs were meant to help define the intensity of the color spectrum and the infinity of the universe. The floral geometrics of Art Deco and the signpost reality images of Pop art also forced a new generation to take a fresh look at an America that seemed to be disappearing. By the 1970s Americans were becoming nostalgic for their lost innocence as well as a "lost America." Unable to cope with what Warhol called "the plastic inevitable," the beginnings of the technological computer age, many began to seek refuge and comfort in the past. Busby Berkeley's zany golddigger musical films; *No, No, Nanette,* starring "Golddiggerdame" Ruby Keeler herself tapdancing the nostalgia revival onto Broadway; and the sweet soprano sounds of Tiny Tim and Ruth Etting played on 33-rpm— all these soothed the weary 1970s nerves. Pure escapist entertainment seemed to help to heal the wounds of the decade. To be sure, the rebellious radicals of the sixties might have recalled the wacky, banjo-strumming youth of the roaring twenties, while the seventies-into-the-eighties now appears to be a time not unlike the

Depression 1930s, a time of economic woe coupled with a need to happily tapdance the blues away, pretending everything was not so bad after all.

From the mid-sixties throughout the seventies and into the eighties, collectibles from this "lost America," particularly from the era of early mass production and marketing—the 1920s and 1930s—took a strong hold throughout the country. Flea markets, huge antique extravaganzas, and specialty shows featuring the ephemera and memorabilia of these earlier "fun" times seemed to challenge but not to threaten bona fide antiques. Up to about 1970, an antique had to be at least one hundred years old to qualify as bona fide, but in the seventies all the decades of the past fifty years seemed to merge into one. This changed the notion of "art" or "antiques." If you chose to hang an old Coca-Cola sign on the living-room wall or a framed poster of Mickey Mouse advertising bread or candy, who was to say this was not "art"? As the 1934 Cole Porter song told us, "Now, Heaven knows, anything goes." Collectibles marketeers preferred what they called "the real thing" (after the Coke slogan) and went about collecting tin-litho soda-pop signs that were often dated and with a litho number in the corner, just like anything you might find in an art gallery. Movie posters, travel posters, and product-advertising posters soon followed this popular parade into the realm of "high art" and with them the many comic-character cartoon artists led by Walt Disney and his staff with—of course—Mickey Mouse.

Lead Mickey Mouse figure, 2½", 1930s.

Mickey Mouse window poster for bread, ca. 1934.

BIRTH OF MICKEY MOUSE MEMORABILIA

The September 1968 issue of *Life* magazine featured an article celebrating Mickey's fortieth birthday, with remarkable photographs of 1930s Mickey Mouse memorabilia from the collections of Mel Birnkrant, Ernest Trova, and Robert Lesser. Along with an illustration of Robert Lesser's Mickey Mouse watches from the 1930s, the article also showed the newer watches offered on the market at the time. These were manufactured by Timex, which had taken over from Ingersoll, at $12.95. The total production, meant to last a year, was sold in less than a month, and it was reported that movie stars, models, and other luminaries, including the zany comic Carol Burnett and TV host Johnny Carson, were all sporting either the new or old, original Mickey watches.

Mickey Mouse Art

In 1969 the O.K. Harris Gallery in New York presented the Mickey Mouse ink drawings, signed lithographs, and paintings of John Fawcett, an art professor at the University of Connecticut. Fawcett's art used comic-character images from his childhood, particularly the early Mickey Mouse. His meticulously crafted, intricate drawings, utilizing collage, rubber stamps, and various bits and pieces of actual Mickey Mouse paper memorabilia, were a new and novel approach to the then current trend in Pop art. Fawcett, himself a Mickey Mouse collector of renown, was later photo-

graphed by *Newsweek* magazine in his special Mickey Mouse–collector attic room, filled to the brim with Mickey Mouse memorabilia. He was quoted as saying, "Polio got my whole comics collection," referring to the paper drives of World War II and the fact that comics were suspected of contamination during polio epidemics and destroyed, along with metal toys and other priceless collectibles.

Comic book issued on Mickey Mouse's twenty-fifth anniversary. Dell Publishing Company, 1953.

Mickey Mouse Is "Camp"

The 1970 Annual Report of Disney Productions carried the following report from its Character Merchandising Division: "Although this was the biggest year in history for our regular line of the more contemporary Mickey Mouse juvenile merchandise, the biggest story rests with the 'camp' Mickey Mouse items—those which feature the original design of Mickey as he appeared in *Steamboat Willie* and other early Disney cartoons."

"*Mickey-nazi-coke*" pen and ink drawing by John Fawcett, 1969.

Newsweek Nostalgia

The "Nostalgia" issue of *Newsweek* magazine (December 28, 1970) featured a Norman Rockwell Santa Claus cover and an in-depth article by Associate Editor John Culhane about the full-blown nostalgia fever that was beginning to sweep the United States. The article coordinated a wide range of reporting from correspondents across the country and featured, in addition to the aforementioned Fawcett photograph, other photographs from the comic-character memorabilia collection of toy designer Mel Birnkrant. Editor Culhane noted that the nostalgia craze—the need to turn back to the comfort of the past—could be an oblique response to the grievous national hurt of the shooting of the President in Dallas, Vietnam, countrywide race riots, the assassinations of Martin Luther King and Bobby Kennedy, and the Chicago demonstrations in 1968. He quoted Pete Smith, Disney's merchandising chief: "Mickey got a whole new lease on life in 1967 when hippies wore the watches to poke fun at the establishment. To everyone's amazement, sales tripled in three years . . . in the last six months of 1970 alone, Mickey Mouse watches and clocks have brought in $7.5 million." It was also noted that a man named Norman Traeger from Columbus, Ohio, had sold $400,000 worth of Mickey Mouse sweatshirts in one month. Culhane predicted—correctly, as it turned out—that the decade of the 1970s was going to be even more nostalgic than the previous one, noting that nostalgia was now certain to be on its way to academic enshrinement: Scholars at places like Ohio's Center for the Study of Popular Culture had begun to think deeply about the phenomenon.

The Great Common Denominator

In 1971 Webster's Third *New International Dictionary*, unabridged, included "mickey mouse" (noting that it was usually capitalized): "'mickey mouse' is an adjective defined as lacking importance or serious meaning." As if to answer this charge, the *Motion Picture Herald* of October 1, 1972, carried the following 1932 quote from movie historian Terry Ramsaye: "Mickey Mouse is the crystalline, concentrated quintessence of that which is peculiarly the motion picture. He is at one with the Great Common Denominator of the great common art of the commonality in terms of expression, while in production he is a logarithmic derivation of the whole of screen technology. . . . The irrepressible Mickey in charmingly typical expression of his own psychology, which is based on the principle of the *triumph of the boob*, the *cosmic victory of the underdog*, the *might of the meek*, has in a very certain sense paid tribute to Mr. Chaplin by becoming his successor in certain considerable sectors of the world of the motion picture."

Mickey Mouse Memorabilia at Parke Bernet, West Coast

On May 14, 1972 in the Los Angeles gallery rooms of the prestigious international auction house of Sotheby Parke Bernet, 170 lots of Disney memorabilia were officially described as "collectors' items" in what is believed to be the first important auction sale of Disneyana. It was

Mickey Mouse bubble gum card #2, produced by the Mickey Mouse Bubble Gum Company, Philadelphia, from 1933 to 1935. The first set ran to 96. A second set of cards ran from 97 to 120 and featured Mickey Mouse with movie stars.

reported in the *New York Times* that a Mickey Mouse and Pluto snow shovel made in 1935 brought $125 at this auction. A 1935 Mickey Mouse watering can went for $70. Sketchbooks, celluloids (final mockups for animated cartoons), and production books brought prices ranging up to several hundred dollars each. The highest price paid for an item at the auction was $2,000 for a 14-by-14-inch ink-wash Claes Oldenburg *Mickey Mouse* (1966), signed with the artist's initials. Bill Prensky, a Los Angeles psychologist and the grandson of Kay Kamen, whose estate supplied many of the Mickey Mouse memorabilia at the auction, told the *Times*, "Mother must have thrown out eight times this much stuff . . . she had no idea it would be worth this much. In fact, she only hoped to make about $500 from this sale. Instead, she earned $4,785." Malcolm Willits, part-owner of a bookstore in Hollywood and a long-time collector of Mickey Mouse memorabilia, attended the auction and was quoted as saying, "Mothers are the great enemies . . . when you become a man, you get a girl and you throw out the comic books. One you do for yourself and the other for your mother." Thus a man is supposed to give up his boyhood dreams and treasures. He also said that the upsurge of interest in things Mickey Mouse began in 1968, when celebrities like Sammy Davis, Jr., began wearing their Mickey Mouse watches in public, perhaps to show that they were proud to be underdogs, perhaps because Mickey Mouse was a survivor, over forty and still going strong.

There were numerous Mickey Mouse watches and clocks in this auction sale, many from the collection of Robert Lesser. There were Disney posters, books, postcards, decals, film celluloids, Big Little Books, paper masks, promotional books, Mickey Mouse magazines, gum cards, Disney studio staff Christmas cards, even a pencil sketch of Peg Leg Pete from the film *The Cactus Kid*. Also featured in the catalogue were Disney comic-character lamps, bisque figurines, radios, toy dishes, rubber figurines, playing cards, a toy grand piano, wooden figures, buttons, a Minnie Mouse ashtray, jewelry, silver forks and spoons, a ceramic mug, a Mickey Mouse movie projector, mechanical toys, a treasure chest bank, a José Carioca wristwatch, a Mickey Mouse Bagatelle game, Castile soap figurines, sets of *Snow White and the Seven Dwarfs* bisques, and a toy telephone bank.

Mickey Mouse play money, promotional give-away from the Norwich Knitting Company, Norwich, N.Y., manufacturer of popular knitted and woven garments featuring Mickey Mouse, 1930s.

Left: *Mickey Mouse pinback button issued in 1973 in conjunction with Lincoln Center festivities celebrating the fiftieth anniversary of the founding of Walt Disney Studios. Right: Pinback button issued for Mickey Mouse's fiftieth birthday, 1978.*

Maurice Sendak, Mickey Mouse Collector

In January 1973 the noted children's book author and illustrator Maurice Sendak was the subject of a *New York Times* article which pictured the author-artist with his prized Mickey Mouse memorabilia collection. Later, in his introduction to *The Disney Poster Book*, published in 1977 by Harmony, Sendak wrote: "For many years, as an adult, I searched for the Mickey Halloween mask. That face, that completely nuts look of fiery, intense animation—the smile, the eyes, the vividness of the characterization—is mind-boggling and still works so beautifully. I have the mask and I look at it now and get the same pleasure I did as a child. Friends come to my house, and it is bestrewn with these glaring Mickey Mouse–joy faces. I never get tired of seeing that face. It just gives me pleasure. What do friends think? Wisely, I never ask."

Lincoln Center Honors Disney Studios at Fifty

The year 1973 was the fiftieth anniversary of the founding of the Walt Disney Studios, and Lincoln Center in New York mounted a comprehensive retrospective showing of Disney films at Alice Tully Hall. July 9 through August 4 was the period chosen for the anniversary celebration of the company originally founded in 1923 by Walt and Roy Disney and their partner, Ub Iwerks. This celebration also marked the first time the Disney Studios had opened their archives and vaults to any organization.

The special events included panel discussions, showings of Disney silent shorts and animated shorts made before 1927, some never seen before (or since); films made during World War II, commercial and educational films; TV shows and films that showed the development of Disneyland and Walt Disney World. More than forty different programs were shown, including the classic black and white and color film cartoons of the 1930s. The celebration became a major cultural event in New York, generating an enormous amount of media attention, quickly becoming a big success and a hot ticket during an especially muggy summer in the city.

Mickey Mouse Predates Pop Art

In a *Time* magazine essay, "Disney; Mousebrow to Highbrow," dated October 15, 1973, and illustrated with posters of Mickey Mouse movies, writer Robert Hughes focused on the "migration of Disney's iconography from masscult to the commercial fringes of 'high' art." He cited the resurrection of the Disney artists and animators Fred Moore, Bill Tytla, and Albert Hurter (*Pinocchio*) by English art critic Christopher Finch in his book *The Art of Walt Disney*, published that year by Harry Abrams. Hughes further stated that "high and low art collapsed into one another" with the appearance of Mickey Mouse in *Fantasia*, clambering up the podium to shake hands with Leopold Stokowski. This gesture, he believed, made Pop art possible twenty years before Roy Lichtenstein painted his first Mickey Mouse picture, entitled "Look, Mickey, I've hooked a big one"; or Claes Oldenburg based his series of vast civic sculptures, multiples, and drawings on "The Mouse." Hughes felt that Disney lost the power to stimulate the imagination and his work became much too bland after the late 1930s (with a few exceptions), deteriorating into "cyclamate guck" with *Cinderella, Alice in Wonderland,* and Disneyland and Disney World. This view was shared by James

A. Michener, who was quoted in the *New York Times* a few years earlier. He called Mickey Mouse "one of the most disastrous cultural influences ever to hit America," referring to Mickey's descent from ebullient 1930s mouse into vapidity and conservatism.

Mickey Mouse Visits Newark for Christmas

In 1973 again, on November 19, the day after Mickey's birthday, an event opened that had far more significance for Mickey Mouse collectors than the Lincoln Center retrospective or *Time* and *Newsweek* essays. The *Times* reported it under a banner headline in the Sunday edition: MICKEY MOUSE IN NEWARK. Bamberger's, Newark, New Jersey's largest and most successful department store, opened its sixth annual holiday art exhibit with the display of a collection of five hundred pieces of Mickey Mouse memorabilia. All over the store giant holiday posters of Mickey Mouse as Santa proclaimed the location of the "Mickey Mouse-eum" on the fifth floor, next to the toy department. The Mickey Mouse memorabilia on exhibit were encased in recessed plexiglass display units incorporated into an ingeniously designed walk-in Mouse-eum, clearly identifiable, with giant graphic wall stripes and a curved entranceway, and brilliantly painted in the familiar Mickey Mouse colors of red, black, and yellow. Entertainment was provided by a Mickey Mouse theater with continuous showings of the twenty-five-minute retrospective film *Fifty Happy Years of Disney*. Window shoppers could watch audio-animatronic mechanical orchestras, with Mickey Mouse conducting his friends playing Disney tunes, while life-size versions of Mickey, Goofy, and Pluto wandered the aisles of the store. These Disney goodwill ambassadors were also driving all over New Jersey in Hertz Rent-a-Cars—Hertz was one of the exhibition's sponsors—making personal appearances in all of the thirteen Bamberger stores and handing out new Mickey Mouse paper masks (alas, this mask had a distinctly pinkish face and a ho-hum expression) to children and adults.

This show really had nothing to do with the fiftieth anniversary of Walt Disney Studios. It actually served as a celebration of Mickey Mouse's forty-fifth birthday and was orchestrated by collector Mel Birnkrant, who used the occasion to show some of his vast collection of Mickey Mouse memorabilia in public for the first time. Just inside the Mouse-eum entrance was a giant, gleaming red-and-blue neon clock, in which Mickey did a complete somersault every minute, while his hands pointed out the time. Specially built life-size cut-out Mickey and Minnie Mouse furniture offered seats for the weary shopper, while giant papier-mâché figures of Clarabelle the Cow and Horace Horsecollar, produced in 1934 by the Old King Cole Display Company, stood grinning on the sidelines. Standing in a central place of honor on a yellow Grecian column, as if it were the *Apollo Belvedere* on display, and enclosed in a thick plexiglass box, was a rare Mickey Mouse cast-iron bank, made in France in 1931. Found in a Paris flea market, it was, according to Birnkrant, the only one of its kind in the world. Rumors have persisted since this show that Birn-

Mickey and Minnie Cut-Out Doll *book, published in 1933 by the Saalfield Publishing Company, Akron, Ohio.*

krant had turned down offers of up to $15,000 for this 9-inch-high, primitive-looking Mickey Mouse icon.

Farther on in this magical, Emerald City–like Mouse-eum were Mickey Mouse masks, the paper ones given away at Mickey Mouse Club matinees in the 1930s, and a chilling English "Mickey Mouse" gas mask issued to all English preschool children during World War II as protection from possible enemy gas attacks. It was known affectionately as a "Mickey Mouse" mask because it bore an eerie resemblance to Mickey.

There were also in the show:

- Halloween false faces.
- Lit-up Noma Christmas tree lights.
- A Pin-the-Tail-on-Mickey game (1934).
- Emerson radios.
- Mickey Mouse lamps.
- Mickey and Minnie toy piano.
- A movie projector actually projecting a Mickey Mouse 16-mm cartoon.
- Limited edition Steiff Mickey and Minnie dolls (1933).
- A numbered 1939 World's Fair Mickey Mouse doll.
- A circus pull-toy (1930).
- China figurines made in Germany (1930).
- Pop-up books.
- Waddle Books (with the Waddle figures amazingly intact, coming right down the ramp).
- Mickey Mouse coloring books.
- Cut-out doll books of Mickey and Minnie.
- A full size Post Toasties cereal box with the Mickey cut-outs intact.
- Disney sheet music.
- Tin teasets.
- Mickey Mouse sodapop bottles (said to be particularly popular in Hollywood in 1931).
- A collection of 135 bisque figurines of Mickey Mouse and Minnie and all the other Disney characters, hand-painted in Japan in the 1930's, in an infinite variety of shapes, sizes, and forms.
- Twenty-five celulloid figurines and wind-up toys.
- A Mickey Mouse tie rack.
- The 1935 circus train (in operation).
- Mickey Mouse banks.
- Mickey Mouse puppets.
- Sieberling Company rubber toys of Mickey, Donald Duck, Pluto, Elmer the Elephant, and Snow White and the Seven Dwarfs.
- Mickey Mouse pencil cases.
- A flash light with Mickey Mouse batteries.
- A Mickey Mouse thermometer.
- A musical Big Bad Wolf pitcher made in 1934, which played "Who's Afraid of the Big Bad Wolf."
- Mickey and Minnie wooden dolls.
- Mickey and Minnie composition dolls.
- A large Mickey Mouse tin top.
- A Mickey Mouse lunch pail.
- Mickey Mouse gum cards.
- Mickey Mouse puzzles.
- An English brass Mickey Mouse statue on a wooden base (1930).
- Mickey and Minnie aluminum cookie cutters.
- An Austrian bronze Mickey Mouse orchestra, which included 10 tiny painted figurines with musical instruments (1930).
- A Mickey Mouse pocket watch (1933).
- A rare Mickey Mouse English pocket watch (1933).
- A handmade Mickey Mouse wood cut-out.
- German Mickey and Minnie saltshakers.
- A wooden Mickey Mouse nodding toy.
- A Mickey Mouse cast-iron doorstop.
- The first Fisher–Price push-toy (1934).
- A Mickey Mouse corn-popper (1936).
- A Minnie Mouse lace purse and an enameled purse (1932).

■ Mickey Mouse socks with the original manufacturer's labels (1934).

■ A Mickey Mouse underwear box (1933).

■ Two German post-war Hummel figurines of Mickey and Minnie.

■ A Mickey lightbulb.

■ Mickey ashtrays.

■ China figurines of Snow White and the Seven Dwarfs and Pinocchio.

■ A Mickey Mouse jam-jar bank (1934).

■ Rare Mickey Mouse wind-up toys.

■ Mickey Mouse blocks.

■ An English china orange-juice squeezer (1936).

■ A Mickey Mouse Rosenthal china candy dish (1931).

Seeing these items in a public exhibit inspired other collectors to search for them at antique shows, shops, and flea markets.

Of his fine collection, Birnkrant stated in the special Bamberger exhibition catalogue, "I think there's a Mickey Mouse in everybody's attic. And somewhere out there, there are a million homeless Mickey Mouses. I want them all. If I were to say what my mission in life would be, it's perhaps to gather together all these homeless, lost little creatures and give them a home where they can remain safe from the ravages of time."

Birnkrant's Mickey Mouse memorabilia were also on the cover of the November–December 1978 issue of *Americana* magazine, which featured a visit with the premier collector at his Mickey Mouse "schoolhouse" in suburban New York. In the article, chock full of color pictures of Mr. Birnkrant's stunning col-

lection, the collector-artist revealed how embarrassed he was by his interest in Mickey Mouse as a beginning enthusiast in 1966. "I was aware that Mickey Mouse was generally thought of as kid stuff . . . then I realized that I wasn't collecting toys, I was collecting art, great art, and there was nothing childish about that." The article went on to mention Birnkrant's favorites: the famous cast-iron Mickey Mouse bank, two large painted wooden Mickey Mouse carousel figures imported from France, and a complete set of 1930s marionette figures, which include Mickey, Minnie, Clarabelle, Horace Horsecollar, Donald Duck, and Pluto.

Business Week Mickey

Taking a serious financial look at the Mickey Mouse market in a special issue entitled "Investment Outlook 1975," the December 21, 1974, issue of *Business Week* magazine noted Disneyana was becoming a standout in the nostalgia marketplace and interviewed collectors and dealers who were claiming 50-percent gains for Mickey collectibles in 1974 alone. The article carried a photograph of a group of Mickey Mouse collectible figurines and wind-ups.

Mickey Mouse at the New School

In 1975 the New School for Social Research in New York presented a course on Walt Disney, featuring a study of Mickey Mouse, called "The Evolution of

LOEW'S WARWICK
Fulton and Jerome Streets
●
SPECIAL KIDDIE SHOW
AND FOR GROWNUPS, TOO!
Saturday Morning, September 28th
AT APPROXIMATELY 10 A. M.

All Walt Disney Revue!

An entire program of
MICKEY MOUSE and
SILLY SYMPHONIES
IN TECHNICOLOR

COME TO MICKEY'S 7th BIRTHDAY PARTY
AND HAVE A BARREL OF FUN!

CHILDREN 10 CENTS — ADULTS 20 CENTS

PACE PRESS, INC., N.Y.C.

Flyer from Loew's Warwick Theatre, 1935.

Mickey Mouse Superstar—Voice Centerfold

June 30, 1975: The internationally distributed Greenwich Village newspaper, the *Village Voice*, offered its full Centerfold guide, then edited by Ali Anderson, for collectors of Mickey Mouse memorabilia. Appropriately illustrated with rare Mickey Mouse tin-litho sandpails and sand sifters from the 1930s, the *Voice* centerfold pointed the way for serious and casual collectors of Mickey Mouse and other Disney character collectibles. The where-to-find-it places listed included Chick Darrow's Fun Antiques, a long-established store on Second Avenue, which that week was selling the Big Bad Wolf and the Three Little Pigs Ingersoll alarm clock for $425; Old Friends, a store that was run for a few years by Russ Phelan, selling rare Mickey Mouse memorabilia right alongside the new and wonderful toys and character merchandise from Disney World and Disneyland (in 1978 Mr. Phelan started a Mickey Mouse collectors' newsletter, now defunct); Grover Van Dexter's store, Second Childhood, at 283 Bleeker Street in New York, where one can still find good toy pieces; and Penny Arcade, a store run by Victor Nelson, now closed. The article was spectacularly illustrated with photographs of the brilliant Mickey Mouse Colorforms pop-up sets, then selling briskly in stores across America. These modern games, designed by Mel Birnkrant, were the first new toys in decades that featured the original look of Mickey Mouse and his early friends, Pluto, Minnie, Clarabelle, Horace, and Donald. According to the centerfold

the Animated Film from Cartoon to Full-Length Feature, 1923–1959." The course, ranging over all of Disney's animation work, was conducted by Gene London, a Mickey Mouse collector and the founder of a Mickey Mouse museum located on Eighth Avenue in the Chelsea section of New York. The museum, now closed, boasted early Disney memorabilia, with hundreds of collectors' items, including original art, cels, Disney artifacts (including the first ring Walt Disney bought, at the age of sixteen with money he earned working in his father's jelly factory), jewelry, dolls, toys, games, a chronology of Mickey Mouse and a tribute to Disney merchandising.

feature, influences that helped create interest in the 1930s Mickey were the shop of Kenny Kneitel, Fandango, Michael Malce's first pop-shop, and the shops of Les Sackin of Sarsaparilla and Betty "Bascha" Lipton of West Orange, New Jersey.

Modern Art Shows *Mickey's Birthday Party*

On Sunday, December 21, 1975, the Museum of Modern Art, in conjunction with the major re-release of *Snow White and the Seven Dwarfs*, presented as part of its Films for Young People "The Evolution of Walt Disney's *Snow White*," with collector-historian Gene London tracing the development of Disney's art and showing the new film *Mickey's Birthday Party*, made by the Disney Studios and following Mickey Mouse from his first appearance in a sound film in 1928 right up through 1975.

Auction Star of 1977— London, England

Mickey Mouse was the favorite auction star of 1977 according to an article in the *New York Times* by Rita Reif. The well-known antiques writer reported that the "rare wind-up version (a German toy) of the 'rodent' as an organ-grinder set a record for a tin toy at auction of $3,105, at Sotheby's in London." The article featured photos of the colorful tin-litho Mickey Mouse toy, with grinning ratlike teeth, along with a $200,000 125-year-old Heriz rug and a $220,000 Fabergé egg. Mickey had arrived in the world of bona-fide antiques.

A toothy, grinning rodent-like Mickey Mouse hurdy-gurdy color litho on tin wind-up action toy made in Germany, early 1930s. Collection of Robert Lesser.

*1930s English
Mickey Mouse Gallery
pages 28, 29 and 30.*

Mickey Mouse post office
bank, litho on metal, marked
" 'Happynak' Series Made in
Gt. Britain."

The English Mickey Mouse Market

Collectors of Mickey Mouse memorabilia are always delighted to find a mouse collectible marked "Made in England" or "Made in Great Britain." Mickey Mouse was greatly admired in Britain and the toys and memorabilia that survived the Second World War have been cherished and preserved by collectors. British antique shops and auctions place great value on Mickey Mouse collectibles and lead the field in the international marketplace, which includes France, Germany, Italy and Japan.

William Banks Levy became Walt Disney's official representative for licensing Mickey Mouse merchandise in Great Britain in June 1930. Mickey proved so popular that within only a few months Levy had signed up dozens of British licensees to manufacture items featuring Mickey Mouse, Minnie Mouse and the other early Disney characters. The products included jewelry, handkerchiefs,

Mickey Mouse birthday party tea set, "Happynak" series.

cushion covers, wallpapers, cretonnes, serviettes, attache cases for boys and "pouchettes" for girls, enamel powder compacts, postcards and calendars, soap, perfume bottles, children's slippers, toothbrushes, and hat ornaments. In February 1936, Levy began publishing the successful *Mickey Mouse Weekly* in partnership with Odhams Press Ltd. Major merchandisers of English Mickey Mouse memorabilia included Lewis Knight Ltd. and Dean's Rag Book Company Ltd., of Elephant & Castle, London. Dean's produced eight sizes of

Mickey Mouse dolls with jointed bodies, pull toys, Mickey Mouse glove toys, a Triketoy, a Mickey Mouse Skater and a Li-Vo Mickey puppet. Johnsons of Hendon Ltd. produced a battery-operated lantern projector using pictures mounted between glass. One of the most popular English items was a Mickey Mouse camera, advertised as "British throughout," produced by Ensign Ltd. Ensign also produced Mickey Mouse printing outfits for developing the Mickey Mouse M10 film used in the camera.

Mickey Mouse child's tea plate, "Happynak" series.

Sharp's Mickey Mouse toffee tin, Edward Sharp & Sons Ltd. Kreemy Works, Maidstone, England. Collection of Robert Lesser.

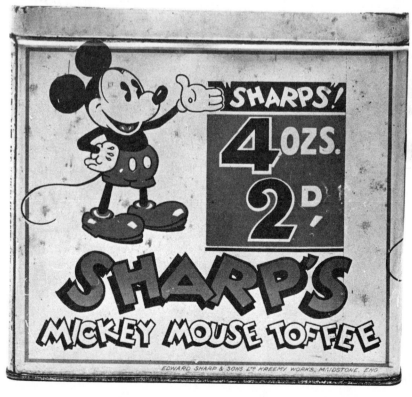

Donald Duck paints Mickey on the lid of a cookie tin. Marked "By Permission of Walt Disney (Mickey Mouse) Ltd."

vember saw six million mailing pieces going to homes with young children; and, of course, Mickey was featured in Macy's Thanksgiving Day Parade. There were thirty thousand point-of-sale displays featuring Happy Birthday sweepstakes, and ten million newsprint flyers featuring "Happy Birthday Mickey" were distributed through mass retailers. On November 19 there was a ninety-minute television special on NBC, composed of clips from Mickey's old films. "Happy Birthday Mickey Week," November 18 through November 25, saw retail promotional gimmicks and birthday parties every day. There was also a special Mickey Mouse birthday party held at the White House.

Mickey Mouse had a personal train touring across the country, beginning at Los Angeles' Union Station on November 13, with ceremonies in Kansas City, November 14; Chicago, November 15; Washington, D.C., November 17; and arriving in New York City on the 18th, where a plaque was placed in the lobby of the Colony Theatre (now called the Broadway) on his birthday, which has been established as the date that *Steamboat Willie*—the first Mickey cartoon—opened.

There were mall celebrations throughout the country in 1978. Typical ones were seen at the Willowbrook Mall and the Paramus Park Mall in New Jersey, where the "Happy Birthday Mickey Mouse Celebration" consisted of a "This Is Your Life, Mickey Mouse" program, a Disney exhibit, and a gallery of current Disney art. Museums across the land had film retrospectives and art exhibits.

An English birthday greeting for Mickey Mouse, postcard printed by Valentine & Sons Ltd., Dundee and London, 1930s.

Mickey Mouse's Fiftieth-Birthday Celebration

Mickey's fiftieth-birthday celebration began in January 1978, with big parades at both Disneyland and Disney World. There were personal appearances by Mickey Mouse in the fifty largest U.S. markets throughout April, $2 million worth of broadcast and print advertising from September through October, and "Happy Birthday Mickey" television film clips went out to stations all across the United States. The months of October and No-

California Hosts First Mickey Mouse Memorabilia Museum Exhibit

The Bowers Museum in Santa Ana, California, is almost a stone's throw from Disneyland and thus was the perfect place for a fully comprehensive exhibition of Mickey Mouse memorabilia on the occasion of Mickey Mouse's fiftieth-birthday celebration. The Mickey exhibition, held from October 20 to December 30, 1978, was dedicated to Walter E. Disney, Ub Iwerks, Floyd Gottfredson, Ward Kimball, and an elite group of animators; to the men behind the scenes through the years at the Disney studios, Les Clark, Wilfred Jackson, and Freddie Moore; and to the serious collectors throughout America, whose "foresight insured the preservation of Mickey Mouse art and memorabilia" that made the exhibition a reality. Henry Mazzeo, Jr., one of the forty lenders to the exhibit, wrote an article for the catalogue, itself now a collectors' item, in which he made it clear that recognition as a Mickey collector had not spoiled the innocent fun of collecting Mickey Mouse for him. "The supply of 'rarities' is ample," Mr. Mazzeo went on to say; "half a century of astute merchandising assures collectors that the older memorabilia will last at least another fifty years. It was never produced in small quantities. And nothing ensures an ongoing interest to collectors like a good supply." He also pointed out that the Disney organization continues to issue limited collector editions, reissues, and new products.

The Bowers exhibit included eighty examples of original art, cels, and posters; twenty-four books and other printed material, including a comic book in Arabic and postage stamps from San Marino; thirty-six sculptures and figurines, sixty-nine toys and dolls; ten examples of watches and clocks; and almost a hundred other diverse Mickey Mouse collectibles, many from the collection of Disney animator Ward Kimball, who ruefully reminisced that he threw into the wastebasket a lot of early toys given to him by Kay Kamen in the 1930s.

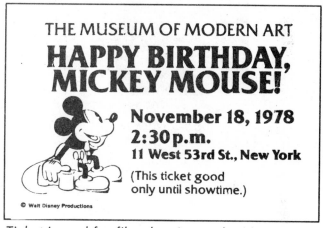

Ticket issued for film showing at the Museum of Modern Art, November 18, 1978.

Museum of Modern Art's Fiftieth-Birthday Tribute to Mickey Mouse

The Department of Film of the Museum of Modern Art began its fiftieth-anniversary tribute to Mickey Mouse appropriately with the showing of *Steamboat Willie* at noon Saturday, November 18, 1978, just fifty years to the day, if not the hour and the minute, after the first appearance of the Mickey Mouse film at the Colony Theatre in New York. The event itself created an exciting aura of celebratory enthusiasm among the hundreds who jammed the Museum of Modern Art theater that historic afternoon to see *Mickey's Follies* (1929, which introduced Mickey's theme song, "Minnie's Yoo Hoo"), *The Pointer* (1939), *Mickey's Birthday Party* (the second one, made in 1942), and *The Simple Things* (1953)—the last Mickey Mouse starrer made. The second program, beginning at 2:30, included *Plane Crazy* (animated entirely by Ub Iwerks in 1928), the first *Birthday Party* (1931), *Gulliver Mickey* (1934), *Mickey's Service Station* (1935)—the first cartoon to feature "the gang," Mickey, Donald, Goofy, and Peg Leg Pete, and one of the last made in black-and-white—and *Thru the Mirror* (1936) in which Mickey Mouse imitates Fred Astaire in Busby Berkeley–type musical numbers.

As if all this excitement were not enough, the 5 p.m. program included the 1946 fairy-tale cartoon segment *Mickey and the Beanstalk* from *Fun and Fancy Free;* the featurette (originally part of the 1941's *The Reluctant Dragon*) *Behind the Scenes* of *Walt Disney Studio*, which demonstrated animation procedures; and *The Sorcerer's Apprentice*, originally planned as a featurette to star Mickey Mouse in 1940. As a result of the enthusiasm of the famous conductor Leopold Stokowski, Disney expanded the production until it grew into the full-length feature film *Fantasia*.

This program was introduced with many celebratory and rakish remarks by Ward Kimball, winner of two Academy awards for *Toot, Whistle, Plunk and Boom* and the film featurette, *It's*

Tough to Be a Bird. Kimball also created the character of Jiminy Cricket and personally animated brilliant sections of *Dumbo* and *The Three Cabelleros*, and directed and produced many Disneyland TV programs and the TV show *The Mouse Factory*. He said, "Hollywood, as well as the rest of the country, was struggling through the Great Depression, but Mickey managed to keep everybody laughing with his many six-minute film escapades. The art of animating Mickey was a very exacting business. Every proportion and shape had to be just right—even the width of a line was important. We always drew his ears as round shapes, no matter which way he turned his head." The Museum of Modern Art opening day anniversary program was certainly a brilliant success for Mickey's fiftieth-birthday party. Subsequent programs, shown on Saturdays and Sundays for a month, included a total of forty-five cartoons. The program issued in conjunction with the celebration is an exceptional instant collectible, featuring an embossed Mickey Mouse on the black matte cover (some of the covers were autographed by Ward Kimball), transparent paper with Disney Mickey Mouse sketches, historical photographs of the Colony Theatre, film stills, and examples of movie posters. A poster was also issued by the museum, as were commemorative Mickey Mouse pinback buttons, most of which disappeared on opening day.

Mickey Mouse mask, color litho on paper, promotional give-away offered at movie theaters through the first Mickey Mouse clubs. Einson-Freeman Company Inc., Long Island City, N.Y. Wholesale price in 1933 was $15 per 1000.

Minnie Mouse color-litho paper premium mask, 1933.

One collector's collection: The Mouseum, exhibited at L. Bamberger's Department Store, Newark, N. J. Christmas 1973. Mel Birnkrant collection.

Octagonal neon industrial display clock featuring an animated somersault Mickey Mouse.

Made in Japan bisque figurine and toothbrush holders featuring a pyramid display of Disney cartoon characters: Snow White and all seven dwarfs, Elmer Elephant, Donald Duck, Mickey and Minnie, Ferdinand the Bull, the Big Bad Wolf, the Three Little Pigs, and characters from Pinocchio.

Rare painted Mickey Mouse cast iron bank, ca. 1930s.

Made in Japan hand-painted 1930s bisque figurines and toothbrush holders, including: Mickey Mouse and Minnie Mouse, some playing instruments or games, some of Pluto and Donald Duck, and an original box in the lower left hand corner.

Painted papier mache figural pencil box produced by Joseph Dixon Crucible Company of Jersey City, N. J., ca. 1934. Collection of Robert Lesser.

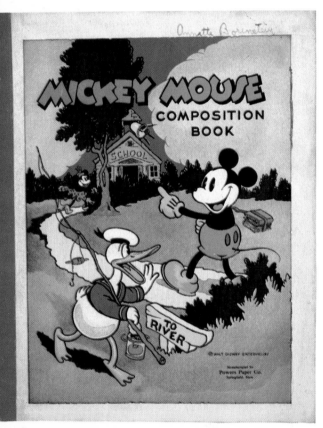

The Mickey Mouse composition book produced by Powers Paper Company, Springfield, Mass., 1935.

Sheet music, "Mickey Mouse's Birthday Party," Irving Berlin, Inc., Music Publishers, New York, 1936.

Birthday card from Hall Brothers, Inc. (now Hallmark), 1933.

Opened birthday card, marked Hall Brothers, Inc., 1933.

"Building a Better Mouse" at the Library of Congress

The exhibition at the Library of Congress in Washington, D.C., from November 21, 1978, to January 30, 1979, called "Fifty Years of Animation—Building a Better Mouse," included over 120 rare and previously unseen examples of Mickey Mouse memorabilia. The Music Division of the Library of Congress provided examples of unpublished sheet music; nu-

merous first editions of Big Little Books in mint condition, rare and valuable comic books, pop-up books, and Waddle Books (including a version of the Three Little Pigs with Braille pictures) came from the Rare Books and Special Collections Division; a colorful map of Mickey's and Donald's race to Treasure Island at the Golden Gate International Exposition in San Francisco Bay in 1939 came from the Geography and Map Division; examples of pen-and-ink drawings, original cels, and posters were loaned from the Prints and Photographs Division; and numerous Disney movie stills and the films themselves were supplied by the Motion Picture, Broadcasting and Recorded Sound Division.

Michael Barrier was the guest curator and author of the comprehensive exhibition catalogue, in which he traced the history of Disney animation, pointing out that it was the monies derived from the merchandising efforts that enabled Disney constantly to create better animation procedures. He noted that the strike of the cartoonists in May 1941 and, later that year, the beginning of U.S. involvement in World War II marked the end of Disney's momentum and success with animation. After the war, of course, the emphasis at Disney Studios was on live-action films, television programs, and theme parks. The exhibition also included many rare items loaned by the Walt Disney Archives, such as the theater program from the world premier of *Fantasia* at the Broadway Theatre in New York, and a 1917 pen-and-ink drawing of the heads of a man and woman by Walt Disney.

November 1978 issue of Life Magazine, with infinity view of Mickey Mouse on his fiftieth birthday.

Mickey Mouse Newsletter

After all the hoopla surrounding Mickey's fiftieth birthday, it was no wonder that in 1979 a national club was founded, called the Mouse Group, for collectors of Disney-character merchandise. The Mouse Group is composed of Mickey Mouse Clubs, which have different chapters for different areas. They have get-togethers for evenings of fun, trading, movies, and the sharing of information about collectibles. The editor of the *Newsletter*, Ed Levin, a self-proclaimed Mickey Mouse junkie, hosted the first Mickey Mouse convention, in August, 1982 in Anaheim, California. To subscribe to *The Mouse Group Newsletter*, write Ed Levin, 13826 Ventura Blvd., Sherman Oaks, CA 91423.

Mickey at Bloomingdale's

Not to be outdone by Bamberger's in Newark, Bloomingdale's department store in New York City became Walt Disney Productions' glittering headquarters in the Big Apple for the entire summer of 1981, in conjunction with the premiere of the new Disney feature animated film, *The Fox and the Hound*.

The Madison Avenue Boys Club performed at a gala party; one-of-a-kind Disney displays of superscale character models, instantly recognizable props, and rare Disney collectibles were displayed in glass cases all over the store. The public and collectors ogled the Mickey Mouse memorabilia from the 1930s, es-pecially a Mickey Mouse streamliner velocipede painted Depression-green, with Mickey's image on it. The most interesting features of this tricycle are the pedals, which were made to resemble Mickey's legs and feet. Manufactured by the Colson Company of Elyria, Ohio, which manufactured Disney-character merchandise for just one year, the tricycle attracted collectors to the store to view this true rarity. A "live" Mickey Mouse appeared every day at the store, and there were beautiful replicas of the original Mickey and Minnie cotton dolls for $20 each. There were also interesting Mickey Mouse cloth pop-up sticks at $5 each. A special Bloomingdale's anniversary poster was also issued and sold as an instant collectible for $1.50.

Museum of Broadcasting— Disneyvision

The Museum of Broadcasting in New York celebrated Walt Disney's "crowded imagination" as it was applied to television during the months of August and September 1981.

"Fantasy Week" showed Mickey films, *Alice in Wonderland*, the Disneyland story, Disney's first TV show in color (1961), Donald Duck films, and the Uncle Remus and Br'er Rabbit adventures. "Nature and Science Week" was followed by "Mouseketeer Week," showing the highlights of the Mickey Mouse Club episodes from the series. *Mickey's 50th*, a ninety-minute extravaganza with more than seventy-five stars paying tribute to Mickey, and *The Mouseketeer Reunion* (November 1980), with Annette Funicello and thirty of the original Mouseketeers celebrating the twenty-fifth anniversary, were the highlights of this historical program. There was also a "Western Week," which featured a showing of the obscure *Elfego Baca* and *Davy Crockett*, and a "Week of Specials," which included *Ben and Me*, *Peter and the Wolf*, *Hans Brinker*, *Treasure Island*, and *Kidnapped*.

T-shirt sold at the Whitney Museum of American Art in conjunction with the Disney Animations and Animators show, June 24–September 6, 1981.

Disney Animation Art at the Whitney

"Disney Animations and Animators" was the title for the greatly admired, much-heralded Whitney Museum of American Art Show, which was held in New York from June through September 1981. More than five hundred thousand visitors viewed the spectacular display of more than fifteen hundred drawings, painted cels, and backgrounds. All segments of the public at large—mothers with baby carriages, students, blue-collar workers, secretaries, waitresses, businessmen, and others—stampeded this exhibit in numbers no other show at the Whitney had drawn. Cartoon screenings were sold out and had to be rescheduled. Special Mickey Mouse T-shirts and posters were sold out immediately. The extensive exhibit explored the special characteristics of Disney animation, tracing the development of well-known cartoon characters and examining the creative process through the work of seventeen animators. Throughout the show, 115 of Disney's films from the 1920s through the 1940s were shown, some for the first time since their initial release. The museum concept was to utilize the various components of cinema—light, darkness, projection, shadow, rhythm, illusion, and movement—to convey the animation process; and the exhibition material, including sequences of drawings, character sketches, layouts, scale models, sketchbooks, test reels, cels, and films, all emphasizing the work of the Disney studio from 1932 to 1942, was presented in the atmosphere of a movie theatre, created with dark walls and silvery lighting. This was indeed a beautiful show and received a great deal of laudatory critical attention.

AUCTIONS IN THE EIGHTIES

Donald Duck Big Bucks

An important Disneyana auction, produced by David Dunham at Phillips Son & Neale, Inc., was held on October 5, 1981, at the famous auction house's Madison Avenue galleries. Attended by many of the top Mickey Mouse collectors, the auction included cels, toys, posters, and original art and featured an abundance of Donald Duck collectibles from the estate of the late Al Taliaferro (one of Disney's top animators). Ephemera and books were first on the auction block, and bidding for them was hot and heavy. A Walt Disney Studios illustrated staff Christmas card from 1935 went for $400; a Blue-Ribbon Mickey Mouse Pop-Up Book for $180; *The Adventures of Donald Duck*, published by Grosset & Dunlap in 1936, with the original dust jacket, for $260; six Mickey Mouse Wee Little Books (1935), published by Whitman, for $275; *Walt Disney's "Snow White and the Seven Dwarfs"*, published by Harper in 1937 and signed by Walt Disney, for $475; *Walt Disney's Comics and Stories*, Volume I, No. 1 (1940) with Donald Duck on the cover, for $650; the first twelve issues of *Walt Disney's Comics and Stories* (1940) bound together in one volume, for $1,900; and a Donald Duck comic book No. 9 (1942), art and story by Carl Barks—*Donald Duck Finds Pirate Gold*—for $500. A 1933 Silly Symphony movie poster, "Father Noah's Ark," brought $2,700. Donald Duck's "Beach Picnic" movie poster (1939) brought $1,700. A *Snow White*

Donald Duck Japanese bisque figurine, 3", 1930s.

movie poster was $1,300, and a *Fantasia* movie poster brought $700.

In the category of animation photostats, drawings, and celluloids, a lithograph of *The Three Caballeros* (1945), signed by Walt Disney and published by Walt Disney Enterprises, brought $550; a sequence of four drawings from *Pinocchio*, showing Jiminy Cricket taking a bow, brought $750; as did three cartoon drawings depicting Katharine Hepburn, Fred Astaire, and Charles Laughton from *Mother Goose Goes Hollywood* (1938). An original drawing in pencil of Donald

Duck and other characters from *The Wise Little Hen* brought $2,600. Ten pencil drawings from *Oswald the Lucky Rabbit* brought $2,500. An animation celluloid of Mickey Mouse, Pluto, and Donald Duck, circa 1943, brought $600; a celluloid of Jiminy Cricket with the original background, $1,400; an animation celluloid of Dumbo with the Courvoisier Galleries' authentication on the reverse, $1,300. Also from Courvoisier (a San Francisco art gallery which contracted with the Disney Studios in 1938 to sell original art and celluloids) was a cel of Mickey Mouse as the Sorcerer's Apprentice atop a mountain,

which went for $1,400. The highest price for a cel was $2,750 for a Donald Duck from *The Band Concert* (1935), showing Donald with a flute (and a very long bill).

Original art of *The Three Little Pigs* (1933), in pen-and-ink, for a Sunday comic strip, by Al Taliaferro, copyright Walt Disney Enterprises, and dated July 24, 1938, brought $1,800. Other Taliaferro original art included a Mickey Mouse four-panel pen-and-ink daily strip from December 24, 1934—$900—and a Donald Duck strip for $600. High prices for original Carl Barks Donald Duck art were realized at this auction, including $8,500 for an oil painting on board done in 1972, called *Christmas Carolers*, and $5,500 for a signed oil portrait of Donald Duck on board.

Three-dimensional collectibles came last on the block, starting off with a 1947 Mickey Mouse wristwatch, which went for $120. A 1930s bisque figure of a double Donald Duck went at $325. Two Donald Duck drinking glasses with decals, one being Donna Duck, went at $70. A Mickey Mouse pocket knife, 1936, was $200. A Mickey and Minnie pillow, 1931, Number 971 in the Vogue Needlecraft Mickey Mouse series fetched $90. A Fisher-Price Donald Duck cart pull-toy sold for $90. Donald Duck soap in the original box took a bid of $200. Children's leather gloves with fringed cuffs and featuring a silkscreened picture of Mickey the Cowboy riding his bronco, 1933, sold at $140. A wind-up tin Donald Duck with key, in the original box, made in Germany by the Schuco Company, went for $225. A Marks Brothers Donald Duck bank, circa 1940s, went

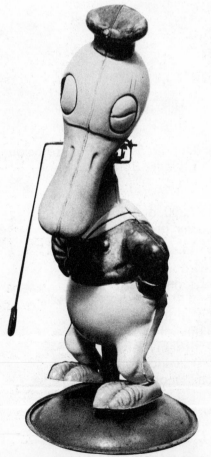

Donald Duck celluloid nodder with wind-up rubber-band action, Japanese, 1934. Collection 'Tiques of Old Bridge, N.J.

for $325. A Mickey Mouse Steiff puppet, 1932, distributed by George Borgfeldt & Company, 8½ inches high, closed bids at $425. A Borgfeldt Mickey Mouse sparkler sold for $425. A French Donald Duck composition toy from the 1940s sold for $425. A 6-inch celluloid Donald Duck toy "nodder" made in Japan in the 1930s, with the original import stamp, went at $425. A Donald Duck celluloid toy on a wind-up metal cart, pulled by a celluloid Pluto, took a top of $900. The Donald Duck Lionel railcar went at $850. A Donald Duck ashtray sold for $900. A 1931 18-inch Mickey Mouse Steiff doll, with a black velvet body and green pants, originally distributed by George Borgfeldt & Company, sold at $1000. This was the last item in a breathless sale that included 314 individual items covering an enormously wide range of Disney collectibles. The emphasis at this sale was definitely on Donald Duck, attesting to the duck's ongoing popularity with a great many collectors.

Mickey Mouse and "Rosebud" Score at Sotheby's

All the international auction houses have collectible departments now, including Sotheby's, Phillips, and Christie's. The smaller houses like Hamilton and Swann Galleries in New York handle ephemera and movie memorabilia, and Mickey Mouse paper collectibles turn up in their varied auctions quite often, including original movie posters, lobby cards, broadsides, and advertising and mer-

The first Mickey Mouse movie poster, 40" x 26", 1929.

chandising ephemera. Sotheby's in particular has made a genuine "collectibles commitment." Twice a year it has a "Collector's Carousel," offering everything imaginable in the collectibles field. Original cels from the films have become a very big item, having increased in value from a price range of $400–$800 in 1978 to $2,500–$3,000 in 1982. Disney cels bring the most interest because they are triple collectibles, appealing to art collectors, movie memorabilia buffs, and Mickey Mouse memorabilia collectors. One such collector is Steven (E.T.) Spielberg, who made international headlines when he purchased the sled "Rosebud" from the Orson Welles film *Citizen Kane* for $60,500 at a Sotheby's Collectors Carousel on June 9, 1982, establishing a new record for a single movie prop. Spielberg, who publicly stated that he "owes his inspiration to Walt Disney," also set a record for a Disney cel at that auction when he purchased the "Wicked Queen" celluloid from *Snow White* for $2,250. He bought four other cels for a total of $4,500, and a Silly Symphony poster, "Just Dogs," for $2,500. George ("*Close Encounters of the Third Kind*") Lucas was another bidder at Sotheby's June 9 auction, purchasing two Disney cels. Lucas has also publicly acknowledged Disney's influence on his own work and has reportedly met several times with representatives of the Disney organization regarding future film projects. Of the 265 collectible lots at this by now famous auction, a movie poster from the 1932 cartoon *Klondike Kid*, starring Mickey Mouse, set the highest record, selling for $7,000.

Collectors Buy Mickey's Birthplace

March 22, 1982: Paul Maher, a Los Angeles Disney buff, auctioned off the garage-studio where Mickey Mouse was born for $8,500. Maher hopes the 18-foot-by-12-foot garage will be used to house a collection of Mickey Mouse memorabilia one day, but a spokesman for the buyers, a group of Walt Disney Productions employees and members of a group called Hollywood Heritage, said that "until its ultimate disposition is decided" it would be stored in a warehouse.

MICKEY MOUSE FACTS AND FIGURES

Walt Disney's life came to an end due to lung cancer on December 15, 1966 when he was sixty-five, during the making of *The Jungle Book*—just six weeks after the removal of one lung. The death of a genius and legend such as Walt Disney is a great loss to the world; but brother Roy Disney remained as president, carrying on the vast undertakings of the company until his retirement in 1968. He continued as chairman of the board and chief executive officer of Walt Disney Productions, and passed away at the age of seventy-eight on December 20, 1971.

The foresighted Disney brothers had made sure to provide for the corporate future of the company, and in 1972 E. Cardon Walker, who started with Disney as a mailboy in 1938, and Donn Tatum, a former West Coast ABC television chief, took over the creative and business aspects of the organization. As of 1983 Card Walker is chairman of the board and chief executive officer, and Ron Miller is president and chief operating officer.

Ub Iwerks, the early Disney partner who had contributed so much to the graphic concept of the early Mickey (Walt Disney was fond of saying that he had never picked up his cartoonist's pen after 1926), also died in the year 1971. Kay Kamen, the merchandising expert, and his wife, Kate, had been long gone, having died in an Air France crash on October 28, 1949, along with thirty-seven other passengers and eleven crewmen. Fortunately, many of the original ani-

Mickey Mouse play money. Promotional give-away for Mickey Mouse cones, ca. 1934.

mators and Disney staff are still with us to provide accurate information about the workings of the studio.

Funny Money Mouse

In a *New York Times Magazine* article dated November 16, 1980, one Disney executive said, "unless somebody does something stupid like selling *Snow White and the Seven Dwarfs* to television, this company will continue to be the nearest thing to a perpetual money machine anybody's ever seen."

In November 1982, at the twenty-fifth anniversary of the listing of Walt Disney Productions on the New York Stock Exchange, who should appear on the floor, to the surprise and delight of the brokers, but Mickey Mouse—"in person." It was announced at this impromptu celebration that in 1957, when Roy Disney was president, Walt had bought the first 100 shares traded on the exchange at a price of 14⅞. Those 100 shares, after adjustments for stock splits and other actions, would have totaled 1,300 shares today, valued at $91,000.

The Disney empire of 1957 was certainly a vastly different one from what it is today. At that time it had assets of $23.8 million and grossed $35.8 million annually, compared to the 1982 reported assets of $2.06 billion and annual sales of $1.03 billion. When stock was first listed, there were 1,500,000 shares outstanding and 5,500 shareholders. At the close of fiscal 1982, there were 33,200,000 shares outstanding and 63,000 shareholders. In 1957, when *The Mickey Mouse Club* was on television and

Zorro was introduced as a series, Disneyland in California had welcomed its ten millionth visitor since opening in July 1955. By the end of fiscal 1982, Disneyland attendance had topped 220 million.

Disney World, the second theme park, which opened in Florida in October 1971, also now includes the Epcot Center (the Experimental Prototype Community of Tomorrow), which got off to a positive start on October 1, 1982. The annual attendance rate at Disney World's Magic Kingdom is approximately twenty-six million. Epcot is said to have been envisioned by Walt Disney—who had been captivated by the 1939 New York World's Fair's "World of Tomorrow"—as a permanent world's fair, which it seems well on the way to becoming.

Tokyo Disneyland opened on April 15, 1983, with ten million projected to attend in its first year of operation. The cost of $600 million was borne by Japanese railway and real-estate interests. Disney did not pay one cent into this new theme-park venture; in addition, the company is paid royalties by Tokyo Disneyland and fifteen of Japan's leading corporations, who showcase their products by sponsoring different attractions. The Tokyo Disneyland official corporate participants include: Coca-Cola (Japan) for Space Mountain, Tomorrowland Terrace, and the Refreshment Corner; Fuji Photo Film Company Ltd. (the Magic Carpet and the Camera Center); Kikkoman Corporation (Polynesian Terrace, Plaza Restaurant); Kodansha Publishers (Mickey Mouse Revue), Matsushita Electrical Industrial Company (Meet the

World); Tomy Kogyo Company, Inc. (Western River Railroad and the Toy Kingdom); and others. Some of the attractions include Cinderella Castle, Pirates of the Caribbean, the Haunted Mansion, Pinocchio's Daring Journey, and Magic Carpet 'Round the World.

In addition to the release of *Who Censored Roger Rabbit?*, a new live-action and animation feature film that introduces a totally new character collectible, Roger Rabbit, to the world of Mickey Mouse memorabilia in 1983, Mickey Mouse returned to the screen in a theatrical featurette costarring Donald Duck, Goofy, Pluto, and other Disney favorites in *Mickey's Christmas Carol*, adapted from the Dickens classic.

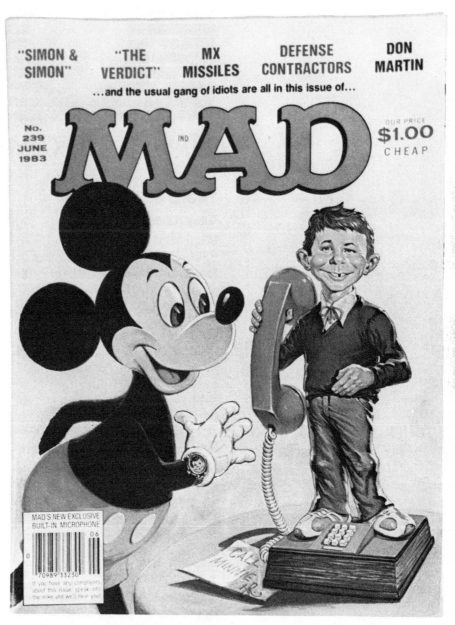

Mickey Mouse wearing an Alfred E. Neuman wristwatch, preparing to call Minnie on an Alfred E. Neuman telephone, on the cover of Mad Magazine, June 1983.

Walt Disney Productions, cable channel logo.

The Disney Channel

The Disney Cable Channel

Walt Disney Productions opened up its own Disney Cable television channel on April 18, 1983, to be transmitted via satellite throughout America. The channel offers Disney classics such as *Dumbo* as well as $100 million worth of new programming for the first three years beamed by satellite to cable subscribers. The company began with over 350 cable system operators, representing five million subscribers to the sixteen-hour-a-day Disney channel, which has its main office at 4111 West Alameda Avenue, Burbank, California 91505.

Re-runs include the popular *Davy Crockett* and *Zorro* series in addition to a new series called *The Mousterpiece Theater*, which shows vintage Disney cartoons. New series line-ups include *Welcome to Pooh Corner*, a daily half-hour of songs and stories for children, starring life-size puppets of the A. A. Milne characters; *Five Mile Creek*, an adventure series based on the tales of Louis L'Amour; *You and Me Kid*, a daily show of activi-

ties for youngsters and their parents, and *Wish Upon a Star*, a program in which young people will be able to live out, via TV, fantasies of becoming a fireman, a marine, a magician, or other grown-up occupations.

Adults watch special magazine-format programs coming directly from Disney's Epcot Center in Florida. Classic feature-length movies with a G-rating such as *Can Can*, *Popeye*, or newer Disney movies fresh from their theatrical releases are being presented, as well as many special Disney films and features, some of which have been buried in the Disney vaults for decades. Top Disney feature-length films like *Bambi*, *Snow White*, *Fantasia*, *Alice in Wonderland*, *Mary Poppins*, and *Lady and the Tramp* continue to be reserved for movie theater showings only, mainly to avoid taping by viewers on their home video-cassette recorders.

The *Disney Channel Magazine* with feature articles, interviews, games, Mickey Mouse activities, and programming, is already an instant collector's item.

MICKEY, THE MOVIE-STAR MOUSE

The 1930s Mickey Mouse has been described by many eminent artists, cartoonists, and collectors as the most perfect graphic symbol and cartoon character ever created. The pure, straight lines with circular constructions and sharp black, white, red and yellow colors appear to have jumped directly out of the Bauhaus or from the Art Deco style of the 1920s which focused primarily on angularity combined with the curvilinear. Ernest Trova, an artist and Mickey Mouse collector, has said that Mickey is one of the three most famous, oft-repeated, and indelible graphic symbols of the twentieth century, the others being the swastika and the Coca-Cola bottle. Mickey is also regarded as one of the three top movie-star personalities of this century, right alongside Marilyn Monroe and Charlie Chaplin, who Disney has said directly influenced his creation. Alva Johnston, in the July 1934 issue of *Woman's Home Companion*, wrote in an article entitled simply "Mickey Mouse": "Chaplin was a kind of godfather to Mickey Mouse. It is now and always has been the aim of Disney to graft the psychology of Chaplin upon

Mickey Mouse in his most characteristic stance as a decal applique made for the Keystone Mickey Mouse movie projector, 1935.

Mickey. The two universal characters have something in common in their approach to their problems. They have the same blend of hero and coward, nitwit and genius, mug and gentleman." She stated further that Mickey's domain was even more extensive than Chaplin's, as he was global and extended "beyond the frontiers of civilization."

It is the early, vintage Mickey, the more primitive imp rodent, that has inspired collectors and artists today. The mischievous mouse that banged on cows' teeth to simulate a xylophone, pulled at a sows' udders as if

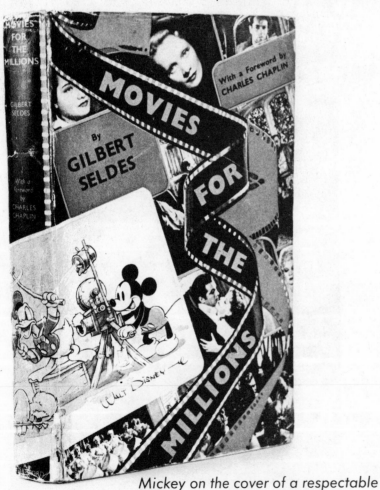

Mickey on the cover of a respectable book of film criticism, Movies for the Millions, by Gilbert Seldes, with a foreword by Charles Chaplin. B. T. Batsford, London, 1937.

they were bagpipes, and twisted and pinched the other barnyard creatures in performing "Turkey in the Straw" as a Silly Symphony, is a far cry from the smiling, pink-faced humanoid mouse that acts as the goodwill ambassador at Disneyland today. Children and adults of the Depression era loved and took to heart this fun-filled mad, bad mouse with big gnashing teeth, rodentlike features, a white face, two black, oval eyes with pie-wedge indentations, a long nose that ended in a black stub, black balloon ears, a red-heart tongue, a skinny tail, stovepipe legs and arms, wearing red shorts held up mysteriously, without suspenders, by two big buttons; clown-sized rounded shoes; and thick four-finger gloves. Disney himself has described his mouse cartoon creation this way: "His head is a circle with an oblong circle for a snout. The ears are also circles so they can be drawn the same, no matter how he turns his head. His body is like a pear with a long tail." These circles and lines that combined to make a mouse were, at the time of early animation, a way of being expedient and economical. However, the talent and genius of Walt Disney and Ub Iwerks in the late 1920s infused this little mouse creature with the sparkle of life—and the public responded with abundant adoration.

When Mickey was just six years old, *Fortune* magazine, the business mind of America, reported in its November 1934 issue: "Mickey Mouse is an international hero, better known than Roosevelt or Hitler, a part of the folklore of the world. It takes more than humor to achieve such renown. It takes quality, real and simple enough to cut deep into the emotions of people everywhere; and that quality, in whatever form you find it, is art."

It was in 1919 that Walter Elias Disney, at the age of eighteen formed the Laugh-O-Gram Studios with Ub Iwerks, to produce animated shorts of such fairy tales as "Goldilocks and the Three Bears," "Jack and the Beanstalk," and "Little Red Riding Hood," but by 1923 these two bright comic artists saw their business, which was based in Kansas City, heading into bankruptcy. At this point, Walt headed for Hollywood, where he began the development of his *Alice in Cartoonland* shorts, which featured a real-life Alice acting with cartoon characters. Roy Disney joined his brother as the business manager for the series; and Ub Iwerks and a staff of artists produced one *Alice* short each month over a period of several years, in which fifty-six of these silent live-action cartoons were produced. By 1927 Walt Disney, who was fond of all the little creatures he remembered as a Kansas farm boy, created a new cartoon character he called Oswald, the Lucky Rabbit. Oswald became the star of a silent series that was distributed by Universal Pictures. The public took to Oswald with the same enthusiasm it had for Felix the Cat, Otto Messmer's successful feline cartoon creation; and after twenty-six Oswald cartoons, Disney headed for New York to try to negotiate a better deal for himself and his new studio. Instead, he was blatantly offered less; and also made the astonishing discovery that a miniclause in his original

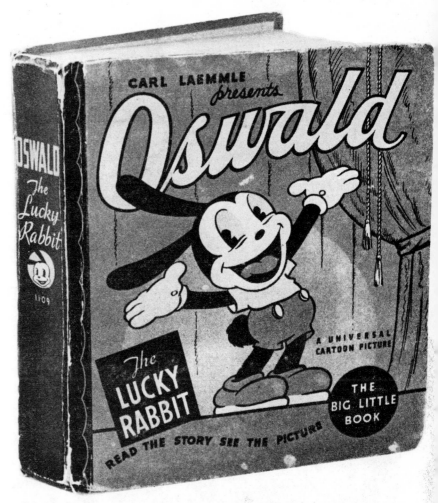

Disney's first successful cartoon character, Oswald the Lucky Rabbit, *Big Little Book*, Whitman Publishing Company, Racine, Wisc., 1934.

contract stated that he did not even own the rights to his rabbit. This seemed to be the end of the line for unlucky cartoonist Walter and his lucky rabbit Oswald. Later, Oswald the Lucky Rabbit was sold to Walter Lantz, who changed his image to one that was less doglike and more bunnyfied.

Feeling disheartened, angry, and embittered at having been manipulated in this way by people he believed he could trust, Walt and his wife, Lillian, boarded a train heading back to sunny Hollywood. It was during

Mickey Mouse gum card #92.

this by-now-famous train ride that Disney began dreaming and doodling with his pencil, as was his habit. At one point in his early days as a cartoonist in Kansas City, Walter had kept some field mice in cages in his office. One particularly bright mouse would almost seem at times to want to speak to master Walt; and so Walt let the mouse come to visit with him at the drawing board, where the two of them would play the game of man and mouse. Legend has it that it was this mouse that Walt remembered fondly during the historic train ride. In any case, before arriving in California, Walt Disney had drawn a new cartoon character that was a cheery little mouse. Disney himself said, "Out of the trouble and confusion stood a mocking, merry little figure. Vague and indefinite at first, it grew and grew, and finally arrived—a mouse. A romping, rollicking little mouse. The idea completely engulfed me. The wheels turned to the tune of it. By the time my train reached the Midwest, I had dressed my dream mouse in a pair of red velvet pants with two huge pearl buttons, had composed my first scenario, and was all set." One legend has it that Walt wanted to call his new-found cartoon creature Mortimer, a name which his wife disliked, finding it too "highbrow." According to his story, Lillian Disney suggested the name Mickey. Another circulating story is that Disney's distributors did not feel the name of Mortimer was commercial enough and asked for a change. In either case, it was on a "choo-choo train heading for better times," going east to west, that a mouse star was born into the Hollywood heavens of make-believe and dreams.

In April 1928 Walt Disney, Ub Iwerks, a new team of animation artists, with brother Roy handling business, began to plunge ahead on the first Mickey Mouse cartoon, which was called *Plane Crazy*. This new short, which had Mickey sporting a ruffled Charles Lindbergh-style "tossled" hairdo, was designed to capitalize on the current national obsession with airplanes and air pilots. Ub Iwerks animated and created the drawings for this film, and many credit him with the look of the early mouse, adding that he may have been the best illustrator of Mickey, although there were other good ones to follow. *Gallopin' Gaucho* followed *Plane Crazy*, but prior to their releases Walt Disney had gone to New York and attended the first "all singing, all-talking" film, *The Jazz Singer* (1927), in which a black-faced Al Jolson cried out longingly in song for his Mammy ("My Mammy") to a movie audience that was awestruck to hear voices coming forth from the silver screen. Walt was so enthralled to see and hear the immortal Jolson that he decided right then and there to add music, voices, animal squeals and

Mickey Mouse as the captain in Steamboat Willie, *the first synchronized sound cartoon, 1928.*

squeaking sounds to his third Mickey Mouse short, *Steamboat Willie*. The first sound cartoon featuring Mickey, Minnie and an assortment of barnyard animals opened at the Colony Theatre in New York on November 18, 1928, in New York and was instantaneously a stupendous success. Crowds hooted and howled to hear a mouse whistle and speak. Walt himself was Mickey's falsetto voice, and, in a sense, from that time forward Walt and Mickey were inseparable pals. The first sound cartoon was moved two weeks later to the larger, more prestigious Roxy Theatre where audiences waited clamorously in line to see the new celebrity on screen. Thus Mickey Mouse became America's first all-talking comic cartoon-character superstar and a bonafide movie star of the first order.

The success of Mickey Mouse enabled Walt to build a new animation studio and to reinvest in more and more cartoons. Mickey Mouse shorts were turned out on a monthly basis during the 1930s.

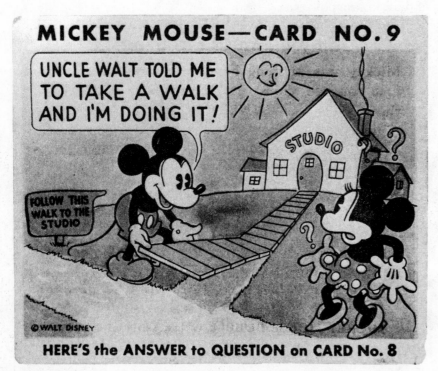

Mickey Mouse gum card #9.

A COMPLETE LIST OF CARTOONS STARRING* MICKEY MOUSE

1928–1929

- Steamboat Willie
- Plane Crazy
- Gallopin' Gaucho
- Barn Dance
- The Opry House
- When the Cat's Away
- Barnyard Battle
- The Plow Boy
- The Karnival Kid
- Mickey's Follies
- El Terrible Toreador
- Mickey's Choo Choo
- The Jazz Fool
- Haunted House
- Wild Waves

1930

- Just Mickey
- The Barnyard Concert
- Cactus Kid
- Fire Fighters
- The Shindig
- The Chain Gang
- Gorilla Mystery
- The Picnic
- Pioneer Days

1931

- Birthday Party
- Traffic Troubles
- The Castaway
- The Moose Hunt
- Delivery Boy
- Mickey Steps Out
- Blue Rhythm
- Fishin' Around
- Barnyard Broadcast
- Beach Party
- Mickey Cuts Up
- Mickey's Orphans

*Mickey Mouse appeared in numerous Donald Duck, Pluto, and Goofy cartoons throughout the 1930s and 1940s.

Mickey Mouse 16-mm film in the original box, Hollywood Film Enterprises, Hollywood, Cal.

1932

- *Duck Hunt*
- *Grocery Boy*
- *Mad Dog*
- *Barnyard Olympics*
- *Mickey's Revue*
- *Musical Farmer*
- *Mickey in Arabia*
- *Mickey's Nightmare*
- *Trader Mickey*
- *The Whoopee Party*
- *Touchdown Mickey*
- *The Wayward Canary*
- *The Klondike Kid*
- *Mickey's Good Deed*

1933

- *Building a Building*
- *The Mad Doctor*
- *Mickey's Pal Pluto*
- *Mickey's Mellerdrammer*
- *Ye Olden Days*
- *The Mail Pilot*
- *Mickey's Mechanical Man*
- *Mickey's Gala Premiere*
- *Puppy Love*
- *The Steeplechase*
- *The Pet Store*
- *Giant Land*

1934

- *Shanghaied*
- *Camping Out*
- *Playful Pluto*
- *Gulliver Mickey*
- *Mickey's Steamroller*
- *Orphan's Benefit*
- *Mickey Plays Papa*
- *The Dog Napper*
- *Two-Gun Mickey*

1935

- *Mickey's Man Friday*
- *The Band Concert (first color)*
- *Mickey's Service Station*
- *Mickey's Kangaroo*
- *Mickey's Garden*
- *Mickey's Fire Brigade*
- *Pluto's Judgement Day*
- *On Ice*

1936

- *Mickey's Polo Team*
- *Orphan's Picnic*
- *Mickey's Grand Opera*
- *Thru the Mirror*
- *Moving Day*
- *Mickey's Rival*
- *Alpine Climbers*
- *Mickey's Circus*
- *Donald and Pluto*
- *Mickey's Elephant*
- *Mother Pluto*

1937

- *The Worm Turns*
- *Don Donald*
- *Magician Mickey*
- *Moose Hunters*
- *Mickey's Amateurs*
- *Modern Inventions*
- *Hawaiian Holiday*
- *Clock Cleaners*
- *Lonesome Ghosts*

1938

- *Boat Builders*
- *Mickey's Trailer*
- *The Whalers*
- *Mickey's Parrot*
- *The Brave Little Tailor*

1939

- *Society Dog Show*
- *The Pointer*

1940

- *Tugboat Mickey*
- *Mr. Mouse Takes a Trip*
- *Fantasia* (the *Sorcerer's Apprentice* segment)

1941

- *The Little Whirlwind*
- *Nifty Nineties*
- *Orphan's Benefit*

1942

- *Mickey's Birthday Party*
- *Symphony Hour*

1946

- *Mickey and the Beanstalk* (segment from *Fun and Fancy Free*)

1947–1953

- *Mickey's Delayed Date*
- *Mickey Down Under*
- *Mickey and the Seal*
- *Pluto's Christmas Tree*
- *The Simple Things*

Mickey adopted many varied occupations in his movie-mouse adventures, including that of a cowboy, gaucho, fireman, fisherman, sailor, detective, tailor, taxicab driver, inventor, storekeeper, boxer, exterminator, hunter, plumber, magician, carpenter, skater, actor, and football player. Mickey was Gulliver in one cartoon, and in his first star-

Society Dog Show, poster featuring Mickey Mouse and Pluto, 1939.

Accompanied by his girl friend Minnie and dog Pluto, the celebrated movie star Mickey Mouse is greeted by friends Goofy, Horace, and Clarabelle on a tin litho child's serving tray from Ohio Art Company, Bryan, Ohio, ca. 1933.

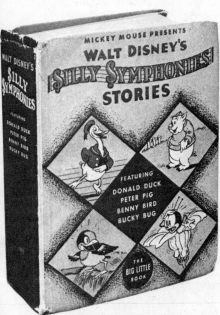

Silly Symphonies Stories, featuring Donald Duck, Peter Pig, Benny Bird, and Bucky Bug. Big Little Book, Whitman Publishing Company, Racine, Wisc. 1936.

Mickey developed a following of fans among notables, including Franklin and Eleanor Roosevelt, who loved to show Mickey cartoons at the White House; Mary Pickford, who said publicly that Mickey Mouse was her very favorite star; and child stars Shirley Temple and Jane Withers, both of whom had collected or been given many early Mickey Mouse dolls. One well-known newspaper reported that England's Queen Mary refused to leave a movie show until she saw the Mickey Mouse cartoon, even though her ladies-in-waiting were urging her to return home to the palace for a high tea for which she was already late. Charles de Gaulle, it has been said, was a collector of mouse memorabilia and amassed an excellent collection before his death.

Mickey today continues to be a global star. He is Miki Kuchi in Japan, Micky Maus in Germany, Topolino in Italy, Musse Pigg in Sweden, Mikel Mus in Greece, Mickey sans Culotte in France, Muku Mayc in Soviet Russia, and in Africa among primitive tribes his image has been used as a charm to ward off evil spirits.*

ring role in a feature film he played the part of a sorcerer's apprentice. Ultimately, after a long career in cartoons and in television of the 1950s, Mickey left his movie career behind to join his Uncle Walt as a goodwill ambassador and symbol, greeting the public-at-large and visiting domestic and foreign dignitaries at Disneyland and Disney World.

The first Silly Symphony, known as a "rhythmic cartoon," was called *The Skeleton Dance*, and the first Silly Symphony cartoon in color was a pastoral epic called *Flowers and Trees*. Opening at Grauman's Chinese Theater on July 30, 1932, this film began with credits that read, "Mickey Mouse Presents A Walt Disney Silly Symphony," which was Mickey's first entrée into the world as a producer-enterpreneur. Disney earned an Academy Award that year for *Flowers and Trees*, as well as a special Academy Award for the creation of Mickey Mouse, movie star.

*Shiva Baba, the founder of the Barahma-Kumaris Raja Yoga World Spiritual Center at 777 U.N. Plaza, New York City, insists that his followers and students only watch Mickey Mouse cartoons. This religious sect believes that Mickey Mouse is very spiritual. B. K. Joy, a Shiva Baba follower, told the authors that if you can stand aside and learn to laugh at your own foibles and anger the way you laugh at a Mickey Mouse cartoon, it can help you to realize the fundamental absurdity of everything in the universe.

FIRST MICKEY MOUSE CLUB

In late 1929 Harry W. Woodin, manager of the Fox Dome Theatre in Ocean Park, California, organized the first Mickey Mouse Club. Roy and Walt Disney fully cooperated with Woodin, as they were very interested, in those early times, in developing the idea of merchandising through clubs, which they felt would also help promote the Mickey cartoons. The original club at Ocean Park was so successful in its first months that Disney persuaded Woodin to work at the studio as general manager of Mickey Mouse Clubs across the country. An *Official Bulletin of the Mickey Mouse Clubs* was published on a semimonthly basis and sent to theater managers to assist them in the promotion of the clubs in their particular towns.

Children's movie matinees were usually held at noon on Saturdays, and the stated purpose of the clubs was to help children learn activities that would build character and inspire patriotism in the midst of the Depression. Local businessmen participated through advertisements in the bulletin; bakeries offered free birthday cakes on Saturday to club children celebrating a birthday; florists sent flowers to sick children who were out of school; dairies offered ice cream to contest winners; banks gave free Mickey savings banks to club members on their birthdays; and department stores gave out free inexpensive Mickey Mouse toys to lure parents into buying more expensive ones. Before long all the stores in town—the candy store, sports store, record shop, stationery shops, shoe stores, the five-and-dimes, the drug-

store, and the jeweler—were involved with the concept of Mickey Mouse through the club; and by participating as advertisers they benefited in their businesses. Parent-teacher associations joined in on the Mickey bandwagon, feeling it promoted good citizenship and kept the children out of trouble after school.

Following the Mickey Mouse cartoon showing at a matinee, the club officers, led by a chief Mickey Mouse and chief Minnie Mouse, would form a circle on the movie stage, and the clubs' credo would be read aloud: "I will be a square shooter in my home, in school and on the playground, wherever I am. I will be truthful and honorable and strive always to make myself a better and more useful citizen. I will respect elders and help the aged, helpless or children smaller than myself. In short, I will be a good American!"

Following this, the audience of children would scream out together, "Mickey Mice do not swear, smoke, cheat, or lie!"

After this histrionic opening, an American flag would be saluted and club members joined in singing "America the Beautiful." Games, stunts, and contests followed, and at the end the kids would yell out:

Handy! Dandy! Sweet as candy!
Happy Kids are we!
Eeenie! Ickie! Minnie! Mickey!
M-O-U-S-E!!

A Mickey Mouse Club Song that was flashed on the screen was then sung in unison—all of this prior to the regular matinee fea-

Pinback button, Mickey Mouse Globe Trotters Member, ca. 1930s.

Pinback button, from the original Mickey Mouse Club, 1928–1930.

tures. By 1930, hundreds of Mickey Mouse Clubs were forming across America and in England, Canada, and other countries as well. In 1932 the clubs boasted over a million members, which was, at that time, more than the combined membership of the Boy Scouts and Girl Scouts of America.

Collectors today search avidly for early Mickey Mouse Club memorabilia, which include 8½-by-8½-inch orange-and-black store signs that read OFFICIAL MICKEY MOUSE STORE, membership club pinback Mickey buttons, birthday cards, membership cards, Mickey Mouse and Minnie Mouse masks, the official club bulletin, newsletter, and the *Mickey Mouse Magazine*, distributed by leading stores through local theaters.

By 1935 Disney considered that the clubs were unwieldy, causing the studio too much work and too many extraneous problems, and he consequently disassociated himself from them. However, many Mickey Mouse movie clubs enthusiastically persisted throughout the 1930s, and some into the war years. The Odeon Theatre Chain in England claimed 160 clubs, attracting 110,000 children each Saturday in 1939. By 1955, when it became apparent that the little rectangular box was to be a fixture in a great many homes, Disney decided to revive the Mickey Mouse Club format for TV, and it became a phenomenon of that era also.

Official Mickey Mouse Club store window card. Black and orange, ca. 1933.

SULLIVAN'S TRAVELS TO MICKEY MOUSE

Preston Sturges, the Hollywood genius director, paid a special tribute to Mickey Mouse in his 1941 Paramount film *Sullivan's Travels*, on which Sturges also took credit for the screenplay. Andrew Sarris and Tom Allen, reviewing this film in their "Revivals in Focus" column in the *Village Voice* (February 1, 1983), called it "just about the funniest, wittiest and wisest movie ever made by Hollywood about Hollywood." On the credits of the movie, Sturges's formal dedication read: "To the motley mountebanks, the clowns, the buffoons, in all times and all nations." In the film, starring Joel McCrea, Veronica Lake, and William Demarest, McCrea portrays Sullivan, a wealthy director of slick Hollywood factory-churned-out comedies meant to cheer up people who were either in Depression breadlines, sleeping in railroad cars, or scraping through by hook or crook. Theoretically, at that time anyone could spare a dime in order to get relief by seeing a "happy" film. Frustrated and feeling he has become a Hollywood phony, Sullivan longs to make strongly stated social-message epics spelling out the truth of what really happened to Americans in a Great Depression. He takes to the road with his Hollywood entourage in a streamliner bus, but later manages to duck them and wander about the country on his own. In a beatific—"Hallelujah, I'm a bum!"—gesture, he hands money out to startled hoboes, one of whom hits him on the head, robbing him of all his money, stealing also his studio identification card, which was hidden in Sullivan's shoe. This robber-hobo is later crushed beyond recognition by an oncoming train, and hence it is reported in the nation's newspaper headlines that the beloved director of comedy—Sullivan—is dead. Meanwhile, a stunned Sullivan awakens in a state of amnesia in a railroad boxcar and is promptly arrested and taken to a prison work-farm with other indigents. While he is in prison and suffering physical brutality at the hands of several sadistic guards, it dawns on him who he really is when, by accident, he reads his own death notice in an old paper; but he is scoffed at and goes unrecognized by the guards and the other prisoners. A film shown for the prisoners turns out to be a Mickey Mouse cartoon, and Sullivan is astonished when the hard-faced, miserable, overwrought, overworked prisoners burst into raucous laughter at Mickey's antics. Through his own tears, he suddenly recognizes that laughter is one of the most important means of escape in a world filled with suffering, tragedy, and despair. Through a series of incidents he manages to escape jail, claims his true identity, reunites joyously with his peek-a-boo-bang girlfriend, Veronica Lake, and vows to make better and better comedies, inspired and reawakened by the one and only Mickey Mouse.

WILLIAM FAULKNER AND MICKEY MOUSE

Mickey Mouse gum card #93.

Unfortunately for Mickey Mouse's fans, no literary giant ever wrote a screenplay just for him alone, but one almost did. Samuel Marx, in his book *Mayer and Thalberg—The Make Believe Saints*, published by Random House in 1975, recalls the story of his first meeting with William Faulkner, who had just been hired by MGM to write screenplays. Marx asked the renowned novelist if he would work on a wrestling story for Wallace Berry. "Who's he?" asked Mr. Faulkner. After Marx explained who Beery was, Faulkner replied, "Never heard of him. I want to write for Mickey Mouse." Marx was sad to report to Faulkner that Mickey Mouse was under contract to another studio.

AN OBSTREPEROUS DUCK

As Mickey Mouse became more and more the top cartoon star at the Disney Studios, he was expected by the American movie-going public of the 1930s to behave as one. Mothers would write angry letters to Disney if the famous mouse did this or that, which would in turn cause havoc at home with the kiddies, who always emulated and imitated Mickey's actions. Mickey could no longer become an angry mouse, gritting his teeth, and had to be assigned to behave only as a good little boy-mouse who wore red shorts should. Walt Disney felt that all this "do-gooder American mouse moralizing" took some of the fun out of the character of Mickey; but, through all the pressure brought to bear by stardom, he recognized that his creation now had to be a Sparkle Plenty creature of goodwill who did not get himself into too much trouble.

As early as 1931, Disney saw that he was "trapped with the mouse," as he put it. Mickey, he said, was on a pedestal and could no longer do off-color things that might be construed as mean or hostile. The answer, as Disney saw it, was to develop new characters who could ex-

DONALD WAS MAD

Color illustration from The Adventures of Donald Duck. Grosset & Dunlap, New York, 1936.

press the rage and anger he knew the masses were feeling during a bleak Depression. "We got Pluto and the Duck," Disney has said. "The Duck could blow his top. Then I tied Pluto and Donald together. The stupid things Pluto would do, along with the Duck, gave us an outlet for our gags."

In Mickey, Disney had created a genuine American Boy Scout type of idol-icon, but it was Donald who was to encompass the more human emotional levels. Donald Duck was wholeheartedly embraced by the filmgoing public and became instantly famous for the exact traits that Mickey would sadly be stripped of. Movie crowds later would project whatever they chose onto Mickey, eventually according him the reverence usually reserved only for heroes and saints. But it was through watching Donald twisting and twirling his feathery form into a blue, white, and orange ball while he released a series of agitated, angry screaming "quacks" or shouted, "I'll getcha, you dargone #*#!#**##!! sum of a . . . !" that audiences could vicariously express their own pent-up frustrations. Donald and Mickey often got together as cartoon duck-mouse sidekicks, Donald being the perfect foil for Mickey's new-found righteousness.

Liberty magazine of May 9, 1942, had a feature article called "Donald Duck's Biggest Moments" by Howard Sharpe, in which a psychiatrist explained Donald's popularity by calling him "epically symbolical of every small frustrated man in an era of frustration." Disney explained in the same article that

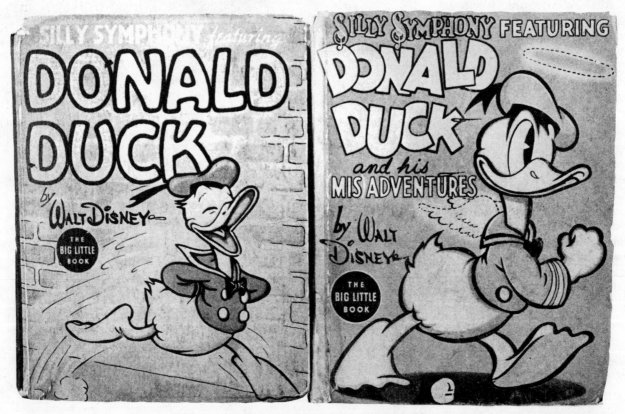

Two Big Little Books featuring Donald Duck. Whitman Publishing Company, Racine, Wisc., 1937.

"Life to Donald is just a hat with a brick underneath waiting for him to come along." Disney often liked to pooh-pooh intellectual probings into his cartoon offspring and was never at home with the idea that what he was doing was high art.

The first appearance of Donald Duck on screen was in 1934,* in *The Wise Little Hen,* and he also made a striking, squawking appearance as a loud, quacking, obstreperous duck in Mickey Mouse's first color cartoon, *The Band Concert* (1935), considered one of Disney's best by critics, featuring Mickey leading the Overture to *William Tell* and "Turkey in the Straw"—together. Donald became part of Mickey's retinue of other early Disney characters, which included Minnie Mouse; Clara Cluck, the operatic hen (the voice of Florence Gill); Goofy, originally called Dippy Dawg; Clarabelle the Cow; Horace Horsecollar; Peter Pig; and Peg Leg Pete. Donald Duck as a cartoon star almost achieved equal status with Mickey, and to some he was and is their very own favorite. Andy Warhol,** interviewed for the *New York Post* in December 1982, by twelve-year-old junior-high-school journalist, Nemo Librizzi, insisted that his favorite actor was Ronald Reagan, his favorite artist was Walt Disney, and his favorite comedian was Donald Duck. (Yet it will always be Mickey Mouse who is king of the barnyard walk.)

*The year 1984 marks Donald Duck's fiftieth birthday.

**Andy Warhol seems to have had a change of mind since the 1982 New York Post interview—at least regarding Ronald Reagan. When author Robert Heide spoke to Warhol in June 1983, Andy stated that his favorite actor is Mickey Mouse, his favorite actress is Minnie Mouse and his very own personal hero is Walt Disney. Donald Duck still remains his favorite comedian.

Painted plaster-of-Paris carnival doll figure of Donald Duck, 14", ca. 1940.

Celluloid and metal wind-up action Donald Duck toy, hand painted in Japan, 1930s.

Painted plaster-of-Paris bookend, marked "W.D. Ent. 1938."

Ceramic figurines of Donald Duck and Daisy Duck, marked "Made in Occupied Japan," 1940s.

A COMPLETE LIST OF CARTOONS STARRING DONALD DUCK

Donald Duck's first film appearance in 1934 in *The Wise Little Hen* was a cameo in a Silly Symphony. He appeared in many of Mickey Mouse's films, but his first starring role did not come until late 1937 in *Donald's Ostrich*.

1938

- *Self Control*
- *Donald's Better Self*
- *Donald's Nephews*
- *Polar Trappers*
- *Good Scouts*
- *The Fox Hunt*
- *Donald's Golf Game*

1939

- *Donald's Lucky Day*
- *Hockey Champ*
- *Donald's Cousin Gus*
- *Beach Picnic*
- *Sea Scouts*
- *Donald's Penguin*
- *The Autograph Hound*
- *Officer Duck*

1940

- *The Riveter*
- *Donald's Dog Laundry*
- *Billposters*
- *Mr. Duck Steps Out*
- *Put-Put Trouble*
- *Donald's Vacation*
- *Window Cleaners*
- *Fire Chief*

1941

- *Timber*
- *Golden Eggs*
- *A Good Time for a Dime*
- *Early to Bed*
- *Truant Officer Donald*
- *Old MacDonald Duck*
- *Donald's Camera*
- *Chef Donald*

1942

- *The Village Smithy*
- *Donald's Snow Fight*
- *Donald Gets Drafted*
- *Donald's Garden*
- *Donald's Gold Mine*
- *The Vanishing Private*
- *Sky Trooper*
- *Bellboy Donald*

1943

- *Der Fuehrer's Face* (Academy Award winner)
- *Donald's Tire Trouble*
- *Flying Jalopy*
- *Fall Out—Fall In*
- *The Old Army Game*
- *Home Defense*

1944

- *Trombone Trouble*
- *Donald Duck and the Gorilla*
- *Contrary Condor*
- *Commando Duck*
- *The Plastics Inventor*
- *Donald's Off Day*

1945

- The Clock Watcher
- The Eyes Have It
- Donald's Crime
- Duck Pimples
- No Sail (this was a co-starrer with Goofy)
- Cured Duck
- Old Sequoia

1946

- Donald's Double Trouble
- Wet Paint
- Dumbbell of the Yukon
- Lighthouse Keeping
- Frank Duck Brings 'Em Back Alive

1947

- Straight Shooters
- Sleepytime Donald
- Clown of the Jungle
- Donald's Dilemma
- Crazy With the Heat (another co-starrer with Goofy)
- Bootle Beetle
- Wide Open Spaces
- Chip 'n' Dale

1948

- Drip Dippy Donald
- Daddy Duck
- Donald's Dream Voice
- The Trial of Donald Duck
- Inferior Decorator
- Soup's On
- Three for Breakfast
- Tea for Two Hundred

1949

- Donald's Happy Birthday
- Sea Salts
- Winter Storage
- Honey Harvester
- All in a Nutshell
- The Greener Yard
- Slide, Donald, Slide
- Toy Tinkers

1950

- Lion Around
- Crazy over Daisy
- Trailer Horn
- Hook, Lion and Sinker
- Bee at the Beach
- Out on a Limb

1951

- Dude Duck
- Corn Chips
- Test Pilot Donald
- A Lucky Number
- Out of Scale
- Bee on Guard

Donald Duck soap figure, shown with the original box, Lightfoot Schultz Company, New York, 1938.

1952

- *Donald Applecore*
- *Let's Stick Together*
- *Uncle Donald's Ants*
- *Trick or Treat*

1953

- *Don's Fountain of Youth*
- *The New Neighbor*
- *Working for Peanuts* (in 3-D)
- *Canvas Back Duck*

1954

- *Spare the Rod*
- *Donald's Diary*
- *The Lone Chipmunks*
- *Dragon Around*
- *Grin and Bear It*
- *The Flying Squirrel*
- *Grand Canyonscope*

1955–1961

- *No Hunting*
- *Lake Titicaca* (from *Saludos Amigos*)
- *Blame It on the Samba* (from *Melody Time*)
- *Bearly Asleep*
- *Beezy Bear*
- *Up a Tree*
- *How to Have an Accident in the Home*
- *Donald in Mathmagic Land*
- *How to Have an Accident at Work*
- *Donald and the Wheel*
- *The Litterbug*

Plastic Donald Duck camera with the original box, made in 1947 by the Herbert George Company of Chicago. The camera uses standard 127 film.

Collectibles from early Mickey Mouse, Donald Duck, Goofy, Pluto, or Silly Symphony films include cels, original art, full-sheet posters from the films, lobby cards and stills. (Some premiums such as the Mickey Mouse paper masks or buttons were given out at movie theaters.) This type of paper memorabilia is highly sought after by collectors and is usually offered only at auction and at extremely high prices.

Of course there are great volumes of Donald Duck merchandise. Most companies that produced Mickey Mouse items also eventually included, and in many cases featured, Donald Duck, who is Walt Disney's second most famous comic character and cartoon star. The merchandise includes dolls, pull-toys, bisque figurines, rubber dolls, celluloid dolls, clocks, watches, masks, costumes, teasets, games, tin-litho toy pails, books, comics, and so forth.

Donald Duck stuffed doll, 17", manufactured in 1938 by Richard G. Krueger, Inc., New York. Collection of Robert Lesser.

Donald Duck bisque figurine with movable arms. Hand-painted and made in Japan for George Borgfeldt Corp., New York, in 1935.

Siamese twin long-billed Donald Duck toothbrush holder. Hand-painted bisque made in Japan for George Borgfeldt Corp., New York, in 1935.

Metal Donald Duck wind-up action toy that walks and opens and closes its bill. Wearing a felt sailor-suit, this desirable toy was manufactured by Schuco Co., Germany, in 1935.

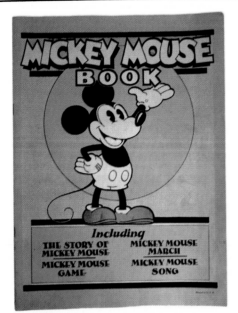

Mickey Mouse Book, featuring the first published fictional account of the origins of Mickey Mouse. Published in 1930 in New York by Bibo and Lang. This rare collectible book is fifteen pages long and is copyrighted "Walter E. Disney." Hake's Americana and Collectibles, York, Pa.

Mickey Mouse and Minnie at Macy's, one of two premium books developed by Walt Disney Studios exclusively for the Christmas season at Macy's in New York. Size 3⁵⁄₁₆″ × 3⁹⁄₁₆″, softcover, glued binding, 144 pages. Copyright 1934. Collection of Robert Lesser.

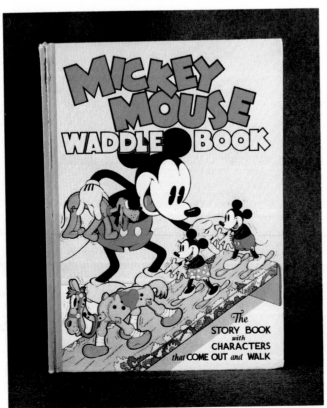

Mickey Mouse Waddle Book, published in New York in 1934 by Blue Ribbon Books, Inc. This book contains punch-out characters to be assembled and made to "waddle" down a ramp.

Mickey Mouse Weekly, volume 2, no. 99, December 25, 1937. This British magazine was created by William B. Levy. Size 11" x 15"; 450,000 copies of each issue were printed.

Topolino Pompiere (Mickey Mouse Fire Brigade), the Grandi Piccoli Libri hardcover sixty-page illustrated book, published with special permission of Walt Disney Enterprises in Italy in 1937.

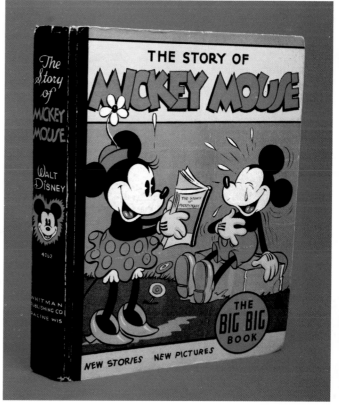

The Story of Mickey Mouse, a Big Big Book, Whitman Publishing Company of Racine, Wisc., 1935.

Volume 1, no. 1 of the third Mickey Mouse magazine and the first to be sold nationally on newsstands. June–August 1935, summer quarterly issue. Published by Hal Horne in association with Walt Disney Enterprises, licensee Kay Kamen. Size 10" x 13½", 42 pages. Cover illustration by John Stanley.

STORYBOOK MICKEY

The very first storybook featuring Mickey was *The Story of Mickey Mouse*, published in 1930 by Bibo and Lange. The story itself, written by Bobette Bibo, the eleven-year-old daughter of the publisher, tells of a strange mouse called "number thirteen." He is expelled from mouse fairyland for playing too many tricks and pranks, such as maliciously pulling the mouse king's whiskers. Thrown out into the heavens, mouse thirteen is hurled through space and eventually falls down a chimney right into the living room of lucky Walt Disney in Hollywood, U.S.A. Disney is enchanted by mouse thirteen and, after the prankster mouse tells him he just ate a wedge of old green cheese, Walt replies, "Now, let me see; green is the color of Ireland. Green, Irish, Mickey! I have it! Mickey Mouse shall be your name!" Mickey Mouse then went on to perform his mouse antics before the Hollywood cameras and, after a few successful cartoon comedies, became a full-fledged movie star. The first storybook text goes on to describe Mickey and Minnie at a big picture-show opening with stars like Clara Bow, Mary Pickford, and Buddy Rogers. This original book also features a Mickey Mouse game, a Mickey Mouse song, and a Mickey Mouse march. One illustration shows the famous mouse

Mickey Mouse Story Book, *published by David McKay Company, New York, 1931.*

Mickey Mouse, a *stand-out book* with a cardboard Mickey cut-out on the cover. *Whitman Publishing Company, Racine, Wisc., 1936.*

The Adventures of Mickey Mouse Book #1, the first of the early books to achieve large sales and distribution, was published in 1931 by the David McKay Company of Philadelphia. Disney originally had difficulty finding a publisher for Mickey Mouse, eventually landing a contract with McKay that was agreeable. This turned out to be quite profitable for all parties and caused other publishers to jump on the bandwagon. (McKay, still in business, now in New York, reissued the original book in a new cover for Mickey's birthday celebration in 1978.) In this bit of early mouse fiction, Mickey is a barnyard rodent who lives "in a cozy nest under the floor of the old barn." His girlfriend, Minnie, in a polka-dot skirt, flowered hat, and oversized pointy shoes, has a home safely hidden somewhere behind a chicken coop. A large, ferocious cat named Claws would sometimes sit for hours staring into the hole-in-the-wall entrance to Mickey's hideaway home, where the clever cat had set up baited mousetraps with cheese. Eventually it is Claws' own paw that gets snapped in the trap, to the squealing delight of Mickey and Minnie, who watch from a safe distance. Other comic characters introduced in this original barnyard tale were Clara Cluck and an extra-long-billed, squat Donald Duck. There was also a literary introduction in the form of a Silly Symphony poem, which describes Mickey playing the drums, the fiddle, the bassoon, the xylophone, the horn, and the saxophone, while Minnie pounds away on a tiny piano.

The third book on Mickey was called *Mickey Mouse Series*

crooning "My Mammy" before the cameras in the manner of Al Jolson in *The Jazz Singer,* the film that originally inspired Disney to add sound to *Steamboat Willie* in 1928. This two-color book, printed in black and green, with many nice Mickey illustrations, is a collector's gem and ranges in price, depending on condition, from $150 up to a high of $800 mint, when it can be found. For collectors, there is nothing like a "number one."

No. 1. It featured fifty-two pages of reprinted newspaper comic strips in black and white, published by McKay in 1931. Series 2 was issued in 1932; Series 3 in 1933, in color from the Sunday funnies; and Series 4, black-and-white, in 1934.

The Mickey Mouse Storybook (McKay, 1931) is the first with illustrations and an accompanying text by the staff of Walt Disney Studios, from the cartoons Traffic Troubles, The Birthday Party, Mickey Steps Out, and Fishin' Around. Walt dedicated this book to "all the little friends of Mickey Mouse throughout the world to whom he hopes to bring more happiness by coming into their homes."

The Adventures of Mickey Mouse, Book 1, published by David McKay Company, New York, 1931. Featuring the adventures of Henry Horse, Carolyn Cow, Patricia Pig, Donald Duck, Clara Cluck, and Robert Rooster, this book was reprinted with a different cover in hardback by McKay in 1978 on the occasion of Mickey Mouse's fiftieth birthday.

The Adventures of Mickey Mouse, Book 1, back cover. David McKay Company, New York, 1931.

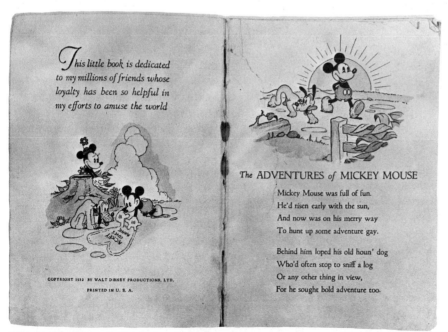

The Adventures of Mickey Mouse, Book 2, first two pages. David McKay Company, New York, 1932.

Mickey Mouse Illustrated Movie-Stories (McKay, 1932) is described in the publisher's catalogue: "This time Mickey and Minnie are in the movies. Eleven exciting scenarios. And when the pages are flipped over Mickey and Minnie dance. $1.00 never bought more fun for any child!"

The Adventures of Mickey Mouse Book #2 (McKay, 1932) features Mickey and Minnie with Pluto the Pup, in an adventure poem-story, running away from the villainous Peg Leg Pete.

Mickey Mouse Stories, *Book #2, softcover book featuring stills from 1931 Mickey Mouse cartoons. Published in 1934 by David McKay Company, New York.*

Mickey Mouse Stories Book #2 (McKay, 1934) has illustrations and text from the cartoons *Pioneer Days, The Moose Hunt, The Castaway,* and *The Delivery Boy.* These early books sold originally for 50 cents and were distributed nationwide.

Mickey Mouse Movie Stories Book #2 (McKay, 1934), copyright Walt Disney Enterprises, a beautiful hardcover book, also has illustrations and stories from twelve cartoons, including *Mickey's Good Deed, The Mail Pilot, The Klondike Kid, The Mad Doctor, Gulliver Mickey, Building a Building, Mickey's Pal Pluto, Touchdown Mickey, Mickey's Mechanical Man, Shanghai'd, Mickey's Steamroller,* and *Ye Olden Days.*

Blue Ribbon Books, Inc., New York, produced some strikingly beautiful pop-up books in 1933, including the *Pop-Up Mickey Mouse* with three splendid pop-up illustrations in full color. This pop-up series included the pop-up *Minnie Mouse Book, Mickey Mouse in King Arthur's Court,* and *Mickey Mouse Presents His Silly Symphonies—Babes in the Woods—King Neptune,* all with pop-up illustrations. The latter two books were bigger than the previous two, "novel size" rather than the smaller, thinner original storybook sizes usually associated with early Mickey Mouse books. In 1934 Blue Ribbon produced the *Mickey Mouse Waddle Book,* which had cut-outs of Mickey, Minnie, Pluto, and Mickey's horse Tanglefoot, "with characters that come out and walk!" It is rare to find this book with the Waddle characters unpunched, but it still represents a top-of-the-line collectible book, even with the cutouts missing.

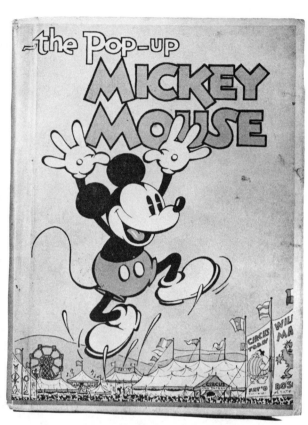

Mickey Mouse Illustrated Movie Stories,
hardcover book with 190 pages of cartoon
stills, David McKay Company, New York, 1932.
The original price of this book was $1.

The Pop-up Mickey Mouse, illustrated story
book with three pop-up pictures. Published by
Blue Ribbon Books, Inc., New York, 1933.

Mickey Mouse Movie Stories, Book 2, hardcover book with
stories and movie stills. Published in 1934 by David McKay
Company, New York.

Mickey Mouse and Pluto, *illustrated hardcover book published by Whitman Publishing Company, Racine, Wisc., 1936.*

Whitman Publishing Company of Racine, Wisconsin, published a great many books on Mickey Mouse and his pals in the early 1930s, including an abbreviated reissue of the David McKay *Mickey Mouse Series 3.* Among the most desirable as collectible Whitman books, and with the best graphic illustrations, are:

- *Mickey Mouse and Pluto the Pup*
- *The Mickey Mouse Mother Goose*
- *The Mickey Mouse Fire Brigade*
- *Mickey Mouse Has a Party— A School Reader*
- *Mickey Mouse in Numberland*
- *Mickey Has a Busy Day*
- *The Three Orphan Kittens*
- *The Wise Little Hen*
- *The Robber Kitten*
- *The Golden Touch*
- *Toby Tortoise and the Hare*
- *Walt Disney's Nursery Stories*
- *Donald Duck*
- *Clarabelle Cow*
- *Dippy the Goof*

All of these were regular or large-size books, and there were big coloring and painting books from Whitman as well, including *The Mickey Mouse Paint Book* and *The Mickey Mouse–Donald Duck Gag Book.* Many of these coloring books were published from the 1930s well into the 1940s. (In the late 1970s, special editions— ''from the 1930s original publications''—were sold again at Woolworth's, this time for 79 cents as opposed to the initial 10-cent price.)

No matter where you went in the five-and-dime stores, department stores, or children's sections of the libraries during the Depression, it seems you could find a beaming Mickey popping out at you from a book.

During the 1930s, Big Little Books also became extremely popular at the dime stores and these are among the top pop-culture collectibles today. These small books measure 3¾ inches to 4 inches wide and 4½ inches high. They are generally 300 to 450 pages in length, with the left-hand page containing the text and the right consisting of a drawing illustrating the text. They were thought of as quite a bargain at a dime in the Depression. Today these might sell, de-pending on condition, at be-tween $5 to $50, depending also on the rarity of the title. Sturdily constructed, with bright, colorful comic graphics on the thick cardboard covers, these "novel-books with illustrations" were designed to fit snugly into a child's jacket pocket, metal Mickey Mouse lunchbox or Mickey Mouse schoolbag. Depression kids looked for-ward to finding a Big Little Book under the Christmas tree, or re-ceiving one as a birthday gift or often just begged Mom to spend a dime on one at the five-and-ten-cents store. Whitman Pub-lishing Company issued over four hundred titles under the Big Little Book banner. They in-cluded Mickey Mouse, of course, and Donald Duck and

A group of Big Little Books featuring Mickey Mouse and one of Pluto. Whitman Publishing Company, Racine, Wisc. 1930s.

Little Orphan Annie, Popeye the Sailor, Dick Tracy, Smilin' Jack, Buck Rogers, Flash Gordon, Junior G-Men, Gang Busters, Green Hornet, the Shadow, the Lone Ranger, Tom Mix, Buck Jones, Red Ryder, Roy Rogers, Gene Autry, Felix the Cat, Skippy, Skeezix, Jackie Cooper, Mickey Rooney, Jane Withers, and Dickie Moore, as well as a host of other comic characters and movie personalities. Competitors in this small-size dimebook publishing marketplace were Fast Action Books from Dell and Five-Star Library and Little Big Books from Saalfield Publishing Company. In the late 1930s, Big Little Books were renamed Better Little Books. Often these were a child's first introduction to the novel form. Whitman also produced a 5-by-5½-inch series with cardboard covers similar to the Big Little Books, featuring Mickey, Minnie, Pluto, Donald, Goofy, Elmer the Elephant, and some of the other Disney characters as the main subjects of the stories. They were much shorter, under a hundred pages.

There were also Wee Little Books, measuring 3½ by 3 inches that were just thirty-eight pages long. Dated 1934, these came in a compact library of six which fit into a small cardboard shelf-container. Finding a whole set of these in an original box is a joy to book collectors. The titles for the Mickey Mouse Wee-Little Books are:

- *Mickey Mouse at the Carnival*
- *Mickey Mouse Wins the Race*
- *Mickey Mouse and Tanglefoot*
- *Mickey Mouse Will Not Quit*
- *Mickey Mouse's Misfortune*
- *Mickey Mouse's Uphill Fight*

Walt Disney's Story of Clarabelle Cow, illustrated hardcover story book published by Whitman Publishing Company, Racine, Wisc. 1938.

Whitman also produced a beautiful Big Big Book called *The Story of Mickey Mouse* (1935), measuring 9½ by 7¾ inches, with 317 pages, fully illustrated in black-and-white. The most complete and up-to-date guide for Big Little Books is *The Collector's Guide to Big Little Books and Similar Books*, written and published by Larry Lowery, P.O. Box 732, Danville, California 94526. The prices quoted for Big Little Books depend a great deal on condition but generally range from $20 to $60 for mint-condition Mickey Mouse titles. Mickey Mouse BLB #1, for instance, is listed at $75 in mint condition, but only $21 in fair condition.

Walt Disney's Story of Pluto the Pup, *Whitman Publishing Company, Racine Wisc., 1938.*

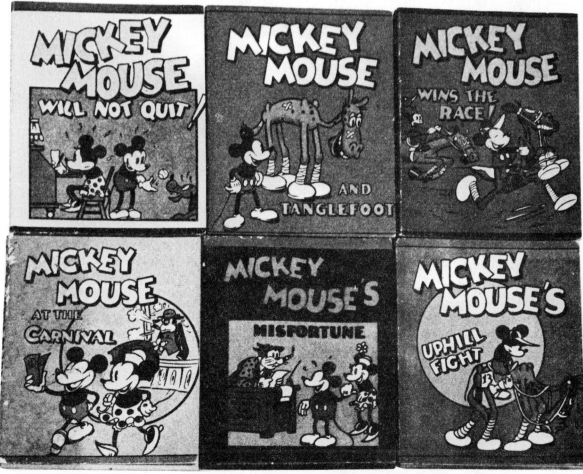

Set of six Wee Little Books, 3" × 3½", forty pages, Whitman Publishing Company, Racine, Wisc., 1934.

The Walt Disney Big Little Book series included these titles:

- *Mickey Mouse* (the first, published in 1933)
- *Mickey Mouse in Blaggard Castle* (1933)
- *Mickey Mouse Sails for Treasure Island* (1933)
- *Mickey Mouse Sails for Treasure Island* (softcover giveaway, 1933)
- *Mickey Mouse the Mail Pilot* (1933)
- *Mickey Mouse the Mail Pilot* (softcover giveaway, 1933)
- *Mickey Mouse the Detective* (1934)
- *Mickey Mouse and the Bat Bandit* (1935)
- *Mickey Mouse and the Bat Bandit* (softcover giveaway, 1935)
- *Mickey Mouse and Bobo the Elephant* (1935)
- *Mickey Mouse and the Sacred Jewel* (1936)
- *Mickey Mouse and Pluto the Racer* (1936)
- *Mickey Mouse Runs His Own Newspaper* (1937)
- *Mickey Mouse in the Race for Riches* (1938)
- *Mickey Mouse and the Pirate Submarine* (1939)
- *Mickey Mouse and the Seven Ghosts* (1940)
- *Mickey Mouse in the Foreign Legion* (1940)
- *Mickey Mouse in the Treasure Hunt* (1941)
- *Mickey Mouse on Sky Island* (1941)
- *Mickey Mouse and the Magic Lamp* (1942)
- *Mickey Mouse and the Dude Ranch Bandits* (1943)
- *Mickey Mouse on the Cave-Man Island* (1944)
- *Mickey Mouse Bell Boy Detective* (1945)

Mickey Mouse, Big Little Book #1, published in 1933 by Whitman Publishing Company, Racine, Wisc.

- *Mickey Mouse and the 'Lectro Box* (1946)
- *Mickey Mouse and the Lazy Daisy Mystery* (1947)
- *Mickey Mouse and the Desert Palace* (1948)
- *Mickey Mouse in the World of Tomorrow* (1948)
- *Mickey Mouse and the Stolen Jewels* (1949)
- *Mickey Mouse on the Haunted Island* (1950)

- *Mickey Mouse Presents Walt Disney Silly Symphony Stories* (featuring Donald Duck, Peter Pig, Benny Bird, and Bucky Bug, 1933, 1936.)
- *Silly Symphonies* (1933)
- *Silly Symphonies* (featuring Donald Duck, 1937)
- *Silly Symphony* (featuring Donald Duck and His Misadventures, 1939)

- *Donald Duck Hunting for Trouble* (1938)
- *Donald Duck Such a Life!* (1939)
- *Donald Duck Forgets to Duck* (1939)
- *Donald Duck Gets Fed Up* (1940)
- *Donald Duck Sees Stars* (1941)
- *Donald Duck Says Such Luck!* (1941)
- *Donald Duck Headed for Trouble* (1942)
- *Donald Duck Off The Beam* (1943)
- *Donald Duck Is Here Again* (1944)
- *Donald Duck Up In the Air* (1945)
- *Donald Duck and Ghost Morgan's Treasure* (1946)
- *Donald Duck and the Green Serpent* (1947)
- *Donald Duck Lays Down the Law* (1948)

- *Donald Duck and the Mystery of the Double X* (1949)
- *Donald Duck in Volcano Valley* (1949)

- *Pluto the Pup* (1938)
- *Snow White and the Seven Dwarfs* (1938)
- *Pinocchio* (1940)
- *Bambi's Children* (1941)
- *Dumbo* (1941)
- *Bambi* (1942)
- *Thumper and the Seven Dwarfs* (1944)
- *Br'er Rabbit* (1945)
- *Cinderella and the Magic Wand* (1947)
- *Br'er Rabbit* (1948)

Tall Comics from Whitman Publishing Company had one Disney title, *Mickey's Dog Pluto*, 8¼ by 3⅓ inches, with 200 pages and black-and-white illustrations, (1943).

In 1949 and 1950 Whitman issued The *New Better Little Books* in a size and length different from other Big Little Books. They measured 3⅛ by 5½ inches and included *Br'er Rabbit, Donald Duck and the Mystery of the Double X, Mickey Mouse on the Haunted Island* and *Cinderella and the Magic Wand.*

Pluto Comics, a *Tall Comic Book,* Whitman Publishing Company, Racine, Wisc., 1943.

Mickey Never Fails, *a hardcover school reader published by D. C. Heath and Company, Boston, 1939.*

Back cover illustration, D.C. Heath & Company, Boston.

In 1939 Whitman issued the Walt Disney Picture-Story Book Series adapted from films. They were given away as premiums or were sold for one penny. They include:

- *The Brave Little Tailor*
- *Donald Duck's Cousin Gus*
- *Donald Duck's Better Self*
- *Donald Duck's Lucky Day*
- *Farmyard Symphony*
- *Goofy and Wilbur*
- *Mickey Mouse's Gold Rush*
- *The Practical Pig*
- *Pluto at the Society Dog Show*
- *The Ugly Duckling*

Foreign editions of Mickey Mouse and Donald Duck Big Little Books were reproduced following World War II and distributed in Mexico, Central and South America with Spanish translations. José Carioca was featured in two of these Spanish collectibles.

Dell Publishing Company produced a series of books, somewhat larger than the Big Little Books, called Fast Action Books. The Disney Fast Actions included:

- *Mickey Mouse in The Sheriff of Nugget Gulch* (1938)
- *Mickey Mouse with Goofy and Mickey's Nephews* (1938)
- *Donald Duck* (1938)
- *Donald Duck and the Ducklings* (1938)
- *Donald Duck Out of Luck* (1940)
- *Pinocchio and Jiminy Cricket* (1940)
- *Donald Duck Takes It on the Chin* (1941)
- *Dumbo, the Flying Elephant* (1941)

Saalfield and Five-Star Library, the other big-little-book-type publishers, issued no Walt Disney titles.

Whitman published a new series of Big Little Books in full color in the 1960s, and they include:

- *Walt Disney's Donald Duck in the Fabulous Diamond Fountain* (1967)
- *Walt Disney's Goofy in Giant Trouble* (1968)
- *Walt Disney's Mickey Mouse in Adventure in Outer Space* (1968)
- *Walt Disney's Donald Duck in Luck of the Ducks* (1969)

The following reissues were published by Whitman in the 1970s and 1980s:

- *Mickey Mouse Adventures in Outer Space*
- *Goofy in Giant Trouble*
- *Donald Duck Fabulous Diamond Fountain*
- *Donald Duck in Volcano Valley*
- *Donald Duck Luck of the Ducks*

and the new titles:

- *Mickey Mouse Mystery at Disneyland*
- *Donald Duck the Lost Jungle City*
- *Mickey Mouse Mystery at Dead Man's Cove*

Another book series of note is the schoolbook-reader series published by D. C. Heath Company of Boston in hardback with color illustrations. These are:

- *Mickey Never Fails*
- *Mickey Sees the U.S.A.*
- *Donald Duck and His Friends*
- *Donald Duck and His Nephews*
- *Donald Duck Sees South America (featuring José Carioca)*
- *Little Pigs Picnic and other Stories*
- *Water Babies Circus and other Stories*
- *School Days in Disneyville*
- *Pinocchio*
- *Bambi*
- *Dumbo*
- *Here They Are*

School Days in Disneyville, by Caroline D. Emerson, published by D.C. Heath & Company, Boston, 1939.

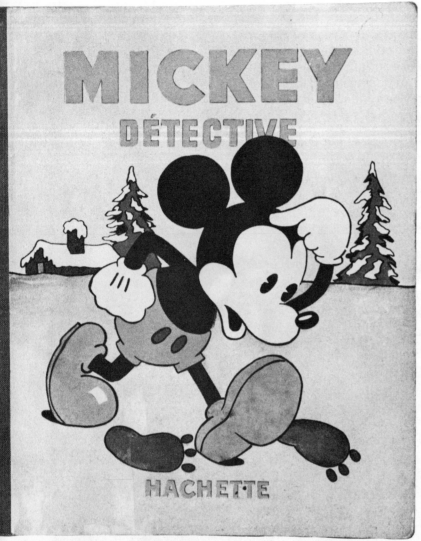

Mickey Detective, 32-page
illustrated book published in
French by Hachette, Paris, 1933.

Hand-painted, handmade wooden primitive bookend, found
in a Paris flea market and made in France.

Mickey Mouse in Giant Land, *hardcover illustrated book published by Collins' Clear-Type Press, London and Glasgow, 1934.*

This series began in the late 1930s and continued into the 1940s. An advertisement from the 1940–1941 Walt Disney merchandise catalogue read: "*Endorsed by Leading Educators*— The wholesome influence of the Walt Disney Characters has been widely recognized by educational authorities. Story Readers with colorful illustrations of these famous personalities have been adopted by school systems in every part of America. Each year large groups of children, through the pages of these books, pleasantly travel the road to knowledge, with their beloved companions daily leading the way."

Many Disney books of note, with color illustrations, came out of England, France, Italy, Canada, and other countries. Prewar foreign storybook editions are highly collectible, as those that made it through the ravages of World War II are scarce.

Over the last fifty years many hundreds of Disney books, storybooks, coloring books, and readers have been published by a number of different publishers. Early ones up through 1938 are usually copyrighted inside with a date and "Walt Disney Enterprises." After 1938 it is "Walt Disney Productions"—making it easy for collectors to spot the earlier editions.

Walt Disney collectible books are sought after not only by Mickey Mouse collectors but by general book collectors as well. Also, book collectors and dealers who specialize in children's books actively seek them out, particularly prizing books of the 1930s, which have come to symbolize a period, namely the era of the Great Depression in America, which for many collectors represents the golden age for Mickey Mouse memorabilia.

Clock Cleaners, *linen-like, sewn softcover book for young children, Whitman Publishing Company, Racine, Wisc., 1938.*

MICKEY MOUSE IN MAGAZINELAND

Mickey Mouse or Minnie Mouse, Pluto the Pup or Donald Duck on a magazine cover makes it an instant collectible. These Disney characters and others have appeared on numerous covers from the golden age of popular culture, usually with inside magazine feature articles. Movie magazines, radio and television periodicals, *Look, Life, Liberty, The Saturday Eve-ning Post, Woman's Home Companion*, and countless other national periodicals with Disney cartoon characters on the cover, or featuring articles inside, are collected assiduously by Disneyana collectors and Pop-culture enthusiasts in general.

The first magazine was produced by Kay Kamen for Walt Disney Enterprises in January 1933. This series, which started with Volume 1, No.1, ending with Volume 1, No.9 in September 1933, was intended as a give-away for movie-theater patrons watching Mickey Mouse cartoons and for shoppers in department stores as well. The magazine featured articles, jokes, stories, puzzles, games, advice and letter columns, with illustrations on most pages. This earliest magazine is a hard-to-find collectible with bright Mickey covers; it measures 7¼ by 5¼ inches.

The new 1938 model being tested by Donald, Mickey, and Goofy at the auto show, on the cover of Collier's magazine, November 6, 1937.

Hal Horne, an advertising director for United Artists, edited a second *Mickey Mouse Magazine*, very similar to the first one in style, size, and format. It was distributed nationally through the dairies, which figured that Mickey could get more kids to drink their milk. This periodical, with a space on its front and back covers to print in the name of the local dairy that distributed it, went from Volume 1, No.1, November, 1933, through Volume 2, No.12, October 1935, consisting of twenty-four issues in all.

The third and last of the Mickey Mouse magazines of the 1930s is thought of by Mickey Mouse memorabiliacs as the most artistic and desirable as a collectible. It was published by Hal Horne as a licensee of Kay Kamen, who by then was handling Disney special publishing rights. Unlike the previous two periodicals, this *Mickey Mouse Magazine* was not a giveaway and was sold at newsstands nationally. Noted for its brightly colored cover depicting a giant Mickey Mouse opening up a large storybook that shows the characters Minnie Mouse, the Three Little Pigs, Donald Duck, Horace Horsecollar, Pluto, Clarabelle, and Goofy spilling out from the pages, the first issue, in an oversized format, used the slogan "A fun book for boys and girls to read to grown-ups." This issue was produced in May 1935 and ran into economic problems immediately, due to overproduction. It was presented as a summer-quarterly issue and sold for 25 cents (a high price in the Depression-era), and Horne ordered a print-run of 300,000. As it turned out, only 150,000 were sold, and readjustments had to

be made. This beautiful 1935 *Mickey Mouse Magazine*, Volume 1, No.1, featured the story "Mickey and the Storks," a poem with illustrations all in color entitled "All Us in Blunderland"—meaning all the Disney characters—a Mickey crossword puzzle, a how-to-draw Minnie, a strange-looking Donald Duck with bright yellow feathers shining a caterpillar's dozens of pairs of shoes, and other funny comic antics; as well as beautiful full-page ads in color, one offering a free Big Little Book premium of *Mickey Mouse Sails for Treasure Island* from Kolynos dental cream; a Lionel Mickey Mouse handcar illustrated in color; and a back page of Mickey Mouse, Pluto and Horace Horsecollar as cutouts in a Post Toasties–General Foods ad that claims: "There's fun on every box!" Often the only toy a child from a poor family in the Depression might have would be a Mickey Mouse cardboard cut-out from the back of a Post Toasties or Corn Flakes box. Sometimes the backs of these boxes with pictures of the Disney characters were cut out and collected to be used as wallpaper in a nursery of a poor home. These cut-outs are among the Mickey Mouse collectibles sought after today, though it is rare indeed to find a box intact.

The *Mickey Mouse Magazine* issues that followed the first one were smaller in size (11 by 8½ inches) and sold at newsstands for 10 cents. Horne published the first nine issues; Summer 1935; October, November, December 1935; February, March, April, May, and June 1936—which was his last issue. Print-order run and distribution for these nine issues were slightly above two million

An irate quacking Donald Duck editor on the cover of Mickey Mouse magazine, May 1936.

Mickey paints a billboard of Donald on the cover of Mickey Mouse magazine, March 1938.

total, while sales were about half that. Horne lost $50,000 personally and went back to work as an associate producer at RKO. He reluctantly turned the magazine rights back to Kay Kamen. Horne, it can be said, set the stage with this excellent Disney juvenile magazine, and Kamen kept it afloat, adding new zest. The magazine sold 500,000 per month from Volume 1, No. 10 through the "transition issue," Volume 5, No. 12, September 1940, a very rare and highly collectible issue, which marked the end of the periodical. By then comics and comic books were taking the lead nationally, and in October 1940 *Walt Disney Comics and Stories* was born.

Other periodicals that are among today's collectibles include *The Official Bulletin of the Mickey Mouse Club*, which began in April 1930. Volume 1 was issued semimonthly from April 15 through December 15, 1931. Volume 2 ran from January 15, 1932, through December 15, 1932. *The Mickey Mouse Melodeon* had four issues, from November 1932 to February 1933, and was a Disney Studios house-organ periodical. *The Mickey Mouse Globe Trotter Weekly*, (size 8½ by 5 inches) had twelve issues in 1937. This was primarily a national bakery advertisement, which also issued pinback buttons of Mickey Mouse in its campaigns. "Travel Tykes Weekly" had a series of twenty issues between January and September of 1939. *The Dumbo Weekly*, with eight issues, was published and distributed by Diamond D-X Service Stations in 1941. A loose-leaf binder made to contain these is-sues was titled *The New Adventures of Walt Disney's Dumbo*, and a special button was issued in this campaign. Two armed-services periodicals, *A Dispatch from Disney* and *Mickey Mouse on the Home Front*, were both published as "one issues" in 1943.

A *Mickey Mouse Weekly*, produced by Bill Levy in London, was a huge success in 1936, with an initial print run of 400,000 copies. It increased its press run with the second issue to 450,000. The Christmas 1937 issue of *Mickey Mouse Weekly* carried the following advertisement entitled "How to Become a Mickey Mouse Chum": "All You have to do is to write your name, address and age VERY CLEARLY on a piece of paper, attach the Little Chums Token you see here, then post it off with 4d in stamps to cover the cost of packing and postage to Mickey Mouse Chums, Enrollment Department, "Mickey Mouse Weekly," 67 Long Acre, London, W.C.2." The French version of *Mickey Mouse Magazine*, beginning with Volume 1, No.1 on October 21, 1934, was called *Le Journal de Mickey*. *Topolino*, the Italian periodical, began publication in December 1932. The size of the French magazine was originally 16½ by 11¼ inches, and *Topolino* started out at 13¾ by 10 inches. Both magazines initially had a comic-strip format for the cover sheet, and are still being published—testimony to the ongoing popularity of Mickey Mouse abroad.

COMIC-BOOK MICKEY

By the end of the 1930s, comic books had invaded the newsstands, building continuously in popularity into the 1940s and 1950s. Comic-book collectors abound, and there is an intensity and voraciousness among collectors who specialize in comic books and attend comic conventions and swap meets. A yearly source book, *The Comic Book Price Guide* (published by Robert M. Overstreet, Overstreet Publications Inc., 780 Hunt Cliff Dr. N.W., Cleveland, TN 37311) lists prices and also serves as a guide for what to look for in this area of collecting.

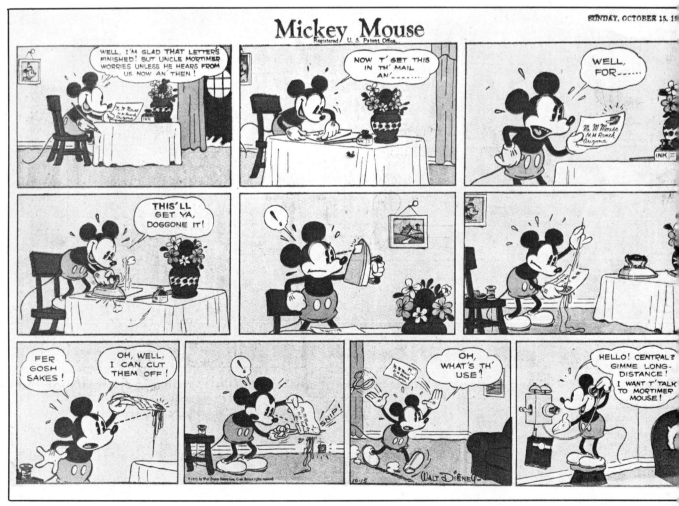

Mickey is trying unsuccessfully to mail a letter to his Uncle Mortimer in Arizona in the Sunday funnies, October 15, 1933.

Prices vary widely with comic books, just as they do with other collectibles, depending mainly on whether the condition is "pristine mint," "mint," "near mint," "very fine," "fine" "very good," "good," "fair," "poor," or "coverless." But paper products, particularly pulp paper, disintegrate rapidly over the years, and it becomes more and more difficult to find them in good condition, without tears or pencil, pen, or crayon marks. One-sheet comic strips from newspapers are also collectible. And, of course, the original art itself, black-and-white ink drawings usually done on Bristol Board "twice up" (twice the size of the printed panels), is highly prized and difficult to obtain. Certain comic books are more desirable than others—such as those featuring the first appearance of a particular character, a limited print run, or a highly regarded artist (such as Carl Barks, who drew Donald Duck, or Floyd Gottfredson, who drew Mickey Mouse), so it is wise to thoroughly investigate comic-book collecting before making an expensive purchase.

Antique dealers often overcharge for old comic books which, in reality, may be worthless. Author and collector Robert Lesser warns comic-book collectors in his book *A Celebration of Comic Art and Memorabilia* (Hawthorn Books, 1975): "Always inspect a comic book very carefully to make sure that no inside pages are missing and that the edges of all pages have not turned brown and brittle, the back cover is intact, the spine is not rolled, and the front cover is not a carefully reproduced copy."

Walt Disney Comics and Stories was first issued in October 1940. It was published monthly by Dell Publishing Company. There were 252,000 copies of Volume 1, No. 1, and by August 1942 Dell was printing 1 million copies per issue; by 1946, 2 million; by 1951, 3 million. By 1952 there were 3,115,000 copies printed per issue. In July 1962 Dell discontinued *Walt Disney Comics and*

Walt Disney's Comics and Stories, March 1947. Cover art and story inside is by renowned Donald Duck artist Carl Barks, whose name appears on the box on the cover. K.K. Publications, Inc.

Stories, but the series continued as *Gold Key Comics*. In 1941 Dell published the first Mickey Mouse comic book, *Mickey Mouse vs. the Phantom Blot*, and this comic book series is still published under the Gold Key imprint. From 1947 until 1951 *Mickey Mouse March of Comics* was printed by Kay Kamen Publications as giveaways. Mickey Mouse was featured in many comic-book series, including *Walt Disney's Christmas Parade* and *Walt Disney Showcase*, and made guest appearances in *Walt Disney's Donald Duck* comic books. The earliest and rarest Disney comics are said to be:

1. A Donald Duck book with a cardboard cover and black-and-white illustrations, published in 1938 by Whitman/K. K. Publications as a limited unnumbered offering. Prices vary widely on this book, but it is listed in the 1982–1983 price guide at $600 mint.

2. A Dell comic book #16 (1940), featuring Donald Duck in black-and-white illustrations from the Sunday newspapers. This book is listed at $1,200 mint.

3. A black-and-white comic paint book (#20), published by Dell in 1941, featuring Donald Duck. Listed at $1,600 mint.

4. A Dell four-color, *Donald Duck Finds Pirate Gold* (1942), listed at $2,200 mint.

The Dell four-color comics featuring Donald Duck and Mickey Mouse in one-shots between 1939 and 1952 are all exceptionally rare and prized comic books. Other one-shot comics in the early 1940s were *The Reluctant Dragon* (1941), *Dumbo* (1942), *Pluto* (1943), *Bambi*

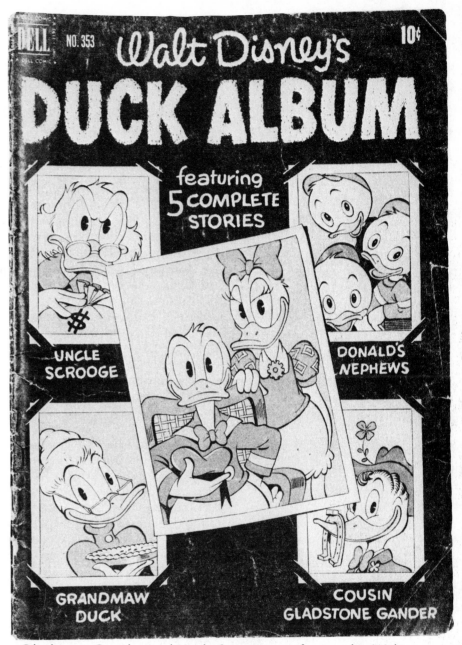

Gladstone Gander and Uncle Scrooge are featured in Walt Disney's Duck Album, *#353. Dell Publishing Company, New York, 1951.*

(1943), *Thumper* (1943), *Bambi's Children* (1944), *Snow White and the Seven Dwarfs* (1945), *The Three Caballeros* (1945), and *Pinocchio* (1945). One-shots had many reprints, and it should be remembered that the first print run is the most desirable.

The most renowned illustrator of Donald Duck comic-book art is Carl Barks, who worked at the Disney Studios, where he developed stories and helped create the drawings for the early Donald Duck cartoons. In the early 1940s Barks quit the studio to try farming, but in 1943 he was asked to illustrate a book featuring Donald in which the Duck was protecting his World War II victory garden against invading crows. So successful was this duck-venture that Barks went on to write and draw Donald Duck comic books through 1966, producing endless pages of interior art, script, and cover art. Barks also developed Uncle Scrooge, who became a wealthy uncle of Donald in his second appearance, in *Walt Disney's Donald Duck* comic book called *The Old Castle's Secret*.

If we associate someone other than Walt Disney with creating Mickey Mouse, it is Disney's early partner, Ub (sometimes called Ubbe) Iwerks, who many connoisseurs feel drew the best Mickey; but it is Floyd Gottfredson who takes the crown with the comic-book (and Big Little Book) Mickey. Carl Barks, most collectors and comic-book fans agree, was the best illustrator of Donald Duck; and his oil paintings of Donald, selling today in art galleries and at auctions for $20,000 to $40,000, attest to his artistic merit and the Duck's on-going popularity.

It should be noted here that the first Mickey Mouse comic strip appeared in the newspapers on January 13, 1930. The single-strip series was drawn by Ub Iwerks and syndicated by King Features. The *Adventure* story strip began on April 1, 1930, and is still running. In 1931 Disney offered a free "autographed" photograph of Mickey Mouse through the strip, and received requests by the thousands for this first Disney mail giveaway. The original strip featured Mickey and Minnie in a Western adventure with horse thieves and lynchings included. Mickey wore a ten-gallon sombrero-style hat and Western boots, and toted a holstered gun. At one point a reward was offered for Mickey Mouse, alias "the Cactus Kid." In this same story an Uncle Mortimer's gold mine is discussed by Mickey and Minnie with Rasmus Rat, who claims he remembers roaming the "blisterin' sands" with their old Uncle Mort. Of course it turns out that he is just trying to get the gold mine and doesn't know their Uncle Mort at all. The name Mortimer Mouse keeps recurring in Disney strips, cartoons, and stories. It is fun for collectors and mouse enthusiasts to discover obscure Disney characters turning up in odd places and situations. For instance, a Mortimer Mouse, a very sleazy ratlike city mouse-dude also is a character in *Mickey's Rival*, a 1936 Mickey Mouse cartoon, in which he battles it out with Mickey for Minnie's affections. Mickey's little mouse nephews are also called Ferdy and Morty. Remember also that Mortimer was once to have been Mickey's name when our mouse was just a gleam in his creator's eye.

MILLION DOLLAR MOUSE AT THE 5 & 10 CENT STORE

Mickey Mouse as a salesman sold $35 million worth of merchandise in 1934, as claimed by this 1935 Kay Kamen promotional broadside.

DISNEY VISITS NEW YORK IN THE GREAT DEPRESSION

Promotional broadside, published by Walt Disney's manufacturer's license representative, Kay Kamen, in 1935.

"Black Thursday," October 24, 1929, was the beginning of a five-day economic plunge downward, ending on "Black Tuesday," October 29, 1929, the day that saw the Wall Street stock market fall into collapse, closing out a decade of fool's prosperity and easy riches in America. Just around the corner, the gaunt gray specter of the decade of the Great Depression stood like a hawk in wait. The New York City that Walt Disney was visiting at this time must have seemed a wild, crazy, up-side-down place. Disney had come to the big city to visit Pat Powers, the distributor of his cartoons, to discuss a new contract after his year of dazzling success stimulated by *Steamboat Willie.* A "talkie" Mickey Mouse had put Walt Disney and his studio on the map, and Disney was beginning to see a composite picture—particularly in this New York visit—of just how much fame he and the mouse had achieved in an America in which many others were sinking under the gloom and doom of the big market crash. Pat Powers had somehow manipulated Disney's chief animator, Ub Iwerks, into signing an exclusive contract with him, and offered to give Iwerks back if Disney signed a new deal. At the same time, Powers also offered Walt more money. Remembering his un-happy legal ordeal with Os-wald, the unlucky Lucky Rabbit, at Universal Pictures, Disney de-cided to hold out for a time, fol-lowing his own instinct. Walt ul-timately did not sign on with eager-beaver Powers, and eventually Iwerks sold back his shares of Disney stock to the brothers Walt and Roy, going on to create Flip the Frog, a new Iwerks cartoon character that enjoyed some success in the days of early animation.

During this same New York visit, Disney had been followed around and pestered by a per-sistent little man who wanted to use the Mickey Mouse image on a school note tablet. After at first resisting the aggressive sales pitch, Walt finally relented when the man offered him $300 in cash. This note tablet is said to be the very first use of Mickey to merchandise a product, and it is—as anyone can imagine—a rare and desirable piece of Mickey Mouse memorabilia when it can be found.

This first Mickey Mouse writing tablet has a picture on its front cover of the grinning mouse sit-ting at his school desk, reading a history book and holding a big red apple for teacher. In bright red, white, and black the cover reads simply, "Mickey Mouse," and, in the bottom right-hand corner: " © 1930 Walter E. Dis-ney."

The interest in using Mickey in this way also piqued Disney's awareness to another area of business potential for his charmed little cartoon creature, and thus a merchant mouse was beginning to emerge.

MICKEY MOUSE—FIRST DOLLS, TOYS AND FIGURINES

A woman named Charlotte Clark, who specialized in creating and selling novelty items to toy and doll manufacturers, was so taken by seeing a Mickey Mouse cartoon that she approached a young artist friend of hers named Bob Clampett to design a stuffed Mickey Mouse doll she felt was marketable. (Bob Clampett went on to draw the very first Merrie Melodies sound cartoon for Warner's, and the first Bugs Bunny cartoon, and also created the cartoon characters Tweety and Puddy Cat.) In January 1930, a sketch was made, and a doll was created that was shown to the Disney brothers, Walt and Roy. They were delighted and immediately decided to set Charlotte up in the full-time business of making and selling Mickey Mouse soft dolls. Bob Clampett, his father, and a group of hired women under the supervision of Charlotte Clark set up a "doll house" factory close to the Disney Studios in Hollywood, where they all began to stuff and sew Mickeys. Youngsters cried for their mothers to buy them, at $5 each, when they saw them standing up in the toy sections of the big department stores across America.* These Charlotte Clark dolls helped Disney to realize even more deeply than he had before that his cartoon characters could all join in the merchandise parade.

Walt Disney is surrounded by the famous Charlotte Clark stuffed Mickey Mouse dolls in this studio photograph, taken in early 1930. The doll with the ratlike teeth, second row, right, is the English Mickey Mouse, produced by Dean's Rag Book Company, Ltd. of London.

*The May Company and Bullock's, two big department stores in Los Angeles, made a deal to sell the first Charlotte Clark dolls, paying $2.50 each—$30 a dozen—and selling them to customers at $5, which was high.

One of the very first products on the Mickey Mouse merchandise market is this cotton handkerchief from the early 1930s, featuring Minnie and Mickey engaged in various domestic activities.

Service for four, children's china tea set made in Japan for the Nifty Toy Company and distributed by George Borgfeldt Corp., New York, 1934.

George Borgfeldt & Company of New York signed a legitimate merchandising contract with Walt Disney Enterprises in 1930 to produce quality items for the marketplace, the first product being a box of Mickey–Minnie Mouse children's handkerchiefs. The first actual toy made by George Borgfeldt & Company was a wooden, jointed Mickey Mouse doll with a painted composition head and a tail made of cloth-covered electrical wire. Heavy-duty elastic held the doll together, and the head was connected by a metal hook. All parts moved, including the head, hands, arms, legs; and the doll could sit or stand. Hand-painted, it was black-and-white, with either red, yellow, or Depression–green shorts and matching shoes. The wooden doll, made in 1930 in two sizes—7½ inches and 9¼ inches—was originally designed for Borgfeldt by the Disney artist Burton Gillett. Along with the original Charlotte Clark dolls, these Borgfeldt "first" Mickey dolls are considered the most desirable among Disney collectors. George Borgfeldt & Company, whose address was 44–60 East 23rd Street in Manhattan, handled the early distribution of the Clark dolls, and by 1931 was producing its own line of stuffed velvet Mickey Mouse dolls, 6, 8½, 11, 13, 15, and 18 inches, including a Charlotte Clark–designed Minnie Mouse.

Other Borgfeldt toys from the early 1930s include a metal sparkler with a Mickey Mouse head, a series of Mickey Mouse metal cricket noisemakers, a 7-inch tin-litho Mickey animated drummer, a 13-inch metal Mickey and Minnie drum, an on-the-war-path Mickey Mouse shooting game, a felt Mickey Mouse hand doll, a Mickey Mouse teaset, a rubber sport ball, and metal-litho Mickey Mouse spinning tops. Borgfeldt also produced toy items featuring Mickey and Minnie in celluloid or bisque. Bisque figurines of Mickey, Minnie, Pluto, Horace, Goofy, and all the other Disney characters that fall under the heading of Mickey Mouse memorabilia were mass-produced in Japan for Borgfeldt, to be sold in the United States as colorful bathroom toothbrush holders; usually one arm of a comic character like Mickey Mouse formed a circle to hold a child's Mickey Mouse toothbrush. Other bisque Disney items, besides those which stood on the bathroom sink, reminding Junior to brush his teeth, included figurines, from the tiniest, such as the ones that might be found as prizes in the catch-tray of a derrick-pick-up candy machine in an amusement park penny arcade, to larger standing figures that might be a few inches in height or several more inches and up to 1 foot—all of which were to be found everywhere from the five-and-dimes to department stores to the local candy stores or ice-cream parlors, where they often were tied with bows atop color-cellophane-wrapped candy.

A celluloid Mickey Mouse doll figurine riding a wooden hobby horse with a tiny bell, made in Japan, distributed by George Borgfeldt Corp., early 1930s.

Handpainted bisque Mickey Mouse toothbrush holder, 5" high, with bisque Pluto figurine. Made in Japan in the 1930s for the George Borgfeldt Corporation.

Mickey Mouse the drummer, handpainted bisque figurine made in Japan for the U.S., 1930s.

Bisque Mickey Mouse the accordionist, Japanese knick-knack, 1930s.

A 1934 George Borgfeldt trade advertisement read: "The American public has established an amazing demand for these miniature bisque dolls of the Disney characters. Children, of course, can't get enough of them to play with and grown-ups are calling for them to be used as favors, bridge prizes, and sophisticated decorative touches for the living room, sun room, and den. Any store showing this line in several departments will re-order constantly."

Many frantic business letters were exchanged between Roy Disney and George Borgfeldt & Company, in which the brothers argued over the various problems concerning the appearance of the Borgfeldt stuffed Mickeys. The Disneys always preferred the very first dolls produced by Charlotte Clark. Since the output ability of Charlotte Clark and her small operation was limited, Roy and Walt began to look for another doll manufacturer who might see things exactly their way and who would be able to supply the increasing demand for the Mickey doll. Another solution was to offer a pattern for the Clark doll through the McCall Company of New York. The pattern—McCall Printed Pattern No. 91—became available to the public at large in America, Canada, and Europe in 1932, and instructions were printed in English, Spanish, and French. From the pattern, containing twenty-seven sections and costing 35 cents, three sizes of Mickey or Minnie Mouse dolls could be made at home—8½, 13½, and 18 inches. Suggested materials to be used were flannel or cotton. The patterns were sold from 1932 to 1939, either at sewing-center stores, the five-and-dime store, or department stores, or through *McCall's* magazine by mail-order. Seamstresses during the Depression who were in need of extra cash began to produce quantities of these dolls at home as a sideline, without Disney's authorization.

Other dolls were created on a wide scale across America as one-shot items made by housewives or grandmothers. If these "home jobs" are well made, they are as highly prized by collectors as a bona fide *manufactured* Charlotte Clark or Borgfeldt item, and are seen as authentic American primitive period pieces by dealers in Americana. Also sought-after in the Mickey Mouse doll market are dolls made by Margarete Steiff & Company, Inc., from Germany, or by Dean's Rag Book Company in England. Excellent examples of Mickey–Minnie dolls from the period, these were both imported to America by Borgfeldt Company.

Charlotte Clark, while continuing to make her own dolls on a limited scale, also designed new and beautiful dolls to be manufactured by the Knickerbocker Toy Company, which in the 1930s was located at 85 Fifth Avenue, New York. These wonderful dolls often had special costumes—such as Mickey in a clown suit, or Mickey in full cowboy regalia, complete with chaps, sombrero, kerchief, lariat, and pistols. Minnie Mouse and Donald Duck dolls were also outfitted with capes and even Mexican serapes. Some of the dolls also featured brightly painted orange or red wooden shoes, making it easier for them to stand. Knickerbocker also produced handsome wood-composition dolls. The Gund Manufacturing Company hired the spirited Charlotte Clark from the early 1940s through 1958 to design Mickey, Minnie, Donald Duck, and Pluto dolls, using a label that read: "A Charlotte Clark Creation." When Mrs. Clark passed away at the age of seventy-six on December 31, 1960, she was like a member of the Disney family. She had helped fulfill the seemingly inexhaustible demand for Mickey Mouse dolls steadily for three decades. She has been called by some the Mother of Mickey Mouse dolls.

Seiberling Latex Products Company of Akron, Ohio, with offices in New York and Chicago, produced hard-rubber molded dolls with movable heads—

Mickey the Cowboy, stuffed doll designed by Charlotte Clark for the Knickerbocker Toy Company, Inc., New York, 1936.

Two-Gun Mickey, stuffed doll designed by Charlotte Clark for Knickerbocker Toy Company, Inc., New York, 1936.

Painted composition Mickey Mouse doll with movable arms, Knickerbocker Toy Company, Inc., New York, 1936.

Painted hard-rubber Mickey Mouse and Donald Duck dolls with movable heads, made by Seiberling Latex Products Company, of Akron, Ohio, 1935.

Stuffed cotton dolls of Minnie and Mickey, 9" tall, not counting Minnie's fanciful hat, designed and made in England for Bloomingdale's Department Store in New York, by Ann Wilkinson Designs, 1980.

Mickey, Pluto, Donald Duck, as well as other Disney comic characters (notably Elmer the Elephant, the Three Little Pigs and a Big Bad Wolf, and later Snow White and the Seven Dwarfs). Softer latex hollow squeeze and whistle playpen models of Disney's characters were also produced. Usually offered in bright-colored boxes featuring the Disney comic characters on the cover, these excellent painted rubber or latex dolls were about 6 inches in height. The Seiberling dolls are carefully wrought, after their on-screen counterparts, and collectors seek the Mickey figure and other characters avidly. Many, however, are found misshapen, overly hardened by time, or distorted in shape by too much exposure to the sun.

Mickey as a plush stuffed doll continues to be manufactured today, but the quality and appearance is considered inferior to those examples that exist from the 1930s. One exception is the cloth stuffed Mickey and Minnie Mouse dolls from Anne Wilkinson Designs, produced in England and sold exclusively in 1981 at Bloomingdale's department store in New York. Measuring 9 inches, these colorful creatures certainly have the look if not the feel, of the old, and were bought up by collectors as instant Mickey collectibles of good design—for investments but probably also, and most important, just for the fun of it. A new doll with the early look of Mickey is a rarity. It should be mentioned that even the early dolls were seen as collectibles in their own time, immediately recognized by whoever owned one as something to be cherished and preserved.

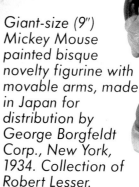

Car mascots—paint on chromium metal figural Mickey Mouse radiator caps, made in England in 1934 by Desmo Corp., sculpted by George Brown. Collection of Robert lesser.

Giant-size (9") Mickey Mouse painted bisque novelty figurine with movable arms, made in Japan for distribution by George Borgfeldt Corp., New York, 1934. Collection of Robert Lesser.

Miniature hand-painted bisque knick-knack figurines of Goofy and Horace Horsecollar, made in Japan for George Borgfeldt Corp., New York, in the mid-1930s.

Hand-painted Mickey, Minnie, and Pluto bisque figurine toothbrush holder, made in Japan and distributed to stores across America by George Borgfeldt Corp., New York, throughout the 1930s.

Stuffed dolls—a 12" Mickey Mouse and a 10" Minnie Mouse—made in the 1930s by Knickerbocker Toy Company, New York. These dolls were said to be Walt Disney's favorites. Collection of Robert Lesser.

The very first American-made Mickey Mouse painted wood doll with jointed hands, arms, legs, square shoes, and with a wire tail. Designed by early Disney artist Burton Gillett and manufactured by George Borgfeldt Corp., New York, 1930. Collection of Robert Lesser.

The second, more improved version of the first Mickey Mouse wood-jointed doll, with movable limbs, a painted composition head, available in three colors, red, yellow, and (as shown) Depression green. Manufactured by George Borgfeldt Corp., New York, in 7¼" and 9¼" sizes in 1931.

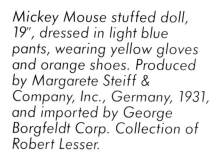

Mickey Mouse stuffed doll, 19", dressed in light blue pants, wearing yellow gloves and orange shoes. Produced by Margarete Steiff & Company, Inc., Germany, 1931, and imported by George Borgfeldt Corp. Collection of Robert Lesser.

The first Mickey Mouse stuffed doll with red pants designed by Charlotte Clark in 1930 for Walt Disney Enterprises. It is 12" high. Collection of Robert Lesser.

Painted composition Mickey Mouse carnival doll made by the Knickerbocker Toy Company, New York. Height one foot, ca. 1930. Posed in front of a reverse-painted-on-glass Art Deco post-prohibition cocktail tray.

Mickey and Minnie celluloid nursery dolls with movable arms, made in Japan in the 1930s. Collection of Robert Lesser.

Five-fingered celluloid wind-up dancing Mickey Mouse toy with metal ears pictured with original box. Made in Germany in 1931. Collection of Robert Lesser.

Mickey and Minnie band set, Mickey playing horn, Minnie with accordion and guitar. Small-sized hand-painted bisque figurines were produced in the millions in Japan for export to the U.S. in the 1930s.

Mickey Mouse slate dancer, color litho on metal animated toy made by Johann Distler, Nuremberg, Germany, ca. 1929. Collection of Robert Lesser.

Mickey Mouse metal drummer by Nifty Toys, distributed by George Borgfeldt Corporation, New York, 1931. Press lever and arms move to beat the drum. Hake's Americana and Collectibles, York, Pa.

Wind-up walker Mickey Mouse toy with grinning rat-like teeth, made for export by Johann Distler in Nuremberg, Germany, ca. 1929. Collection of Robert Lesser.

Tin litho wind-up toy featuring Minnie Mouse and a seated Felix the Cat in carriage with umbrella. Manufactured in Spain in 1929. Collection of Robert Lesser.

Rare Mickey and Minnie on a motorcycle wind-up tin litho toy, manufactured by the Tipp Company, Germany, 1928, for the English market. Collection of Robert Lesser.

Mickey the Musical Mouse—color litho on metal toy featuring Minnie and Mickey with baby carriage complete with baby Mickey playing horn, and a hurdy-gurdy Mickey, all with animated heads. Made in Germany for export in 1928. Collection of Robert Lesser.

Mickey Mouse and Felix the Cat light their cigars on sparks generated by friction of flint on sandpaper. Rare litho on metal sparkler toy made in Spain in 1929. Collection of Robert Lesser.

The first Mickey Mouse watch with chrome-plated wristband, shown with the original box, manufactured by the Ingersoll-Waterbury Clock Company, Waterbury, Conn., in 1933.

The first Mickey Mouse Ingersoll electric clock, 1933. Original price was $1.50. Collection of Robert Lesser.

One of the rarest of all the Mickey Mouse timepieces is this Art Deco wind-up desk clock, only 2" high, featuring a celluloid front-face cover. From Ingersoll, 1934. Collection of Robert Lesser.

The 1935 Mickey Mouse Ingersoll wristwatch with leather band, shown in the original box. This watch is exactly the same as the 1933 watch except for the leather wristband.

MOUSE MERCHANT

So many requests were coming in from various businesses all over the world to produce "something Mickey Mouse" or to utilize a Disney character as part of an advertising campaign that Disney found it necessary to hire someone full-time. He chose Herman (Kay) Kamen, a top-level promotional man and former hat salesman from Kansas City, to be in charge of that area of Walt Disney Enterprises which handled ancillary activities—mainly, the licensing of the use of names and images of characters on merchandise. On July 1, 1932, Kay Kamen signed a contract to represent the studio in all its merchandising deals, and to insure not only that a Disney character was represented on a quality product, but that the image of the famous mouse and his original family of friends was well drawn or developed as a toy or figurine. A Disney character also had to remain untainted in behavioral attitude; for instance, Mickey could never have anything to do with advertising cigarettes, laxatives, or alcoholic beverages, even though a Mickey Mouse ashtray is seen often in the collectibles field. Prestigious firms eagerly paid royalties of 2½ to 10 percent for a Mickey Mouse, who always cheered up a populace otherwise bogged down by Old Man Depression.

One of Kamen's first actions was to enlist United Artists Pictures Corporation to publish a forty-eight-page campaign catalogue to be mailed to fifteen thousand film exhibitors. Outlining various merchandise tie-ins with local stores or creating special lobby decorations during a Mickey Mouse or Silly Symphony movie showing, offering special premiums such as the paper Mickey and Minnie Mouse masks, balloons, booklets, or pinback buttons as giveaways were the kind of promotional gimmicks Kay Kamen was a specialist in. This 1932 campaign book led the way for the publication by Kamen of his famous Disney merchandise catalogues, numbering seven in all—1934, 1935, 1936–1937, 1938–1939, 1940–1941, 1947–1948 and 1949–1950.

A page from Kay Kamen's merchandising magazine which was sent to movie theatre managers offering box office aids, including Mickey Mouse buttons, balloons, masks, books, and magazines.

Salesman Mickey Mouse ringing up sales in this Kay Kamen promotional broadside, 1935.

Mickey Mouse comic cookies: a litho-on-cardboard hat advertising give-away for bakeries, 1933.

Mickey speeds along with a tankful of Nu-Blue Sunoco gasoline in this gas-station blotter premium given away at gas stations in 1940.

These catalogues were produced by the thousands but are difficult to obtain today and always command a respectable price from collectors, as they are excellent sourcebooks for Mickey Mouse–Disney merchandise. The first, produced in 1934, is the hardest to find, since it was sent to only twenty-five thousand film exhibitors, merchants, salesmen, and manufacturers.

Under Kamen's able leadership, merchandise sales jumped several million dollars in 1933, the worst year of the Depression. One lucrative enterprise was the deal Kamen made with the National Dairy Company, which sold ten million Mickey Mouse ice-cream cones. Cheese products were also included in this deal, and an affiliate called Southern Dairies made ice cream in a cup, featuring Mickey Mouse on the container lid. Six million cups of this product were sold in the first five weeks on the market. Eventually, in the world of food products, there appeared Mickey Mouse soda pop; Mickey Mouse bread; Mickey Mouse chocolate bars; Mickey Mouse jujubes (molded candy figures); Mickey gum; figural chocolates of Mickey, Donald, Pluto, and Minnie from the Comet Candy Company; Smith and Peters Lozenge Wafers and Hearts; Mickey Mouse butter creams; Mickey Mouse cookies and wafers from National Biscuit Company; and Mickey Mouse jam from Glaser Crandell Company. Donald Duck's image and name was also leased to sell bread, orange and grapefruit juice (still on the market), chocolate syrup, coffee, popcorn, macaroni and egg noodles, tomato juice, catsup, cocktail sauce, rice, Donald Duck Cola, and other products, including Nu-Blu Sunoco Oil (Mickey also advertised this product). The Post Toasties breakfast cereals from General Foods Corporation employed Mickey, Donald, and the ongoing parade of characters as picture cut-outs on the back of the cereal box. In the 1940s, pocket-sized thirty-two-page comic books were included in boxes of Cheerios as premiums. In 1954 Cheerios offered 3-D comic giveaways in the box, but you had to send away for the 3-D glasses. There were also Wheaties premiums featuring Mickey and his friends, none of whom ever became the super cereal salesmen that the famous 1950s cowboys, Roy Rogers, Gene Autry, Hopalong Cassidy, and the Lone Ranger were. H. J. Heinz Soup company of Pittsburgh, Pennsylvania, made "soup for kids" in 10¾ ounce cans. These "Happy Soups" included a Mickey Mouse cream of tomato soup, as well as other varieties featuring Donald Duck and Pluto.

Kay Kamen was certainly busy during the 1930s and 1940s, and a 1935 merchandising poster from Disney Enterprises attests to that, calling Mickey Mouse "the world's greatest salesman" and bragging about his ability to ring up $35 million at the sales register in one year.

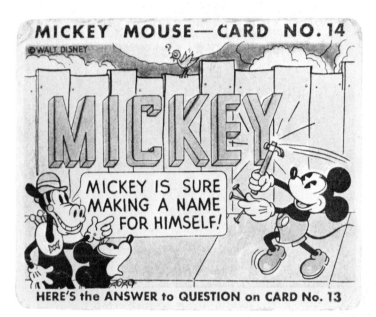

Mickey Mouse gum card #14, 1930s.

Official Mickey Mouse money, 1930s. Kay Kamen, Inc., promotional give-away for Mickey Mouse cones.

Heinz Happy Soup for kids, with noodle pictures and "fun and games inside" the label, ca. 1950.

Wherever you went in 1930s or 1940s America, be it the movies, a five-and-dime store, a department store, toy shop, dry-goods store, music shop, bookstore, grocery, soda shop, or candy store, you would find an endless variety of toys and merchandise. These featured Mickey Mouse or one of his cartoon pals, Minnie Mouse, Donald Duck, Horace Horsecollar, Clarabelle the Cow, Peter Pig, Peg Leg Pete, the Three Little Pigs—(Fiddler, Fifer, and Drummer), the Big Bad Wolf, and the Three Little Wolves. There was also Baby Mickey and Baby Minnie, Morty and Ferdy (Mickey's nephews), Huey, Dewey, and Louie (Donald's nephews), Daisy Duck, Donna Duck, Gus Goose, Gladstone Gander, Uncle Scrooge, and Gyro Geerloose (who didn't show up until the early 1950s). Other friends included Snow White and Doc, Grumpy, Bashful, Sneezy, Sleepy, Dopey, Happy (the Seven Dwarfs), Pluto the Pup, Goofy (originally called Dippy Dog, later named Dippy the Goof, and finally Goofy), Clara Cluck the operatic hen, El-

Canned products featuring Donald Duck, ca. 1950. The orange and grapefruit juices are still being marketed by Citrus World, Inc., Florida.

mer the Elephant, Dumbo, Timothy Mouse, Pinocchio, Jiminy Cricket, Cleo the fish, Figaro the cat, and the Blue Fairy. Other characters with special followings included Lampwick, Stromboli, J. Worthington Foulfellow (Honest John), the sly fox, Gideon the Cat, Monstro the Whale, Gepetto, Bambi, Faline, Thumper, Flower, Friend Owl, the Three Orphan Kittens (Fluffy, Muffy, and Tuffy), the Robber Kitten, Toby Tortoise, Miss Cottontail, the Funny Bunnies, Lucky Pup, Chip 'n' Dale, Bucky Bug, Billie Beetle, Br'er Rabbit, Br'er Fox, Br'er Bear, Polly, Pablo, and Peter Penguin, Tillie Tiger, Little Hiawatha, and Bongo. And there were many more, some less known, some popular, to be discovered as Walt Disney collectibles.

These Mickey Mouse characters of yesteryear that had so much appeal to Depression—World War II kids continue to hold the same fascination for collectors. This early merchandise is the chief Mickey Mouse memorabilia of today.

Mothers and children alike love products endorsed by Mickey Mouse, and here he works up a sweat as he brings customers into the store. Promotional broadside, Kay Kamen, 1935.

"Kids can't get enough Post Toasties when Mickey Mouse toys and games are featured on the back of the box." Cut-out from Post Toasties cereal box, General Foods, ca. 1934.

Mickey runs in terror from the Big Bad Wolf on the back of a Post Toasties cereal box, 1934.

Post Toasties cut-out of Mickey Mouse and his dog Pluto, 1933.

This first Post Toasties advertisement appeared in the Sunday funnies in 1933.

MICKEY MOUSE MEMORIES

For 30¢ Kent Dental Laboratories would send you an extra-large tube of Mickey Mouse tooth paste and an application blank for the Mickey Mouse tooth paste "Didja" contest. Advertisement from a Mickey Mouse magazine, January 1936.

Mickey Mouse milk of magnesia tooth paste in the original box. Kent Dental Laboratories, Philadelphia, 1936.

For a meatless meal, Sealtest's Sheffield Farms Milk Company offered cottage cheese in glasses featuring Walt Disney's All-Star Parade of characters. Recipe booklet dates from 1939.

Mickey and Minnie decorate an All-Star-Parade drinking glass, 1939.

BABY'S FIRST MICKEY

Babies were introduced to Mickey Mouse in the crib, with a celluloid Mickey Mouse rattle. Other toys included metal-litho spinning tops with Mickey and Minnie racing around, and Mickey pull- and push-toys. Most of these were originally from George Borgfeldt & Company. The Bryant Electric Company–Hemco Molding Division made beetleware handle mugs, plates, and cereal bowls as breakfast sets for feeding babies. A two-color-process Mickey was on each piece, and the basic colors available were green, red, and yellow. A special baby's first gift often was a silver Mickey Mouse baby spoon, a Mickey Mouse baby fork, a larger cereal spoon, or a Mickey Mouse sterling silver cup (sometimes engraved with the date of birth and the name of the infant), all from William Rogers & Son of International Silver, Meriden, Connecticut. In the early 1930s the William Rogers cereal spoon was a Post Toasties in-the-box premium. There were also Mickey Mouse rockers, with large images of "the rodent"—for baby to rock in. Seiberling Latex Products Company produced baby hot-water bottles in the shape of a baby Mickey in a nightie, inflated rubber bouncing balls for baby to play with in his pen, and latex squeeze-whistle soft dolls.

Some of the finest chinaware for infants—plates, cups, divided three-compartment plates, cereal bowls, and mugs—was produced by the Salem China Company of Salem, Ohio, featuring brilliant "in color" graphics of Mickey Mouse, Pluto, and the

Minnie is jumping for joy on this painted wooden alphabet safety block manufactured by Halsam Products Company, Chicago, 1935.

A Hallmark card, dated 1935, with Mickey Mouse's best wishes for baby on his third birthday.

The famous Mickey Mouse silverplate spoon, William Rogers Manufacturing Company, 1937.

Three Little Pigs, and always attractively packaged in stunning gift boxes.

For wee tots, the Toy Craft Company of Wooster, Ohio, made hand-painted wooden pull- and push-toys that were predecessors of the famous Fisher–Price pull-toys. Baby bibs, towels, washcloths, pillowcases, and blankets featuring imprints of Mickey and his friends were manufactured by various companies and distributed through Smith, Hogg & Company, Inc.; and Latexeen baby panties were available, made of "genuine latex," from the American Latex Corporation of New York, which claimed that "a nationwide chorus of happy babies gurgle and coo their approval"—all providing an indelible image of Mickey Mouse, which was set in a child's mind during the most impressionable period of development.

A 1935 international newspaper report stated that the very first toys given to the Dionne Quintuplets—Yvonne, Cecile, Emilie, Annette, and Marie—were celluloid Mickey Mouse baby rattles, which were the Quints' favorite playthings. These five famous babies, born on May 28, 1934, in Callander, Ontario, went on to lend their names and images to everything in the marketplace from Karo syrup to soup and margarine products, following their hero, Mickey Mouse, into the wide world of merchandising.

David Bain describes an experiment he made with his infant son Peterson, in his book *Mickey Mouse—Fifty Happy Years* (Harmony Books, 1977). He held up a movie title card from his collection, of Mickey's head, aglow with yellow sunbeams in the background, before the baby. As soon as Peterson saw Mickey's happy smiling face, he smiled gleefully and reached out to touch the mouse. Editor-author Bain suggests that parents duplicate this experiment, which, he says, will prove baby always loves Mickey Mouse.

Post-O, the new wheat cereal from General Foods, offers the Mickey Mouse silverplate spoon for only 10 cents and a box top. Advertising blotter, 1937.

Child's first utensil set, silverplate Mickey fork and Minnie spoon marked "Fairfield Silverplate" on reverse, ca. 1934.

Mickey Mouse is embossed on this child's drinking cup, sterling silver, from International Silver Company, 1934.

Child's sectional dinner plate, featuring Mickey and Pluto, manufactured by the Salem China Company, Salem, Ohio, ca. 1935.

Beetleware mug, from a child's meal-time set, which included cereal bowls and feeding dishes as well as miniature play tea sets in green, red, and yellow, manufactured by Hemco Molding Division of Bryant Electric, Bridgeport, Conn., 1935.

BACK TO SCHOOL WITH MICKEY MOUSE

Bristle hairbrush with an enameled metal band, shown with the original box; made by Hughes-Autograf Brush Company, Inc., New York, 1938.

For a school kid in the Depression who was lucky, there were many Mickey Mouse items that were cheaply priced, relating to the direct needs of attending class. These colorful Disney products helped to keep that sunny-side-up, happy disposition so necessary for a kid in hard times. Mother herself was especially fond of the Mickey Mouse family and was only too happy to reward a good child with some kind of "useful item" that featured the Disney characters—and America's manufacturers made sure that everybody got what he wanted, by fulfilling the demand!

Upon waking up and shutting off his Mickey Mouse alarm clock, a child who might also be sleeping under a Mickey Mouse blanket—as well as wearing pajamas with Mickey imprints on them—would go into the bath-

room to brush his teeth with a Mickey Mouse sterilized toothbrush from the Henry L. Hughes Company, Inc., which was held in a Mickey (or Donald Duck) bisque toothbrush holder. He could wash his hands and face with soap molded into the shape of Mickey Mouse, Pluto, Donald Duck, Peter Pig, or the Funny Bunnies (produced by the Lightfoot Schultz Company). For hair grooming there were Mickey mouse hard-rubber combs from the American Hard Rubber Company of New York and Mickey Mouse enamel-chrome-base brushes from Henry L. Hughes Company, which were always attractively boxed. Later, eating Post Toasties (with Mickey cut-outs on the back of the box) in a Mickey cereal bowl, with a Mickey spoon, the child would drink down his milk in, naturally, a Mickey Mouse glass tumbler.

Donald Duck tries walking on stilts and drawing pictures of his friends Mickey and Minnie on Martex towels, ca. 1935.

Mickey Mouse washclothes, towels, bibs, and pillowcases were made by Martex Division, Wellington Sears Company, New York, and sold and distributed exclusively by Smith Hogg & Company, Inc., with offices in Boston, New York, and Chicago.

EARLY MICKEY WEARABLES

Just after Labor Day in September, the Saturday before school was due to open, Mother took the kiddies shopping to a local dry-goods store—or a big city department store—for their back-to-school outfits. Shirts, shoes, pants, jackets, sweaters, hats, dresses, blouses, skirts, rubbers and galoshes, plus all kinds of accessories, paraphernalia—and even a few frills—were the order of the day. In the children's clothing section of most stores could be found items featuring Mickey Mouse; and any of these "soft goods" would be highly prized today by antique-clothing collectors and Disney collectors alike. Books, toys, and other similar collectibles were often saved; but a pair of socks, mittens, a sleepsuit, or a Mickey Mouse umbrella usually has been worn out or discarded long ago. However, when Mickey Mouse clothing or accessories turn up at an antiques show—and they do—it is a fun-for-all. The following is a list of clothing and other unusual items licensed by Kay Kamen for Walt Disney Enterprises in the 1930s that, if found today in good condition and bearing an original label, would be greeted with joy by any Disney collector.

Cotton fabric used on crib blankets and sheets, ca. 1934. Collection of 'Tiques of Old Bridge, N.J.

Mickey Mouse kiddie necklace, bakelite jewelry, made by Cohn & Rosenberg, Inc., New York, 1935.

1. Mickey Mouse moccasins—The Athletic Shoe Company of Chicago, Illinois.

2. Mickey Mouse rubber boots—Converse Rubber Company, Malden, Massachusetts.

3. Play togs (overall jumpsuits) with a Mickey Mouse emblem—The Crown Overall Manufacturing Company of Cincinnati, Ohio.

4. Boxed sets of handkerchiefs featuring all the Disney characters—the Herrmann Handkerchief Company, 2 Park Avenue, New York. The Borgfeldt Company also produced children's hankies (among the very first manufactured Mickey Mouse collectibles).

5. Mickey Mouse boys' belts with Mickey on the buckle and as an imprint on the leather—Hickok, Rochester, New York.

6. Children's and young misses' Mickey Mouse miniature pocketbooks—King Innovations in New York.

7. All-wool Mickey Mouse sweaters featuring Pluto with Mickey, Donald Duck with Mickey, and Mickey by himself as "Casey at the Bat"—Langer Knitting Mills of North Bergen, New Jersey. The company slogan was "Youngsters will go for them—and by youngsters, we mean *millions!*"

8. Mickey Mouse boys' ties from D. H. Neumann & Company of New York, which also offered all wool Mickey mufflers and Mickey cotton handkerchiefs. Mickey ties were also produced by Capitol Cravat Company of New York.

9. Mickey Mouse sweatshirts and polo shirts and a Donald Duck jacket—Norwich Knitting Company of Norwich, New York.

10. Mickey and Minnie hair ribbons, bands, and barrettes for young girls—Stark Bros. Ribbon Corporation.

11. Boys' Mickey Mouse caps—Charles Tobias Brothers of Cincinnati, Ohio.

12. Mickey Mouse fabric for pajamas, shirts, blouses, kerchiefs, and dresses—Cone Export and Commission Company of New York.

13. Children's umbrellas featuring Mickey, Donald, or Elmer the Elephant figurines as ornamental handles—Louis Weiss, New York.

14. Mickey Mouse costume jewelry for little girls, a mesh 1920s-style pursette, enamel-on-metal coin purses, a charm bracelet featuring all the Disney characters, rings, and slip-on metal bracelets—Cohn & Rosenberg, Inc., of 47 West 34th Street, New York. Another company, Brier Mfg. of Providence, R.I., also made plastic comic-character jewelry, rings, buttons, brooches, and bracelets, to retail for 10 cents at the five-and-dime store.

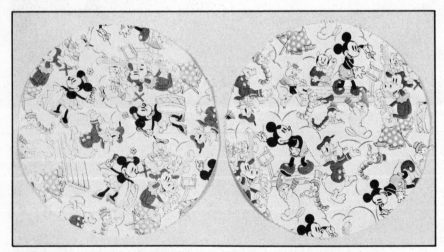

Circular sample patches of rayon fabric featuring Disney characters playing instruments, orchestrated by bandleader Mickey Mouse, ca. 1938.

Mickey Mouse lands a big fish on this rayon boys' tie from D. H. Neumann Company, New York, late 1930s.

MICKEY BACK-TO-SCHOOL PRACTICAL NECESSITIES

HAVE YOU SEEN THE MICKEY MOUSE PENCIL BOXES AT THE BIG SCHOOL SALE?

Yours truly

MICKEY MOUSE

Color litho on cardboard store and school sale stand-up advertising display piece used in conjunction with Mickey Mouse pencil boxes from Joseph Dixon Crucible Company, Jersey City, N.J., ca. 1932.

Joseph Dixon Crucible Company of Jersey City, New Jersey, manufactured a variety of Mickey Mouse pencil boxes in the 1930s, usually stamped "A Dixon Product" or "Dixon U.S.A." and "Walt Disney Enterprises." Sturdy cardboard snapshut boxes with handsome, fun-action scenes depicting Mickey and his friends at play and school, these came in one-section, two-drawer, and three-drawer sizes, and included pencils, pens, pen holder, an eraser, a Mickey Mouse ruler (itself a prized collectible today), crayons, a compass, a miniature bank, a Mickey Mouse map of the United States—"just about everything a youngster can use at a school-room desk." One Dixon series featured a two-dimensional sculptured Mickey Mouse school pencil box container, and children loved having one of these little organizers to carry to and from school. Another 1936 pencil-box set was called a "Mickey Mouse Mystery Art Set," with additional color pencils and art tools included. Dixon pencil boxes are fun to collect, are relatively reasonable in price, and have excellent graphics, making them interesting collector display items.

Mickey Mouse pencils were manufactured in 1934 by Dixon; and in 1949 Hassenfeld Brothers, Inc., of Pawtucket, Rhode Island, also made Mickey Mouse pencils, Donald Duck pencils, and Pluto pencils that sold at the five-and-ten-cents store, three

Two slim-line Mickey Mouse school pencil boxes of different design, one depicting Mickey on the radio, the other showing Mickey and Minnie in Scottish high jinx. Both from Joseph Dixon Crucible Company, Jersey City, N.J., 1936.

Mickey Mouse, Goofy, and Pluto take off for outer space a la Buck Rogers in this blue, gold, and black litho on simulated cowhide cardboard school pencilbox. Large size (9" × 5½") pencil box produced in 1936 by Joseph Dixon Crucible Company, Jersey City, N.J.

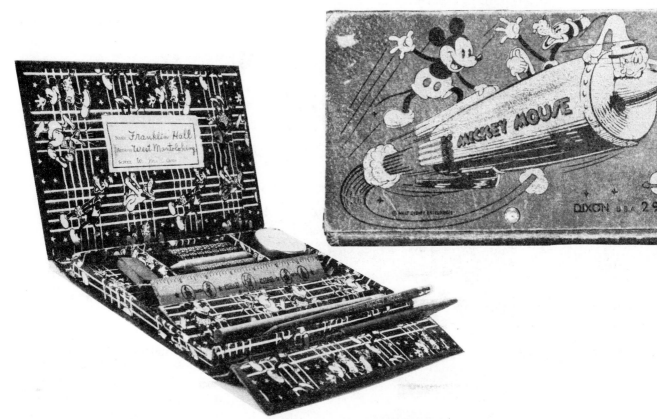

The same 1936 Mickey Mouse rocketship pencil box opened up to show the early Disney character decoration. Included in the school set is a Mickey Mouse ruler, Mickey Mouse pencils, crayons, an eraser, a pen, and a penny bank. Some pencil boxes included the hard to find Joseph Dixon Company Mickey Mouse map of the United States.

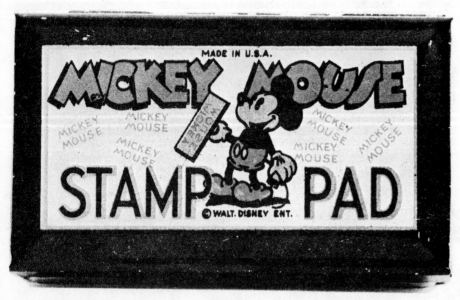

Litho on metal stamp pad box, Fulton Specialty Company, Elizabeth, N.J., 1935.

A rare enamel-embossed litho on metal top of a child's at-home study desk from 1925. This "Micky" character with the "e" left out of the name was a pre-Disney comic character, indicating that someone somewhere in play-product land had the same notion for a rodent with an Irish nickname. Colors for this 20" × 16" desk-tabletop are brown simulated wood with a nile-green Micky.

for a dime. Small yellow, green, red, or orange Catalin pencil sharpeners with bright decals of Mickey, Donald, or Minnie sold for 10 cents from Plastic Novelties, Inc., of New York. This company also produced Mickey and Donald Catalin napkin rings and continued to produce these items into the 1940s.

Companies that produced children's standing blackboards with Mickey Mouse brought into the design were the Richmond School Furniture Company of Muncie, Indiana (1930s), and the Barricks Manufacturing Company of Chicago, featuring twelve different styles (1940s).

A fortunate little schoolboy or -girl might be presented with an InkoGraph Company Ink-D-Cator fountain pen that cost $1.00 if he or she achieved high grades in penmanship. The company's slogan, "Made with the same care as the high priced pens," and the image of Mickey on the pen (sometimes with his head on the top) helped create wide sales. Today fountain-pen collectors and Disney collectors will pay a pretty penny for one of these early, back-to-school kids' fountain pens.

The Mickey Mouse lunch kit, with a metal eating tray, was the first of many, but probably one of the most beautiful children's lunchboxes ever produced. Mickey is shown on the lid, rushing to school, a book strapped to his arm and carrying his own Mickey lunch kit. The characters on the side, who appear to be marching off to a picnic, include Horace Horsecollar, Clara Cluck, Minnie Mouse, and the two mouse twins, Morty and Ferdy. Made of heavy tin plate in an oval shape, and attractively lithographed in four colors, this lunchbox is now an expensive collectors' piece that would sell in the hundreds of dollars in good condition. (Lee Garner, editor of *The Paileontologist's Report*, a newsletter devoted to the collection of lunchpails, reports that the few examples that have come to light have sold at national auction for $500. To receive the newsletter, write to Lee Garner, 3608 Chelwood NE, Albuquerque, NM 07111.) These were produced by the Geuder, Paeschke and Frey Company of Milwaukee, which also manufactured other beautiful tin and sheet-metal lithographed items "with a Mickey Mouse design," such as wastepaper containers, breadboxes, children's eating trays, metal flowerpots, cake covers, and pet-food platters.

A color litho on cardboard novelty Mickey Mouse pencil box from Joseph Dixon Crucible Company, Jersey City, N.J., 1934.

Mickey Mouse-Donald Duck crayon set in color litho on metal box, made by Transogram Company, Inc. of New York in 1946.

Mickey Mouse Has A Party, a 1940 school reader, Whitman Publishing Company, Racine, Wisc.

A Mickey Mouse Alphabet Book for youngsters and now for collectors. Whitman Publishing Company, Racine, Wisc., 1936

TRICKY MICKEY ON HALLOWEEN

Dressing up for Halloween as Mickey Mouse, Minnie Mouse, Clarabelle the Cow, Horace Horsecollar, or Donald Duck was a special "fun" event for kids in the thirties. A child would usually first be taken by his mother into Woolworth's (or one of the other dime stores), where the first order of the day was a red-hot frankfurter smeared with yellow mustard, and a glass of Hire's Root Beer from the chrome and marble-topped luncheon counter. After this 10-cent lunch, a mother and her child would head directly for the toy-counter section, which by October was filled with brilliant orange papier-mâché trick-or-treat pumpkins with demon faces that lit up, orange-and-black metal-and-wood rattles and scary-sounding horns with witches on broomsticks, owls, or skeletons emblazoned on them. Black witch costumes with green face masks always had their appeal, and after the movie *Snow White and the Seven Dwarfs* was released, there were many "wicked witches" on All Hallows Eve, as well as Snow White and all seven of her dwarfs. The Big Bad Wolf, a frightening creature, and all Three Little Pigs were also represented at the dime-store toy counter on Halloween, as fearful symbols of the Great Depression. Masks were not made of plastic, as they would be today, but of a stiffened net fabric of a cheesecloth consistency, molded into the shape of Mickey or one of the other creatures. These face masks could have an almost eerie look; they

A molded stiff-cheesecloth Mickey Mouse Halloween mask which is stamped "Wornova" inside; license from Walt Disney. Wornova Manufacturing Company, New York, 1934.

Donald Duck stiff cloth Halloween mask from the late 1930s.

Painted stiff net cloth Halloween mask of the dwarf Bashful, from Snow White and the Seven Dwarfs, 1940.

Mickey Mouse and Minnie Mouse Stiff Cloth mask; cambric waist and pants or skirt. Felt gloves. Pants or skirt have a long black rubber tail attached! Shipping wt., 12 oz.

Mickey Mouse 49 F 4502
$1.49

Minnie Mouse 49 F 4503
$1.49

Advertisement from a 1935 Sears-Roebuck catalogue offering complete Mickey and Minnie Halloween outfits.

A Grumpy lithographed paper give-away mask from Kay Kamen's Disney Character Merchandise. These masks of Snow White, the witch, all seven dwarfs, the three little pigs and the wolf, Mickey, Minnie and Pinocchio were offered as premiums through the Camay Soap Company, Gillette Razor Blade Company, and other firms in the 1930s and 1940s.

were not intended just to be cute, but to frighten and bedevil.

Whichever Disney character Dick or Jane picked out to masquerade as, you can be sure these little Mickeys or Minnies got plenty of attention at the houses and stores they trick-or-treated at. Passers-by would shout out, "Hi, Mickey! Hi, Donald! Hiya, Minnie!" or sing out in a high soprano, "Yoo hoo-oo-ooo!" after the popular song "Minnie's Yoo Hoo."

The wind blew brightly colored falling leaves everywhere as you headed home with your apples, candies, pennies, and other treasures. Going into the house, it was hard to have to take off your disguise. For a little while you had actually been—Mickey Mouse! After an exciting, spooky night like this, having supper with the family around the kitchen table as just your plain old self, and having to go to bed, did not seem like much fun at all.

These colorful Halloween cartoon character costumes were licensed by Kay Kamen to be produced by the Wornova Manufacturing Company of New York. Their suggestion to stores was "to keep an ample stock of this Disney line at all times." Mickey could also turn up—"in person"—at birthday parties and special school celebrations. The somewhat perishable cloth Mickey Mouse masks have become very desirable pieces of Mickey Mouse memorabilia. If a collector finds the entire costume—red shorts with a long tail for Mickey or a polka-dot skirt with a long tail for Minnie—so much the better, particularly if it is still in the original box. However, the mask all by itself looks very fine indeed in a deep-box frame or on display in a glass case. Often the masks are mangled or squashed, so to find one in good shape is the trick (and treat).

A costumed Mickey Mouse has since become a fixture at Disneyland and Walt Disney World, and many children who see him there shaking hands think of him not as a fantasy but as the real thing.

Movie photo still from Snow White and the Seven Dwarfs depicting Disney's Wicked Witch, who inspired many Halloween costumes in 1940.

A MICKEY MOUSE CHRISTMAS

Christmas in the 1930s was still the season to be jolly and spread joy, good fun, and holiday cheer, even though many Americans and their families were facing hard times and some were standing in breadlines, milklines, or soup kitchens, waiting to be fed. If some of the folks were singing the popular Depression hit songs like "Make Way for Kid Prosperity" or "Brother, Can You Spare a Dime?" as they dunked doughnuts into cups of coffee while staring out of the window of a diner, dreaming of a job, there was still a large percentage of middle-class families, the backbone of the American economy, who remained safe and sound in their wood, brick, or stucco homes—providing Dad could keep at work—usually struggling even then to make ends meet. If a family was poor, there was somehow, with the approach of Christmastime, always miraculously enough money in Mother's Depression budget book to buy a tree, and also to head downtown on the trolley to shop for gifts at the department stores and the five-and-dime.

Certainly the Christmas season was the time toy manufacturers pushed their products full-force ahead, and in the 1930s it was Mickey Mouse that captivated and was as much a star of the toy market as of the movies. He was everywhere to be found. Often a Mickey Mouse tin wind-up costing just a single dime was the very thing that could brighten up a child's Christmas in those dark days. Children whose parents could afford to spend more might receive a store-bought Mickey or Minnie stuffed velvet

Mickey Mouse magazine, volume 3, no. 3, December 1937. This holiday issue, published by Kay Kamen Publications, Inc., New York, depicts a Mickey Santa with a bag full of toys for children of the Depression.

THE NIGHT BEFORE CHRISTMAS
Walt Disney's friends join Santa Claus in wishing you a merry Christmas.

E. C. STASHINSKI
DISTRIBUTOR OF
○ SUNSHINE ○
BEER · ALE · PORTER
MT. CARMEL, PA. — PHONE 446
Service with a Smile

doll, or perhaps one that had been hand-sewn by an aunt or cousin from a McCall's sewing pattern. A father who could stretch a couple of dollars might give a Lionel train set to a son who was the apple of his eye—and, of course, would play train-man himself once he set it up under the tree.

During the Depression, Mickey Mouse made his first appearance of the holiday season as a gigantic inflated-rubber balloon in the Macy's Thanksgiving Day Parade, along with Santa Claus and his twelve reindeer. Mickey himself often popped up at this time on magazine covers and in the comics, wearing a Santa suit and with a white beard. For Disney and his family of cartoon characters in the 1930s—and

ever afterwards—the Christmas season was an abundant and fun time; there was plenty of yuletide joy to be spread around in the form of games, toys, dolls, puzzles, books, and other novelty Mickey Mouse items.

In 1932 Disney produced a Silly Symphony cartoon called *Santa's Workshop*, in which one of Santa's special toys was—"yes, Virginia"—a Mickey Mouse! Another Silly Symphony Christmas cartoon which brought joy to the worst year of the Depression—1933—was *The Night before Christmas*.

In 1935 R. H. Macy & Company, Inc., New York, produced a charming book in the style of a Big Little Book as a giveaway from Macy's Santa Claus.

English Mickey Mouse Christmas card made in Great Britain by Valentine & Sons, Ltd. in 1937.

A rare calendar for 1938 offers Sunshine Beer, Ale, and Porter, products not usually endorsed by Mickey Mouse or Walt Disney. The illustration for December's Silly Symphony calendar is a scene from the popular color-cartoon The Night Before Christmas (1933), showing a Disney Santa with other Silly Symphony characters.

English Christmas card opens to reveal a jubilant Minnie and Mickey, 1937.

Called *Mickey Mouse and Minnie March to Macy's*, it naturally encouraged families to do their toy shopping at the big store. The story in the book centered around the landing of the Pilgrims and "the big Thanksgiving–Christmas Parade of 1935." There were Walt Disney illustrations of Santa and his reindeer on his float, as well as cartoon renderings of the giant Mickey balloon, a giant Pluto the Pup balloon, a giant Donald Duck, and a gigantic Big Bad Wolf balloon, all floating over the crowds on Thirty-fourth Street. This 3½-by-3½-inch, 143-page book had the salutation "Merry Christmas to you from Santa Claus at Macy's—the World's Largest Store" on the back cover. This store premium is much sought after as a collectible—and, naturally, harder to find than the other Big Little Books children always received under the Christmas tree, as it was a limited giveaway. Another book, a premium developed for Macy's in 1934, entitled *Mickey Mouse and Minnie at Macy's*, is even harder to find.

When the family decorated the tree, they could light it with a set of "Mickey Mouse Lights by Noma"—or, for that matter, with "Walt Disney's Silly Symphony Lights"—both from Noma Electric Corporation of New York. Each light on the set has a bright-colored Catalin shade with decal appliqués of Mickey, Minnie, Donald, and the others acting out holiday scenes such as decorating a tree, building snowmen, sledding, or singing carols. These sets are particularly desirable collectibles due to the brightly colored cartoon graphics on the boxes, which measure 16¼ by 6¼ inches.

Mickey Mouse and Minnie March to Macy's, *published by R. H. Macy & Company, Inc., New York. This Big-Little type book was a Macy's Santa Claus give-away for children in 1935. It is a very rare collectible even when not in good condition.*

Mickey Mouse Christmas light set by Noma Electric Corporation used Mazda lamps and colorful beetleware shades with decal appliques of the Disney characters in holiday scenes. Shown with the original box, the set was sold in 1936 to add Mickey Mouse cheer to tree trimmings.

A musical decal applique used on one of the beetleware Christmas shades by the Noma Electric Corporation of New York, showing mice, duck, and dog caroling, 1936.

NEW MICKEY MOUSE CIRCUS TRAIN
With Mechanical Motor $1.79

Lionel Product

SOLD BY MAIL ONLY BY SEARS

MICKEY STOKES HIS ENGINE   DESIGNS BY WALT DISNEY

Mickey Stokes the New Commodore Vanderbilt Locomotive

30-inch train, 84 inches of track—a whole circus. Gay 20x9x11 inch high cardboard circus tent, filling station and 5-inch composition Mickey figure. Strong clockwork motor hauls this big circus train with Mickey's kingdom of animals lithographed in beautiful colors on sides of cars. **Headlight flashes, bell rings, Mickey stokes engine!** 7-inch new Commodore Vanderbilt Streamlined engine with brake; tender, circus diner, animal car and band car. Battery included. Shpg. wt., 6 lbs. 6 oz.

49 K 5103—Complete Outfit..................................**$1.79**

A Sears-Roebuck catalogue advertisement for the Mickey Mouse Lionel circus train set, selling in 1935 for $1.79.

Under the tree, Dad might have set up the tracks for the Mickey Mouse Circus Train, which featured a bright red Lionel engine, a figurine of Mickey Mouse stoking coal into the engine, a Mickey Mouse band car, a circus-dining car, and a circus-animal car made of steel and brightly lithographed with Mickey, Clarabelle, Horace, Minnie, Donald, the Pigs, and an elephant with a sad expression. This train is one of the most exceptional Mickey Mouse pieces ever produced, and it is avidly sought after by toy-train collectors as well as Mickey Mouse collectors. The complete set includes a painted compressed-wood Mickey Mouse "circus barker" figurine, and, to put in the middle of the circle of tracks, a cardboard circus tent called "The Mickey Mouse Circus," a miniature gas station, a miniature road sign featuring Mickey as a clown saying, "This way to the circus—fill up with Blue Sunoco," and a cardboard of Mickey and Minnie rushing past a sign reading TO THE CIRCUS with frantic glee. The color-litho cardboard tent also features a 999-pound hippo called "the largest girl in the world," plus Minnie riding atop an elephant.

When this set can be found at a show or in auction, it can cost thousands of dollars, depending on condition and whether or not it has the cardboard tent set up. Many frantic collectors who have the train search for the cardboard assemblage. Retail price for this set in 1935, complete, from the Lionel Corporation of New York (which had factories in the 1930s in Irvington, New Jersey), was $2.00.

Probably one of the most famous pieces from Lionel Corporation—and a very desirable Mickey Mouse collectible—is the Mickey Mouse handcar. It featured painted composition figurines of Mickey and girlpal Minnie Mouse moving up and down with a seesaw effect as it glided along on tracks under the Christmas tree. In May 1934 the Lionel Company began to manufacture these action-toy Mickey handcars to attract the 1934 Christmas holiday shoppers. The train toys were an instantaneous success, and Lionel immediately received 350,000 orders. It was able to fill only 253,000 in the first year of production, but publicly thanked Mickey Mouse for helping it out of receivership and saving the company from bankruptcy in the Depression. *Fortune* magazine also congratulated Mickey for having kept the wolf from the Lionel Company door, in its March 1935 issue; and Lionel went on with great success, continuing to produce the Mickey–Minnie handcar, which originally sold for $1.00. It also added others to the handcar line; there were an Easter Bunny handcar, a Santa Claus handcar with a small toy Mickey Mouse peering out of Santa's sack, and a popular Donald Duck-and-Pluto-in-the-Doghouse handcar—all

helping to keep American kids happy in gloomy times. Today these handcars usually sell for over $500 in good condition; and if they are still to be found in the original box, this is a plus. Hard-core toy collectors are always in search of "the original box"—which often has beautiful graphics itself—feeling that the box really completes the toy. It might also indicate that the toy was kept in good condition or—if never used—in mint condition. Some collectors, of course, can live without the box if they have the item itself on their shelves.

As the family gathered around the glimmering tree on Christmas Eve or Christmas morning, perhaps listening to a favorite radio show or Christmas carols on the phonograph, there was, as there always is, an air of excitement and anticipation, particularly in the eyes of the kiddies, all wondering what Santa brought them. The following is a special Santa Claus list of toys, games, and other items from the 1930s, all featuring Mickey Mouse or one of his friends. Any

Mickey and Minnie Mouse Take a Ride!
Sold by mail only by Sears. Wind up strong clockwork motor, release brake and away they go. Their attractively colored shaped composition bodies pump away like mad while bell rings. 9-in. metal handcar and 6 ft. of circular track. **94c**
49 K 5105—Shpg. wt..2 lbs. 7 oz. **94c**

Sears-Roebuck advertisement for the Mickey Mouse handcar from Lionel Trains. Marked down to 94 cents in the catalogue, this item originally sold for $1 in 1934.

of these would do under the tree even today, but be warned as you stalk antique shops and the "fleas"—none of these is any longer a nickel, dime, quarter, or dollar. And alas, you would no longer give them to a child to play with. They are now in the domain of adult collectors, all of whom would like to play with them—and some do. For many they are an important link to the past; to others they might be the gift to themselves that was never received in childhood. Most toy collectors, whatever their psychological motivation for collecting, also have come to recognize these items as fine art pieces, as a real aspect of the art of Walt Disney, or sometimes as bona fide Mickey Mouse art. That these things were once mass-produced does not matter, for they were manufactured under the watchful eye of Disney himself at a time when the studio was in its most creative period. The collector toys, Mickey Mouse memorabilia, games, and household items that were originally designed for children and found under a Christmas tree are listed under their manufacturers.

Red, white, and blue cardboard box for the original 1934 Lionel Trains Mickey Mouse handcar.

Aluminum Specialty Company, Manitowoc, Wisconsin
- Perco set, including a Mickey Mouse coffee pot, coffee cups, plates, and saucers;
- Baking set, including egg-beaters, measuring cups, frying pans and baking pans, rolling board and pin;
- Mickey Mouse and Minnie Mouse aluminum cookie cutter set.

Automatic Recording Safe Company, Chicago
- Savings banks.

Fisher–Price Toys, Inc., East Aurora, New York
- Mickey Mouse beating a drum, clashing cymbals; a Mickey Mouse railroad engine with ringing bell; and a Donald Duck xylophone, all made of wood with metal parts.

Fulton Specialty Company, Elizabeth, New Jersey
- Be-Your-Own-Printer set, Mickey Mouse's Print Shop, Mickey Mouse's Picture Printing Set.

N. N. Hill Brass Company, East Hampton, Connecticut
- Mickey Mouse telephone;
- Donald Duck telephone;
- Mickey-Tanglefoot pull-toy;
- Elmer the Elephant pull-toy;
- Horace Horsecollar pull-toy;
- Donald Duck and Pluto pull-toy.

Halsam Products Company, Chicago
- Mickey Mouse safety blocks came in sets with nine blocks, sixteen, twenty, and thirty blocks, beautifully packaged in colorful boxes.

Mickey Mouse Print Shop set from Fulton Specialty Company, Elizabeth, N.J., ca. 1935. Hake's Americana and Collectibles, York, Pa.

Mickey Mouse picture printing set from Fulton Specialty Company of Elizabeth, N.J., ca. 1935. Hake's Americana and Collectibles, York, Pa.

"Merry Christmas from Mickey and Minnie Mouse"—a special holiday page by Walt Disney from Delineator magazine, December 1932.

Kilgore Manufacturing Company, Westerville, Ohio

■ Mickey Mouse Bubblebuster with rubber bubblettes (in sheets), which were inserted into the Bubblebuster and made loud noises.

Marks Brothers Company, Boston, Massachusetts

■ Mickey Mouse large and small target game sets, with handguns, darts, and a wooden stand;

■ Mickey and Minnie miniature piano;

■ Mickey Mouse Bagatelle;

■ Mickey Mouse circus game;

■ Mickey Mouse cardboard soldier set-target game with rifle and corks;

■ Target game with the Big Bad Wolf, Clarabelle, the Three Little Pigs, Pluto, Minnie, and Mickey, all holding miniature targets, with rifle and corks;

■ Miniature Mickey pinball games;

■ Mickey Mouse Scatter-Ball game;

■ Mickey Mouse picture puzzles, Mickey Mouse pin-the-tail-on-Mickey, Mickey Mouse noisemakers, Mickey Mouse kite, Mickey Mouse beanbag game, Mickey Mouse squeeze toy, Mickey Mouse Roll 'em game.

The Ohio Art Company, Bryan, Ohio

■ Colorful tin lithographed toy teasets of Mickey Mouse and friends with dishes, cups and saucers, creamer, sugar bowl, teapot, and serving tray;

■ Pails, sand sifters, sand shovels, snow shovels, carpet sweepers, and a play washing-machine.

Sears-Roebuck catalogue page, 1935, featuring Marks Brothers Company of Boston, games that originally sold in the department stores and five-and-dimes in the Depression.

Sears-Roebuck advertisement for the Mickey Mouse target game, only 89 cents, from Marks Brothers Company of Boston, 1934.

The Most Popular Mickey Mouse Toys for Little Tots

You Play and They Dance
Brand new 10-in. red enameled wood piano. **$1.00** Cardboard Mickey and Minnie Mouse, famous movie characters, are so attached that they dance when the 8 accurately tuned keys are played. The Big Bad Wolf and Three Little Pigs are lithographed on the background. Shipping weight, 1 pound 14 ounces.
49 K 2421 .... **$1.00**

Mickey Mouse Baby Grand Pianos
Sold by Mail Only by Sears. Accurately tuned chime-like **98c** sounding notes. Dark oak **9-Key** hardwood case. Enameled black and white keys look like natural flats and sharps.
9-Keys, Size 10¼x7¾ In.
49 K 2423—Shpg. wt., 3 lbs. **98c**
12-Keys, Size 10⅝x10½ In.
49 K 2424—Shipping weight, 3 pounds 5 ounces.......... **$1.49**

10 Mickey Balloons
Big value. You can inflate **19c** Mickey to 8 inches tall and he has cardboard feet, too. Long ones inflate to 15 in. round shapes to about 9 in. diam. One has squawker. Shipping weight, 4 ounces.
49 K 9114
10 Balloons for....... **19c**

New Mickey Mouse Blocks
Non-poisonous Halsam enameled round cornered safety **45c** blocks. Embossed **15 Pcs.** with colorful genuine characters.
30—1¾-in. Blocks
49 K 3674—Shipping wt., 3 lbs. **89c**
15—1¾-in. Blocks
49 K 3675—Shipping wt., 1 lb. 9 oz. **45c**

Mickey Mouse Play Balls
Newest thing. Inflated rubber in colors. **10c** Design is in rubber, not just stenciled. **3-in.**
49 K 7715—4½-in. Diam.
Shpg. wt., 8 oz. **22c**
49 K 7731—6-in. Diam.
Shpg. wt., 1 lb. 5 oz. **47c**
Solid Sponge Rubber
49 K 7701—3-in. Diam.
Shpg. wt., 1 lb. 12 oz. **10c**

Brand New Mickey Mouse Band
Push it or pull it . . . and Mickey's one arm beats the metal drum; with **89c** the other he strikes the metal cymbal on Pluto's tail. It's a picnic. The cutest wood toy you've ever seen, brightly colored, 12 in. long. 16-in. Push handle.
49 K 5430—Shpg. wt., 2 lbs. 4 oz...**89c**

Watch Mickey Pop Up
Lift the receiver—Mickey jumps up big as life. Dial your number—phone rings. A big 8½-in. French type phone enameled bright red, with nickeled trim and felt base, size 6⅝ in. Green cord attached to metal receiver and mouth piece. Looks just like a regular phone. Shipping weight, 1 pound 9 ounces.
49 K 2457....... **49c**

Hear it Ring
Mickey grins at you as you dial your number and the bell rings. Nickel plated dial, mouthpiece and receiver hook; enameled metal base. Height, 8 in. Wood receiver. Shpg. wt., 14 oz.
49 K 2455....... **25c**

Mickey Mouse Tops **Easy to Spin**
Brightly lithographed Mickey, Minnie and Pluto figures. One musical chord. Just pull up bright red knob and push down.
Large 8-in. Size
49 K 2378—Shpg. wt., 1 lb. 10 oz. **47c**
Junior 6½-in. Size
49 K 2377—Shipping weight, 1 pound 2 ounces.......... **23c**

Mickey Mouse Rolling Chime
There is Mickey Mouse —big as life on top of the **29c** nickel plated bell. Lots of fun for little tots. Red enameled metal. 21 in. long, 8 in. high. Shpg. wt., 1 lb. 8 oz.
49 K 2434 .... **29c**

Assortment of children's Christmas toys that would please any collector today: Mickey Mouse pianos, balloons, safety wood blocks, play balls, pull toy, toy phone, spin top, and chime pull toy. Sears-Roebuck catalogue, 1935.

Brier Manufacturing Company, Providence, Rhode Island
- Mickey Mouse rings and pins;
- Donald Duck rings and pins;

Crown Toy Manufacturing Company, Inc., Brooklyn, New York
- Figurine coin banks of Mickey Mouse and Donald Duck.

La Mode Studios, New York
- Mickey Mouse and Donald Duck lamps and bookends, including hang-up lamps, radio-lamps, and nightlights. Shades were made by Doris Lampshades Co., Inc., of New York.

Micro-Lite Company, Inc., New York
- Infant battery lamps called Kiddie Lites, featuring Mickey Mouse and Donald Duck.

Parker Brothers, Inc., Salem, Massachusetts
- Donald Duck's Own Game.

American Toy Works, New York
- Walt Disney, Mickey Mouse Ski-Jump Target Game;
- Walt Disney Game Parade— Academy Award Winners.

Standard Toy Kraft Products Inc., Brooklyn, New York
- Mickey Mouse Movie Studio, to color and erect.

Mickey Mouse turnabout painted kitchen cookie jar, Leeds China Company, 1947. Minnie Mouse is the turnabout on the reverse side.

The Mickey Mouse wood and metal sled was manufactured by the makers of the famous Flexible Flyer, S. L. Allen & Company, Inc., Philadelphia, in 1935. It is 30" long.

Two hundred and fifty-three thousand of these metal and composition wind-up handcars were sold for $1 in 1934, saving the manufacturer, Lionel Corporation, from bankruptcy in the Depression. Measuring 7½" long, the Mickey Mouse handcar came in a box with eight sections of curved metal track to form a 27" circle.

The Santa Claus handcar (with a cute Mickey Mouse toy peering out of Santa's sack) manufactured by the Lionel Corporation of New York was on the market for Christmas 1935. Collection of Robert Lesser.

The Mickey Mouse circus train featured a red wind-up Commander Vanderbilt engine car stoked by a coal-shoveling Mickey Mouse with three brightly colored litho on metal adjoining cars, a band car, a circus car and a dining car. The set came with a painted composition Mickey Mouse circus barker figurine (shown with the original box) and a heavy cardboard tent and miniature Sunoco Service gas station. The retail price in 1935 from the Lionel Corporation was $2. Collection of Robert Lesser.

The Donald Duck railcar, shown with its original box, featured a composition Duck with a Pluto the Pup in a metal doghouse. Manufactured by Lionel Corporation in 1936.

Mickey and Minnie caught in the rain. Framed pillowcase, #98 Mickey Mouse Series, Vogue Needlecraft, 1931. Embroidered by Olga Heitke of Irvington, N. J.

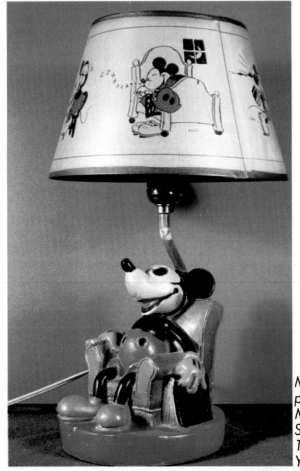

Art Deco glazed ceramic flower vase from Vernon Kiln, created by Walt Disney in 1942 to commemorate the film Fantasia. The design element features the goddess Artemis appearing in the night sky, from the "Pastoral" segment.

Mickey Mouse armchair lamp. Painted plaster of Paris with the original paper Mickey Mouse shade, manufactured by Soreng-Manegold Company of Chicago in 1936. Hake's Americana and Collectibles, York, Pa.

Snow White and the Seven Dwarfs table model radio in pressed Syroco wood; the retail price in 1938 was $14.95. Emerson Radio & Phonograph Corp., New York.

Cover of Modern Mechanix magazine, depicting Disney animation at work for the home hobbyist. January 1937.

Mickey Mouse 16-millimeter movie projector model #E-18, manufactured in 1935 by the Keystone Manufacturing Company of Boston.

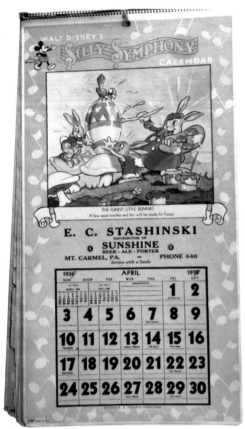

The Funny Little Bunnies are featured in April on Walt Disney's 1938 Silly Symphony advertising calendar.

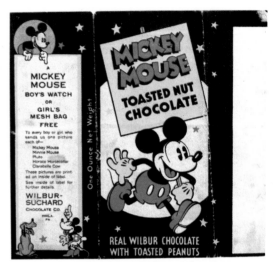

Wrapper from 5¢ Mickey Mouse Toasted Nut Chocolate Bar, made by Wilbur-Suchard Chocolate Company, Philadelphia, 1934. Children saved the handsome wrappers in order to get a Mickey Mouse watch, a Minnie Mouse mesh handbag, or other early Disney collectibles.

Chromo-litho metal advertising sign for Donald Duck bread, 1940s.

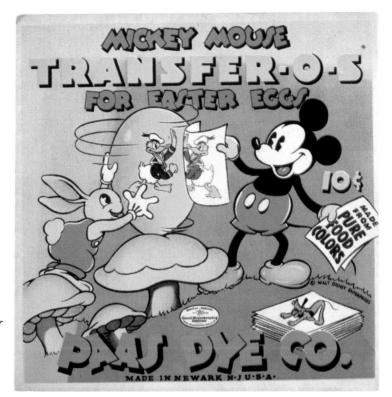

Mickey Mouse Transfer-Ons for Easter eggs. Paas Dye Company, Newark, N. J., ca. 1935.

Paper litho grocery store bread advertisement for Mickey Mouse Globetrotter's Club, ca. 1932.

Mickey Mouse cookies; 1937 lithographed store poster from National Biscuit Company featuring on the cookie box Mickey Mouse, Donald Duck, Max Hare, Pluto the Pup, and Clara Cluck.

Brayton-Laguna Pottery, Laguna Beach, California
- Ceramic figurines of Mickey Mouse, Minnie Mouse, Donald Duck, Pluto, and others.

Evan K. Shaw Pottery Company
- Figurines in ceramic of José Carioca, Panchito, Donald Duck, Pluto, Pinocchio and his friends, Dumbo, Bambi, Flower, and Thumper.

Zell Products Corporation, New York
- Leatherette and metal savings banks.

Soreng-Manegold Company, Chicago
- Disney-character lamps and shades of Mickey Mouse and Donald Duck.

U.S. Electric Manufacturing Company, New York
- Mickey Mouse flashlight.

Sun Rubber Company, Barberton, Ohio
- Rubber toys with movable wheels, featuring Mickey Mouse in a plane, in a fire engine, in a tractor and Donald Duck in a convertible.

Joseph Schneider, Inc., New York
- Speedway Cars, sold individually to make up a set, which included a game board and a phonograph machine.

Previously mentioned were paintbooks, Big Little Books, Big Big Books, Wee Little Books, coloring books, and readers from Whitman Publishing Company. (They also produced boxed paint sets, crayon sets, and games with Mickey Mouse.) Borgfeldt Company of New York (see "Mickey Mouse—First Dolls, Toys, and Figurines") also offered miniature Mickey Mouse and Minnie Mouse wood dolls, a 9-inch wood dancer Mickey Mouse, a wood Mickey squeak toy, a wood Mickey express wagon, and a wood Mickey walker. Kay Kamen giveaways, which came from his headquarters in Rockefeller Center, included, in addition to items mentioned in the "Mouse Merchant" section, a *Mickey Mouse and the Magic Carpet* book.

Mickey Mouse cardboard soldier carrying a bayonet gun. From the Mickey Mouse soldier set game from Marks Brothers Company, Boston, 1934.

The popular pin-the-tail on Mickey party game contains a linen Mickey target and linen tails. Marks Brothers Company, Boston, ca. 1935.

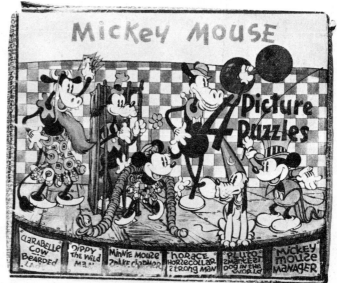

Box containing four different Mickey Mouse picture puzzles manufactured by the Einson-Freeman Publishing Corporation, New York, in 1933. Collection 'Tiques of Old Bridge, N.J.

Mickey Mouse miniature, standard deck playing cards in red, white, and blue box, produced by Whitman Publishing Company, Racine, Wisc., 1938.

Two Library of Games card sets, individually boxed and packaged in cardboard containers. Russell Manufacturing Company, Leicester, Mass., 1940s.

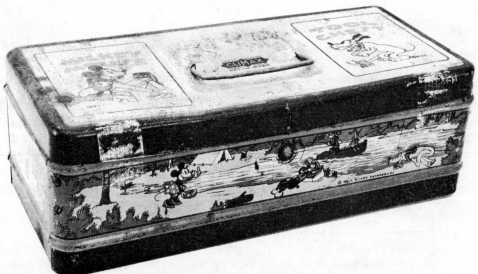

Lithographed metal Mickey Mouse tool chest came with a child-sized hammer, hatchet, screwdriver, and other tools. Hamilton Metal Products Company, Hamilton, Ohio, 1935.

The "Disney Flivver" friction car driven by an imperious Donald Duck. Litho on metal toy made in Japan for Linemar Company, Inc., 1940s.

Tin litho wiggling Mickey wind-up toy with felt ears and plastic tubular tail. Made in Japan for Linemar Company, Inc., 1940s.

Tin litho wiggling Goofy wind-up action toy, Linemar Company, Inc., 1940s.

Tin litho wind-up stretchy Pluto action toy shown with original box, Linemar Company, Inc., 1940s.

Mickey teaches his nephews about how dimes add up to dollars in this 1939 Mickey Mouse dime register bank which held $5.

MICKEY AT PLAY IN WINTER

Once Christmas and the New Year festivities are over and the heavy snows begin to fall, children traditionally, after all the holiday merrymaking, must return to the classroom; but as Old Man Winter settles in, there is also time for fun in the snow. If a child's Christmas gifts included a Mickey Mouse snowsuit from Mayfair Togs Inc. of New York, Mickey Mouse mittens, Mickey Mouse rubber boots, or a Mickey Mouse scarf, then he could romp about in style and warmth in a fully guaranteed Mickey product. For indoor fun, a child could play with his Christmas gift toys and games; for play on the frozen iceponds there were the ice skates, and, for gliding down a snowbank, a Mickey Mouse or Donald Duck sled from S. L. Allen and Company, Inc. of Philadelphia. This company boasted in its merchandise advertisements: "The makers of the famous Flexible Flyer now include a complete line of sleds incorporating the designs and names of the outstanding Walt Disney characters." The Mickey Mouse sled came in 30-inch and 32-inch sizes, and the Donald Duck model, showing Donald with Huey, Dewey, and Louie, was 36 inches long. Later a Snow White and the Seven Dwarfs model was added for bigger children—40 inches long. These snow-sleds were sturdily constructed of wood and steel and were sold in great volume in the 1930s.

Mickey or Donald often appeared on film cavorting in winter activities and sports just like any other kid, and one of the best of these Mickey wintertime cartoons is called *On Ice* (1935). In paintbooks, games, and stories, the Disney characters always seemed to enjoy winter fun—and the world enjoyed it with them.

Mickey Mouse having winter fun on ice in a 10½" × 14" Mickey Mouse Book for Coloring, Saalfield Publishing Company, Akron, Ohio, 1936.

Mickey Mouse Ski Jumping,
glass box miniature pinball
game, 4" × 6", Marks Brothers
Company, Boston, ca. 1932.

Mickey Mouse bubble gum card #77.

A MICKEY MOUSE WATCH ON GRADUATION DAY

A boy in the Depression was oftentimes required to dress for school in a shirt and tie (sometimes a Mickey Mouse tie), usually worn with knickers, high socks held up by garters, and spit-shine-polished shoes. He also wore a matching jacket and vest or a cardigan sweater with pockets. Often this natty outfit was set off by a tweed cap set atop vaseline-slicked-down hair, which was the style of the day. Growing up in the 1930s, a boy anxiously looked forward to graduation day, sometime in June, when finally he could trade in his knickers for a pair of long pants. Pants meant that he was now a young man in the eyes of the world, and no longer just Mommy and Daddy's little boy.

On graduation day it was traditional for parents to present their "grown-up" youngster with a wristwatch or pocket watch; and in the year 1933, to the surprise and delight of many graduates, the watch turned out to be the first Mickey Mouse Ingersoll. Probably the most popular use of the mouse image ever made is a Mickey Mouse comic-character watch, and the first one ever produced was made by the Ingersoll—Waterbury Clock Company of Waterbury, Connecticut, in mid-1933. Retailing at $2.98 (later, in the Sears, Roebuck catalogue, at the bargain price of $2.69), 11,000 Mickey wristwatches were sold at Macy's in New York the very first day of their release. They were packaged in bright orange cardboard boxes that featured imprints of Mickey, Minnie, Horace, Pluto, and Clarabelle run-

Advertisement on back cover of Mickey Mouse magazine, March 1938, for "new" 1938 Mickey rectangular watch from Ingersoll-Waterbury Company, Waterbury, Conn.

Sears-Roebuck catalogue offering the original Mickey wristwatch, pocketwatch, and wagging-head Mickey clock, 1935.

A five-fingered Mickey Mouse pocket watch made in England featured the first pink-faced mouse. Ingersoll Ltd., 1933. Collection of Robert Lesser.

ning around. Originally made from World War I Army surplus watches purchased cheaply from the government, Ingersoll–Waterbury's Mickey Mouse watch was another instance in which a company was saved from bankruptcy in the Depression by Mickey. After only eight weeks of production, the Mickey Mouse watch No. 1 became such a success that Ingersoll added 2,700 people to its 300-employee force. Two and one-half million of these Ingersolls were sold between June 1933 and June 1935, and by 1939 Mickey Mouse pointing out the time on a watch had become such an integral part of American mythology that one was put in a permanently sealed time capsule at the New York World's Fair (1939–1940). In 1957 Walt Disney himself was presented with the twenty-five millionth Mickey Mouse watch in special ceremonies at Disneyland.

Animated character timepieces originated over one hundred years ago in both the United States and Germany. Clocks and watches depicted boys shining shoes, women fanning themselves, dogs performing sit-up tricks, and swinging trapeze artists. The earliest dated animated clock of this kind, other than the ubiquitous German pop-out-of-the-door cuckoo clocks, was patented on September 11, 1877, by the Waterbury Clock Company, which is the very same company that later produced the first Mickey Mouse watch.

Ingersoll–Waterbury also produced, as well as the original wristwatch in 1933, a Mickey Mouse pocket watch with a fob, which sold for $1.50. Robert Lesser, author and noted Mickey Mouse collector and timepiece collector, makes the important

point to collectors that the back of this particular pocket watch must have a die-embossed figure of Mickey Mouse enclosed in two circles near the outer rim, with the legend inscribed, "Ingersoll–Mickey Mouse," to be the authentic first Mickey pocket watch. Since there are many Mickey Mouse pocket watch reproductions on the market, and since prices on comic-character pocket watches can be very high (into the hundreds of dollars), it is wise to look at the reverse side for the proper imprint if you want this one. The wristwatch has no imprint on its back, but it usually has a chromium-link wristband with two Mickey figures cut into two of the links. A rare Mickey Mouse pocket watch, sought after by collectors, is the Mickey Mouse Ingersoll Ltd. from England. There were two different styles of the English Mickey Mouse pocket watch produced, as well as an English wristwatch. These pocket watches from Great Britain *do not have the die-embossed back*, unlike the American counterpart.

Ingersoll also made two table-model clocks in 1933, a Mickey Mouse wind-up clock and a Mickey Mouse electric clock. These were made of metal spray-painted in Depression green (a gray-Nile-green color) and have a pot-bellied, pie-eyed, white-faced Mickey figure with his hands pointing to the hour and the minute. Between his legs is a round second-hand insert that has three tiny Mickey Mouse figures chasing after one another. (This design is exactly the same as the one on the Mickey Mouse No. 1 wristwatch from Ingersoll, including the three tinier Mickeys.) The clocks often have a paper band with Mickey Mouse and his family of early characters pasted on the side, although this is sometimes absent from the piece. However, not all clocks had this appliqué on them, so it is certainly not regarded as an essential element by collectors.

The original watch, the pocket watch, and the electric and wind-up clocks constitute the first four Mickey Mouse time-pieces produced by Ingersoll for sale in America, and collectors actively seek them out. There is also a very small, rare desk clock (2 inches square, circa 1934) with the same design as the wind-up clock—painted the same green—but this must have had a very short production, as few are known to exist today.

The first two Ingersoll clocks of 1933 sold extremely well and were very popular for children's rooms as well as with early Mickey Mouse enthusiast-collectors, who put them right into their dens or living rooms. By 1934, however, the Ingersoll Company discovered that it had made one important sales error in the manufacturing of these clocks—not having added alarms. So for the 1934 clock season a "wake-up alarm system" was added to the new clock. Another delightful design feature was the addition of Mickey wagging his head every second. This was the first "wagging-head" animated Mickey clock. It was manufactured round rather than square like the two previous clocks, because it was believed that shoppers preferred the round shape for an alarm clock. These watches and clocks were prominently displayed at the special Ingersoll exhibit, along with the other timepieces available from the company, at the Century of Progress World's Fair of 1933–1934 held in Chicago, where a

Advertisement from inside cover of Mickey Mouse magazine, December 1938, showing a variety of watches from Ingersoll.

special Century of Progress commemorative watch was also being offered to the public. It was reported, however, that sales of the Mickey Mouse watch at this exhibit were three times more than those of the World's Fair commemorative watch, and Ingersoll boasted at the fair that it was producing 5,000 of the Mickey watches and clocks per day to meet the increasing demand. These 1933 timepieces are all "musts" for those who collect Mickey Mouse or early watches and clocks in general.

Mickey Mouse and other Disney cartoon-character watches and clocks were manufactured from the 1930s up through the late 1960s and include the following important collector timepieces:

1. The first Mickey Mouse wristwatch from Ingersoll, dated 1933.

2. The first Mickey Mouse pocket watch, with both the fob and die-embossed back of the watch featuring an imprint of Mickey Mouse, from Ingersoll, 1933.

3. The first Mickey Mouse wind-up clock from Ingersoll, 1933.

4. The first Mickey Mouse electric clock from Ingersoll, 1933.

5. Mickey Mouse "wagging-head" alarm clock from Ingersoll, 1934. Choice of red or green case.

6. Mickey Mouse desk clock (2 inches) from Ingersoll, 1934— painted green in Art Deco case.

7. English Mickey Mouse wristwatch from Ingersoll Ltd., 1933.

8. English Mickey Mouse pocket watch No. 1 from Ingersoll Ltd., 1933.

9. English Mickey Mouse pocket watch No. 2 from Ingersoll Ltd., 1933.

10. English Mickey Mouse wind-up clock from Ingersoll Ltd., 1933.

11. English Mickey Mouse alarm clock from Ingersoll Ltd., 1933.

12. In 1934 Ingersoll produced a beautiful, bright red Three Little Pigs—Big Bad Wolf alarm clock (4⅜ inches). The hungry wolf, his animated jaws clicking open and shut with each tick of the clock, is at the center of the clock face. In a running position, the wolf is chasing the three pigs, who are also prominent on the clock face. With his furry arms pointing to the time, this ferocious character must have seemed indeed frightening to young tots. This fine collectors' piece, which now sells for over $500, is a striking example of mass-produced comic-charac-

WHO'S AFRAID OF THE BIG BAD WOLF

Big Bad Wolf Wrist Watch—$3.75 Value

With each tick of the watch the Bad Wolf's evil eye is winking at the three little pigs on a bright colored dial. Center opening metal wrist band; decorated with Bad Wolf and Little Pigs. Thin model Chromium plated case. Nonbreakable crystal. Stem wind and stem set. Made by Ingersoll. Shpg. wt., 6 oz.

Metal Band	Leather Band
4 F 952	4 F 953
$2.98	$2.98

Big Bad Wolf Watch and Fob

With each tick of the watch the Bad Wolf winks at Three Little Pigs on bright colored dial. Dangling from black leather strap is a nickel plated fob with Three Pigs in bright colors. Message from Walt Disney on back of watch. Ingersoll, thin model nickel-plated case. Unbreakable crystal. Shpg. wt., 6 oz.
4 F 1651.........**$1.39**

Big Bad Wolf Alarm Clock

Three Little Pigs Alarm Clock. Ferocious jaws of Bad Wolf open and close with each tick of the clock. Bright red case and dial; little pigs and bad wolf in lifelike colors. Genuine Ingersoll 30-hour movement model. Case 4⅜ in. high with 3⅜-in. dial. Shpg. wt., 1 lb. 8 oz.
5 F 8519.........**$1.39**

Advertisement from the Sears-Roebuck catalogue featuring Big Bad Wolf timepieces, 1935.

ter-popular-culture Pop art in itself. It originally came in a colorful cardboard display container showing the three pigs building their houses—after the 1933 Disney Silly Symphony cartoon—and written on the box was the famous phrase "Who's afraid of the big bad wolf?"

13. A Three Little Pigs—Big Bad Wolf wristwatch from Ingersoll, 1934, with similar graphics on the front face (just the wolf's head, not his body) and, on the metal band, the wolf and pigs. The Sears, Roebuck catalogue in 1934 described it this way: "With each tick of the watch the Big Bad Wolf's evil-eye is winking at the Three Little Pigs."

14. The Three Little Pigs—Big Bad Wolf pocket watch (1934) is similar in style to the wristwatch, only larger and with a black-leather strap and nickel-plated fob showing the pigs singing and playing their instruments. This pocket watch is die-embossed on the back with the message "May the Big Bad Wolf Never Come to Your Door—Walt Disney."

15. A Donald Duck No. 1 wristwatch was first produced in 1936 by Ingersoll. It featured three Mickeys from the Mickey watch on the second hand, and Mickey was also on the strap. These Donald Duck watches did not sell with the volume the Mickeys did but are considered very collectible today. Striking pocket watches featuring Donald also were produced in 1939.

16. A French Mickey Mouse alarm clock from the Bayard Company of France was produced from 1936 through 1969, with the exact same graphics and style during its entire run. This alarm clock was similar to the early "wagging-head" alarm clock of Ingersoll except

Bayard Company (made in France) Mickey Mouse wagging head wind-up alarm clock came in a bright red case. Mickey's gloves and shorts are red and his clown-sized shoes are yellow. This clock was produced continuously by Bayard without change from 1936 to 1969.

that the French "wagging-head" Mickey figure appeared to be jumping or running rather than just walking to time. Many collectors consider this imported Mickey wind-up alarm to be among the most beautiful of the Mickey timepieces, and because it was produced for so many years it is still affordable to new collectors when it turns up.

17. The Mickey Mouse lapel watch was manufactured by Ingersoll in 1937, selling for $1.50. It came in a striking royal-blue box with a figure of Mickey in red and yellow on the cover and on the inside. This watch was encased in black, and as well as Mickey on the face front, there was a full Mickey in colored enamel on the reverse side. Attached to the lapel by a cloth rope, it was meant to rest in a suit or shirt pocket, ticking its time along with the owner's heartbeat.

The 1937 lapel watch, reverse side in color enamel and watch front face both featuring Mickey. This Ingersoll product, which sold for $1.50, is a rarity today. Hake's Americana and Collectibles, York, Pa.

18. Snow White wristwatch from Ingersoll, 1940.

19. Another Donald Duck wristwatch from Ingersoll, 1947.

20. José Carioca, the South American parrot, wristwatch from Ingersoll, 1948.

21. The 1948 Ingersoll Mickey Mouse watch showed a changed mouse with a pink face, looking like a good little boy-mouse rather than a funny improdent. This rectangular watch with a red band sold for $6.95.

22. Daisy Duck wristwatch from Ingersoll, 1948.

23. Huey, one of the nephews of Donald Duck, wristwatch from Ingersoll, 1949.

24. Pluto wristwatch from Ingersoll, 1948.

25. Pinocchio wristwatch from Ingersoll, 1948.

26. Bongo the Bear wristwatch from Ingersoll, 1948.

27. Bambi wristwatch from Ingersoll, 1948.

28. Dopey wristwatch from Ingersoll, 1948.

29. Jiminy Cricket wristwatch from Ingersoll, 1948.

30. Cinderella wristwatch from Ingersoll, 1950.

31. Alice In Wonderland wristwatch from Ingersoll, 1950.

32. Pinocchio alarm clock produced in France by Bayard, 1969.

33. A beautiful Snow White—*Blanche Neige*—alarm clock was also produced by Bayard Company of France, with an animated bluebird on Snow White's hand, all seven Dwarfs, and two small redbirds on each clock hand, 1969.

34. A Pluto alarm clock from Bayard of France, 1969.

35. Ingersoll produced alarm clocks from 1947 to 1949 with a pink-faced Mickey, in ivory-white plastic cases and with luminous hands that are attractive but certainly not with the appeal we see in the 1930s timepieces. By the late 1940s Mickey seems loosely drawn, with egg-shaped eyes, droopy drawers for shorts, and a half-smirk replacing the wide grin of the mischievous rodent mouse-collectors hold so dear to their hearts.

The beautiful Blanche Neige alarm clock from Bayard Company of France. This clock, with an animated bluebird and two red birds on the clock's hands, was produced in 1969.

Mickey Mouse wristwatches continue to be produced by companies like Bradley Time (a division of Elgin National Industries), some featuring a more mousy Mickey. These, as well as a Minnie Mouse watch, have sold extremely well throughout the years. Timex produced a large-sized, very attractive water-resistant Mickey Mouse watch with Mickey having a flesh-colored orange face that is similar to the 1940s Mickey on Ingersoll; and these watches from the late 1960s and early 1970s, are collectible today. A 1970 "electric" Timex Mickey Mouse wristwatch is now a hard-to-find rarity, as it had a very limited run of a few months. What sold for $20 in 1970 is valued at ten times more today. A jeweler named Charles Weutweiler of Austin, Texas, adds 14-carat gold and thirty-six diamond studs to this watch and sells it for $12,500. For this price you also get improved internal movements. Japan has produced some digital animated Mickey watches that collectors prize as new instant collectibles. In conjunction with the Walt Disney Studios fiftieth-anniversary celebration in 1973, there were a Mickey Mouse bubble wristwatch and bubble pendant watch selling for $16.00, and a Mickey Mouse travel alarm clock for $10.75. In 1978, Mickey's fiftieth year, Bradley Company issued a Limited Edition Mickey Mouse Birthday Watch in three different sizes: a child's small size, a square adult medium size with imitation alligator band, and a round adult size— all for $19.95 each.

There is little doubt that the original "collectible" watches and clocks were cheaply manufactured, and to repair one today

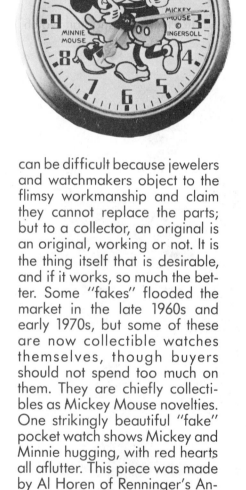

One-of-a-kind love mice "Mickey-Minnie" pocketwatch. This beautiful and unique timepiece was made originally by artist Al Horen as a production model in the 1960s, for the "nostalgia" marketplace. Unfortunately, it was never mass-produced.

can be difficult because jewelers and watchmakers object to the flimsy workmanship and claim they cannot replace the parts; but to a collector, an original is an original, working or not. It is the thing itself that is desirable, and if it works, so much the better. Some "fakes" flooded the market in the late 1960s and early 1970s, but some of these are now collectible watches themselves, though buyers should not spend too much on them. They are chiefly collectibles as Mickey Mouse novelties. One strikingly beautiful "fake" pocket watch shows Mickey and Minnie hugging, with red hearts all aflutter. This piece was made by Al Horen of Renninger's Antique Market in Adamstown, Pennsylvania, and one was sold at a California Parke Bernet auction. These watches are fun novelty pieces to add to any collection, but one timepiece usually abhorred by serious collectors or students of Pop culture and the Disney Studios is an animated pornographic Mickey watch, manufactured illegally.

Other comic characters followed Mickey and his gang into watch- and clockland. Some were popular, but none rivaled the *Mickey Mouse* watch, which has become a symbol of America itself. These other comic-character timepieces include Popeye the Sailor, Buck Rogers, Orphan Annie, Dick Tracy, Superman, Captain Marvel, Porky Pig, Felix the Cat, Bugs Bunny, Flash Gordon, Smitty, Betty Boop, Joe Palooka, Woody Woodpecker, and Smokey Stover. Western wristwatches featuring Tom Mix, the Lone Ranger, Roy Rogers, Dale Evans, Hopalong Cassidy, Gene Autry, and Howdy Doody were popular, particularly in the 1950s.

A *Mickey Mouse* wristwatch, whether a graduation present or given at any other time of the year, was the favorite—and it still is with collectors, celebrities, and practically anybody living in the twentieth century.

Sears-Roebuck catalogue offers a Mickey Mouse original wristwatch in the box for $2.69 in 1936. Any buyers?

MICKEY'S SUMMER FUN

Summer vacation was another spectacular time for Mickey Mouse, his friends, and all the kids who loved to play outdoors, go on picnics, or head out with the family to the beaches. Mickey would drive off for summer excursions with Minnie and the nephews, Morty and Ferdy, in his little Mickey Mouse car, which had a streamlined aerodynamic trailer attachment. Of course, a summer day with this mouse family could involve a lot of crazy situations, antics, and pranks, particularly if Donald Duck and *his* nephews turned up at the same spot on the beach.

More Post Toasties fun. Mickey at summer play throws a mean curve.

Mickey at the bat, a litho cardboard cut-out toy from the back of a 1930s Post Toasties cereal box, General Foods Corp.

Mickey Mouse beach postcard from England has Mickey on summer vacation emptying his pockets to show that he has spent all his shillings. Valentine & Sons Ltd., Dundee and London, late 1930s.

THIS IS ME——BY THE SEA.

WE'RE BRINGING HOME THE ROCK!

Postcard from Great Britain featuring Mickey and Donald carrying a giant saltwater taffy near what appear to be the White Cliffs of Dover. Valentine & Sons Ltd., Dundee and London, 1930s.

Some of the collectibles that relate to summertime fun include the brightly lithographed metal pails, usually featuring action-at-the-beach scenes, showing Mickey and Minnie playing ball, Mickey splashing Clarabelle, Mickey and Minnie squirting a dumbfounded Horace Horsecollar, Donald Duck fishing, or Goofy selling ice cream. Many beautiful color-litho-on-metal sandpails, sand sifters, waterpump toys, and sand shovels were produced by the Ohio Art Company, which originally sold them in a sand set. In the 1930s a pail, a watering can, and a shovel sold for 10 cents to 50 cents, a sieve for 10 cents, and pails and shovels for 5 cents to 25 cents. An Ohio Art Company advertisement from the 1930s read: "Make sales while the sun shines. Sand kits in attractive display boxes, sand sieve sets and sand pails, various sizes with shovels, make strong appeal to all children—especially when decorated with scenes and characters from Disney motion pictures. All gaily lithographed on metal."

Mickey Mouse serenades Minnie and Pluto on this tin litho child's watering can. Ohio Art Company, Bryan, Ohio, 1933.

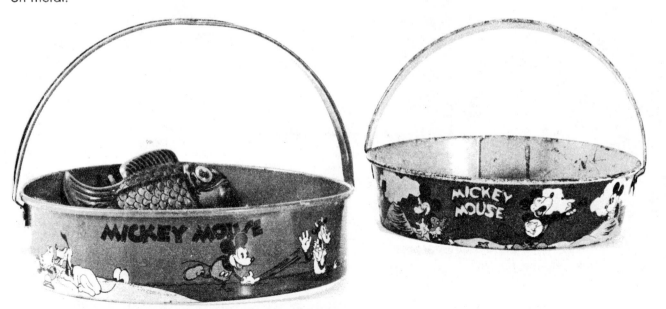

Tin litho sand sifters (with a metal fish-sand-mold), Ohio Art Company, Bryan, Ohio, 1934. From Marianne Short, Turn of the Century Antiques, Point Pleasant, N. J.

Mickey Mouse fishing kit, litho on metal, a side panel view showing Mickey, Minnie, Clarabelle, Donald, Pluto, and Horace camping out, made in 1935 by Hamilton Metal Products Company, Hamilton, Ohio.

Mickey Mouse fishing kits, beautiful color-litho on metal boxes from the Hamilton Metal Products Company of Hamilton, Ohio, which also produced children's tool kits featuring Disney characters, were just the thing to teach children how to fish, particularly since the tools and materials were included inside.

Minnie and Mickey at the beach engraved on a 1½" x 1½" painted metal matchbox container, ca. 1933.

Beach balls featuring Mickey Mouse on one side and Minnie Mouse on the other were produced in the 1930s in great volume in diameters of 4, 5, 6, 7, and 8 inches by Sieberling Latex Products Company of Akron, Ohio. The Eagle Rubber Company, Inc., also produced 4-, 5-, and 6-inch-diameter beach balls. Plastic inflatable dolls of Mickey, Donald, and Dumbo that floated in water were produced in 12 gauge vinylite in 1949 by Vanguard Corporation of Chicopee, Massachusetts. This company also produced beach balls featuring Mickey, Pluto, and Donald Duck at the beach with Huey, Dewey, and Louie. On the beach or in the country, Mom and Dad could bring along the Mickey Mouse popcorn popper made in 1936 by Empire Product Corporation of Two Rivers, Wisconsin. Today all these examples of summer Mickey Mouse memorabilia are collectible for their distinct color lithography and graphic design.

If Mom and Pop took the family on a summer outing to the amusement boardwalks at oceanside places like Asbury Park, New Jersey; Atlantic City, New Jersey; Seaside Heights, New Jersey; or to big amusement parks like the ones at Rye Beach, Rockaway, or Coney Island in New York, or Olympic Park or Palisades Park in New Jersey, they just might become lucky enough to win a painted plaster Mickey or Donald doll with glitter, a Mickey Mouse celluloid or bisque figurine, or a Mickey Mouse bank at a 5-cent game of chance. If Mom or Pop's luck were really working, a child of the 1930s might walk home with a big stuffed Mickey or Minnie doll.

Tin litho Donald Duck pail made in 1935 by Ohio Art Company, Bryan, Ohio.

Mickey Mouse does the hula on a tin litho summer sand pail and dives into a roaring surf on a sand shovel, both made in 1934 by the Ohio Art Company, Bryan, Ohio.

Large-size Mickey-Minnie-Pluto sand pail dated 1938, from Ohio Art Company, Bryan, Ohio.

Donald tests the water on this large metal lithographed shovel, dated 1939. Ohio Art Company, Bryan, Ohio.

MICKEY MOUSE AT HOME IN THE DEPRESSION

Father sits in his favorite over-stuffed chair, studying a *Modern Mechanix* hobby magazine. Perhaps he is planning to make that Mickey Mouse wood jigsaw home cut-out doorstop, as he promised. Puffing on a Lucky Strike, he drops the cigarette ashes into a Japanese-import Mickey Mouse ashtray, which sits on a blue-mirror side table. Mother is busily embroidering a decorative Mickey and Minnie Mouse pillowcase from a Mc-Call's home pattern, under a bridge lamp with a 25-watt bulb. Sister is at the piano, playing one of the merry tunes from her Silly Symphony Song Folio, while Junior reads a Mickey Mouse Big Little Book adventure story and devours a box of Mickey Mouse cookies. One of the worst snowstorms of the 1930s is falling outside, but everyone feels safe and protected in the living room of this middle-class American dream house.

"In Conference," a 1932 puzzle within a puzzle, Einson-Freeman Company, New York. Three boys at play in the dining room, two in shirt and tie and one in his Mickey Mouse pullover sweatshirt, which was probably designed and manufactured by the Norwich Knitting Company of Norwich, N.Y.

A framed original American primitive "Home-Sweet-Home" painting in the best Disney manner. A henpecking angry Clarabelle the Cow is snarling after Horace Horsecollar, perhaps demanding he find work. This was domestic bliss in the Depression , ca. 1934. From Ralph Frame, Point Pleasant, N.J.

"Waterproof" and "sun-tested" Mickey Mouse wallpaper (shown framed) for the children's room. United Wallpaper Factories, Inc., Jersey City, N. J., ca. 1935.

In this dream house of the past, if you wandered into Junior's bedroom, you would notice that the walls were decorated with Mickey Mouse wallpaper from United Wall Paper Factories Inc. of Jersey City, New Jersey. On the floor there could be a 27-by-48-inch Mickey Mouse rug from Alexander Smith and Sons Carpet Company, of Yonkers, New York. The original ads described these rugs as "perfectly knock-out designs—in delightful colors—created by Walt Disney exclusively for Alexander Smith." Of course Disney "art" might be hung on the walls; but not art as we would think of it today—i.e., cels or original studio drawings. These would be simply wall plaques of Mickey, Minnie, Donald, Pluto, or Clara Cluck, which came in a box from Kerk Guild, Inc. Disney characters in full color in antiqued frames from Artisto, Inc., sold for 39 cents in 1938 at the dime store. Today these washable pictures, while not art in the true sense, would certainly be thought of as good graphics and collectible Mickey Mouse memorabilia. Some companies offered glow-in-the-dark Disney pictures, suggesting that a glowing Mickey Mouse would help Junior to get to sleep more easily.

McCall's applique design iron-on transfers (in package) to be embroidered on pillowcases, curtains, bibs, or bedspreads, 1934.

The 1933 four-tube Emerson "baby model" table radio, with Mickey playing musical instruments on all four sides, made of pressed wood syroco.

Naturally Mickey toys would be carefully tucked away in a wood-framed cardboard-and-fabric Mickey Mouse toy chest and children's seat, made by Odoro Company, Inc., of New York, and on a side table you would see a Mickey Mouse metal night-light lamp with a Mickey-decorated paper-parchment shade from the So-reng-Manegold Company of Chicago. Another lamp from the same company had a plaster Mickey relaxing in an over-stuffed armchair, and another featured Donald Duck on a lamppost. (The hard part for collectors is to find the matching Mickey or Donald shade.) Right next to the bedroom lamp might be a Mickey Mouse Emerson baby-model table radio (manufactured in 1933) of wood Syroco. This tiny radio with wood-sculpture relief images of Mickey Mouse playing musical instruments just as he would in a Silly Symphony—the tuba, the piano, the bass fiddle, and the flute—could be tuned in to the *Mickey Mouse Theater of the Air.* The popular radio show was

Cloth-covered wooden top of Mickey Mouse toy chest, which doubled as a children's seat. Odora Company, Inc., New York, 1935.

Wood frame litho on cardboard Mickey Mouse toy chest, 26" x 13" x 16", from the Odora Company, Inc., New York, ca. 1935.

Throw rug, 48" × 27", with a gallopin' cowboy Mickey manufactured by Alexander Smith & Company of Yonkers, N.Y.

Mickey and Donald adorning the cover art of Radio Mirror, April 19, 1938. Mickey Mouse, with the voice of Walt Disney himself, had his very own radio show in the 1930s, called "Mickey Mouse Theater of the Air."

first heard over NBC in 1937, featuring Walt Disney as Mickey Mouse, Thelma Boardman as Minnie Mouse, Clarence Nash as Donald Duck, Stuart Buchanan as Goofy, and Florence Gill as Clarabelle Cow and Clara Cluck. Heard also on this radio program were the Felix Mills Orchestra and Donald Duck's Swing Band and the Minnie Mouse Woodland Choir.

Emerson four-tube baby radios were very popular in the 1930s and the Emerson Radio and Phonograph Corporation of New York, which described itself as "makers of the world's biggest selling little radios," put out, in addition to the Syroco radio described earlier, a cream-color-and-green-painted model with a color-litho-metal figure of Mickey on the speaker. There were four smaller Mickeys in the four corners. This style also came in black and silver. Emerson also produced a Snow White and the Seven Dwarfs radio in two sizes, made of Syroco (a pressed-wood composition), and a Three Little Pigs radio—

Give-away pinback button for the Mickey Mouse Emerson radio, ca. 1934.

all manufactured throughout the 1930s. A Mickey Mouse wind-up portable phonograph was also produced by this company. Today one of these Emerson radios would be valued in the hundreds of dollars, but radios—even baby models—were never cheap, even in their own time.

If the family was spending the evening at home together, they could play a game of cards; one handsome double set of cards in green and orange from Whitman Publishers of Racine, Wisconsin, had Mickey gazing lovingly at a framed picture of Minnie, while the other pack showed Minnie looking at a picture of her boyfriend Mickey on her wall. The playing-card set of two decks came with a Mickey–Minnie bridge scorepad and tallies. Another card game from Whitman that could be played by Sis and Junior was The Mickey Mouse Old Maid Cards, which came in a beautiful cardboard box; each card featured a color-litho of a different Disney character.

Mickey Mouse standard-size bridge playing cards (colors green, orange, and black), from Whitman Publishing Company, Racine, Wisc., 1935.

Package of playing cards featuring Minnie Mouse. Whitman Publishing Company, Racine, Wisc., 1935.

Mickey Mouse talley card from the Whitman card set, which also included a bridge score pad.

These painted Noritake oddball Mickey Mouse lookalike knick-knacks, planters, pin cushions, and ashtray-match containers were made in porcelain in the millions in Japan and sold at the five-and-dimes in the 1930s, probably without Disney licensing.

$1.98

Sold by Mail Only by Sears

New Mickey Mouse Talkie Jector
Clockwork Motor—Electric Lighted

Imagine hearing voices or music with your movie show! Just wind strong spring motor which operates and keeps both record and film synchronized. Clear, flickerless, cartoon-type moving pictures in colors. Can be shown on any blank wall. Made of metal with Mickey Mouse decoration. 13x7½x12 in. Operates on 110-volt A.C. current Use regular house bulb. Record, films, bulb or electric cord and plug not included. See below.
79 K 6841—Shipping weight, 4 pounds.. **$1.98**

**Sets of two 39 In. Colored Films and one
Double-faced 6-In. Record**

Music by Irving Berlin. Each film shows story for one side of record. **42c**
Especially prepared for the little tots. Shipping weight, 1 pound each.

49 K 6960 — Mickey in "Dude Ranch" and "Home Run"......42c	**49 K 6962**—Mickey in "Winning" and "Pal Pluto"...............42c	**49 K 6964** — "Sandman" and "Funny Bunnies"...........42c
49 K 6961 — Mickey in "Flying Mail" and "Haunted House"...42c	**49 K 6963** — Silly Symphony — "Penguin Land"and"Two Bears"42c	**49 K 6965**—"Idle Hour" and "Birds in Spring".........42c

Hand Crank Mickey Mouse Movie Jector

Like **79 K 6841**, except no talkie attachment and no motor. Use ordinary house bulb. Bulb, cord, plug and film not included. See below.
49 K 6842—Size, 10x9x7½ in. high. Shipping weight, 12 ounces............ **98c**
39-In. Mickey Mouse Films in Color. Shpg. wt., 2 oz. **54-In. Films in Color**
49 K 6950—Mickey in "Mickey's Pal Pluto"...10c **49 K 6952**—"Hansel and Gretel"..............9c
49 K 6951—Mickey in "The Haunted House"...10c **49 K 6953**—"Treasure Island".................9c
20 K 671—6-foot Cord and Plug for Talkie or Movie. Shipping weight, 7 ounces **17c**

The 1935 Sears-Roebuck catalogue offered the Mickey Mouse "at home" movie jector. Mickey Mouse and Silly Symphony films in color were also available with a 6" record featuring music by Irving Berlin. From Movie Jector Company, Inc., New York.

Another pastime might find the family watching their own Mickey Mouse movie shorts on the Keystone Mickey Mouse electric projector, a green metal movie-machine with a striking Mickey decal-image appliqué. It came with "cine-art" Mickey Mouse 16 millimeter films in attractive Mickey boxes from Keystone Manufacturing Company of Boston. A Mickey Mouse Movie Jector from Movie Jector, Inc., of New York offered six Silly Symphony films, and also a Talkie Jector made by the same company, which included a phonograph attachment to the "jector" to provide sound to these home movies.

Other Mickey Mouse items found in the home would include ceramics, pottery pieces, and bisque figurines used as decoratives and receptacles for various purposes. Some of these were distributed by companies like George Borgfeldt & Company of New York, National Porcelain Company of Trenton, the Laguna Pottery Company or American Pottery Company of Los Angeles; but a good many might be of the Noritake made-in-Japan variety, which were marketed as ashtrays, cigarette containers, planters, or pincushion holders and sold by the millions in dime stores across America. These seem to have been unlicensed pieces, but they are unusual interpretations of Mickey Mouse. In that they did not exactly resemble Disney's cartoon mouse, they somehow avoided the usual requirement of Kay Kamen licensing.

In the kitchen, Mother might serve the kiddies Mickey Mouse strawberry jam from Glaser, Crandell Company of Chicago. The jar, with Mickey and Minnie on the glass, itself later served as a bank, which is now a fine early collectible. Milk might be served—or, if the children preferred, Mickey Mouse soda—in a premium glass tumbler with a Disney character embossed on it. These glass tumblers were produced by Libbey Glass—Owens—Illinois Glass Company of Toledo, Ohio, and were called safedge tumblers. This joint company also produced milk bottles with Disney characters, and metal lunchboxes. From 1947 to 1949, Leeds China Company produced for the kitchen some wonderful Siamese-twin ceramic painted cookie jars to contain Mickey Mouse cookies. Called Turnabouts, they included a Mickey–Minnie (one figure on each side), a José Carioca–Donald Duck, a Dumbo–Donald Duck, a Pluto–Donald Duck, as well as some of the characters—mostly Donald or Thumper, the rabbit from *Bambi*—all by themselves as cookie jars. The company also produced charming ceramic painted kitchen planters featuring Mickey, Donald, Dumbo, or Dopey the Dwarf. Kitchen penny-saving banks, as well as countless pairs of salt and pepper shakers—a Mickey–Minnie set, a Donald Duck set, a Pluto set, a Dumbo set—were also popular in the home. Collectors prize these pieces, as they represent good quality pottery items that could be purchased originally from the dime store.

Other items found in the kitchen include children's china sets, the most notable coming from the Salem China Company of Ohio, and the Schumann Company of New York, which also produced kitchen ashtrays; and, of course, the famous Mickey Mouse silver spoons from William Rogers and other silverware manufacturers. To complete a Disney kitchen, Mother might also serve Donald Duck orange or grapefruit juice for breakfast, with Donald Duck bread toast, Mickey Mouse marmalade, and Donald Duck coffee.

Mickey Mouse Band
Minnie poses with her violin, Mickey a Sax, a little mouse with accordian, another with a mandolin. Minnie and Mickey 5½ inches tall, little mice in proportion. Colored porcelain. Shpg. wt., 1 lb. 4 oz.
49 F 9110 4 for **29C**

These figurines advertised in the 1934 Sears-Roebuck catalogue were in reality handpainted made-in-Japan bisques (not porcelain).

A Minnie Mouse china figurine with kitchen broom. This housewife-like Minnie was produced in 1947 by the American Pottery Company of Los Angeles.

Mickey Mouse and Donald Duck napkin rings made of Catalin plastic with decal appliques. Plastic Novelties, Inc., New York, 1937.

Minnie Mouse-Mickey Mouse glass tumblers were produced by the Libbey Glass Company, Toledo, Ohio in 1938.

Mickey Mouse and Minnie Mouse handpainted china ashtray set. This rare and beautiful pair were made in Japan in 1932.

A two-cup chinaware teapot was made in Japan for the George Borgfeldt Corporation of New York in 1933.

Turnabout Minnie Mouse cookie jar with Mickey Mouse on the other side. Made by the Leeds China Company, Chicago, 1947.

MICKEY MOUSE MUSIC

The sheet music and Disney Song Folios found on the upright living-room piano might have been purchased either from the music store or from the sheet-music counter at the five-and-dime store. At these establishments in the 1930s, an attractive piano-playing vocalist with flame-red lips, mascaraed eyes, and permanent-waved hair might be found crooning "Minnie's Yoo Hoo" in her best high soprano. Copies of this sheet music—Mickey Mouse's theme song, first introduced in the 1929 cartoon *Mickey's Follies*—were given to lucky members of the first Mickey Mouse Clubs in 1930. Other Mickey Mouse songs the dime-store crooner might sing and play for you would include "Mickey Mouse's Birthday Party," "Mickey Mouse and Minnie's in Town," "The Wedding of Mister Mickey Mouse," or "What! No Mickey Mouse? What Kind of a Party is This?" by Irving Caesar. The latter song was rerecorded in 1970 by Phil Harris with some lyric variation:

"Vote for Mickey Mouse,
And make him our next
     President;
To Congress he is sure to say,
"Meow, meow, okay, okay,
Ja, ja, yes, yes, si, si, oui, oui,
How dry I am, have one on
     me,"
And then he'll cry,
"Give me the facts,
Give me my ax,
I'll cut your tax."
He'll show us all what can be
     done,
When he's in Washington,
So, let's give Nixon's house,
To that slicky, wacki, wicki,
Tacki, tricky Mickey Mouse.
Mickey Mouse!
Mickey Mouse!*

*Copyright 1932 Walt Disney Music Company. Copyright renewed 1959 Walt Disney Music Company.

Large pinback button of a musical mouse duo singing the Mickey Mouse theme song, "Minnie's Yoo Hoo!" Made in England for the "early" Mickey Mouse nostalgia revival in the late 1960s.

Minnie Mouse with banjo and Mickey Mouse with a harmonica are cut-out toys from the back of a Post Toasties cereal box. General Foods Corp., 1934.

Full-sheet advertisement for Folio of Songs, volume II, from Walt Disney's famous pictures. Irving Berlin, Inc., Music Publishers, New York, 1935.

Sheet music "You'r Nothin' But a Nothin,'" from the Silly Symphony The Flying Mouse, Irving Berlin, Inc., Music Publishers, New York, 1934.

Sheet music "Brazil," from Saludos Amigos featuring Donald Duck and a cigar-smoking Disney parrot named José (Joe) Carioca. Southern Music Publishing Company, Inc., New York. Title page copyright 1942.

"Blue Shadows on the Trail," sheet music from Melody Time, which featured the animated stories of Pecos Bill, Little Toot, and Johnny Appleseed, 1948.

Some early Silly Symphony Song Folio hits were "Lullaby of Nowhere," "Funny Little Bunnies," "The Penguin Is a Very Funny Creature," "The Wise Little Hen," "Ferdinand the Bull," "Rats" from Pied Piper, "You're Nothin' but a Nothin'" from The Flying Mouse, or the most famous Silly Symphony song of all time, "Who's Afraid of the Big Bad Wolf" from The Three Little Pigs, which was so popular it became the anthem-theme song of the Great Depression. The most popular all-time favorite songs from Walt Disney films include:

- "Some Day My Prince Will Come" from Snow White and the Seven Dwarfs
- "Whistle While You Work" from Snow White and the Seven Dwarfs
- "Heigh Ho" from Snow White and the Seven Dwarfs
- "When You Wish upon a Star" from Pinocchio
- "Give a Little Whistle," Jiminy Cricket's song, from Pinocchio
- "Hi Diddle Dee Dee" from Pinocchio
- "Der Fuehrer's Face" from the short Der Fuehrer's Face, subtitled Donald Duck in Nutzi Land
- "You Belong to My Heart" from The Three Caballeros
- "Zip-a-Dee-Doo-Dah" from Song of the South
- "Bibbidi-Bobbidi-Boo" from Cinderella
- "A Dream Is a Wish Your Heart Makes" from Cinderella.

Three songs that won Academy Awards were: "When You Wish upon a Star" (1940), "Zip-a-Dee-Doo-Dah" (1946), "Chim Chim Cher-ee" (Mary Poppins, 1964).

Disney sheet music is highly collectible for the splendid graphics, which are perfect inside a picture frame to be hung on the wall in a den, living room, collectibles room, or music room. It is not as remote as posters, lobby cards, or original photographic stills, as it was produced and sold in the millions (and, prior to television) everyone in a family seemed to play the piano, accordion, or some other instrument. Sheet music falls into the category of ephemera, and is to be found today at paper collectibles shows, antique shows, flea markets, nostalgia conventions, and antiquarian book shows.

The Disney music publishers included Villa Morét Inc., Music Publishers from San Francisco, California; Irving Caesar, Inc.; and the major publisher of the 1930s decade, Bourne Music Publishers, sometimes also called Irving Berlin, Inc., New York. A variety of publishers were used by Disney from 1940 up to the present.

Sheet music "What! No Mickey Mouse? What Kind of a Party Is This?" by Irving Caesar, Irving Caesar, Inc., Music Publishers, New York, 1932.

"A March for Mickey Mouse," sheet music by C. Franz Koehler, the Boston Music Co., Boston, 1934.

Record collectors search with great intensity for the early Disney 78-rpms. In 1934 the RCA Victor Company, Inc., of Camden, New Jersey, produced one of the first Disney records, using Frank Luther and his orchestra to perform the Mickey hits. Many dance bands performed songs from Disney movies that were recorded. One recently released long-playing 33 from EMI (record number SH268) uses fifteen cuts "from the Golden Age of British dance bands series" called *Great Songs from Disney Movies*, which is a wonderful record to listen to as background music for Disney collectors while they dust or polish their collectibles. Original 78-rpm record albums from the films are very desirable, particularly those from *Snow White and the Seven Dwarfs*, *Pinocchio*, *The Three Caballeros*, *Dumbo*, *Saludos Amigos*, and *Song of the South*. Today most of these are also available on 33-rpms and in specially packaged Disney sets.

Rare 78 rpm orthophonic recording of "Mickey Mouse and Minnie's in Town," subtitled "El Ratoncito Mickey y Minnie," song by Ann Ronell, performed by Don Bestor and his orchestra, vocal refrain by the De Marco Girls and Frank Sherry. R.C.A. Victor Company, Inc., Camden, N. J., 1934.

Mickey Mouse bubble gum card #76, featuring Mickey Mouse tootin' his horn, ostensibly for Minnie.

The Big Bad Wolf and Little Red Riding Hood *book published by Blue Ribbon Books, 1934.*

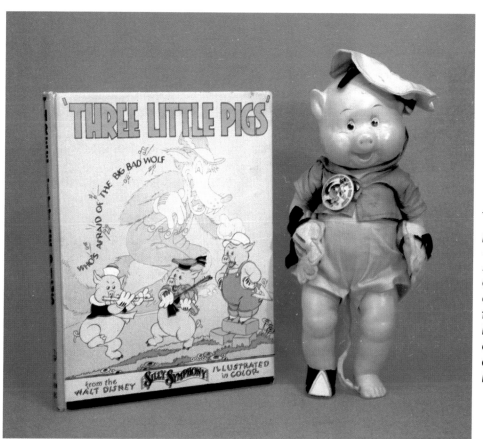

Three Little Pigs *book published by Blue Ribbon Books, 1933. Madame Alexander doll reveals the astonishing fact that there is a child's foot beneath the cute cloven-hoofed black and white shoe of this little pig.*

Three Little Pigs-Big Bad Wolf
wind-up alarm clock, manufactured
by the Ingersoll-Waterbury Clock
Company in 1934. Measuring 4⅜",
the Wolf's animated jaws click
open and shut with each tick of the
clock.

Three Little Pigs painted bisque toothbrush
holder, made in Japan, 1934.

Drummer Pig, Fiddler Pig, and Fifer Pig, felt on tin toys with wind-up
motors, 5" tall, made in the mid-thirties in Germany by the Schuco
Company. Collection of Robert Lesser.

Three Little Pigs laundry set included a lithographed metal washtub, a metal washing board and a clothesline with clothespins. Manufactured by the Ohio Art Company, Bryan, Ohio, in 1934.

Three Little Pigs lithographed metal sand pails. Ohio Art Company of Bryan, Ohio, in 1934.

Post Toasties cereal box cardboard cut-outs of the Three Little Pigs and the Big Bad Wolf. These back-of-the-box cut-outs, which featured a great variety of Disney cartoon characters throughout the 1930s and early 1940s, were sometimes the only playthings a Depression child had. General Foods, ca. 1934.

The perfect touch for Christmas in the Depression was this Silly Symphony Christmas tree light set, with beetleware shades featuring decals of Silly Symphony characters. Pictured with the original box. Made by the Noma Electric Company of New York, 1936.

The term "Mickey Mouse music" was derived from the ricky-tick sound of the early Disney cartoon soundtrack music, much of it written by a former organist and theater orchestra conductor, Carl Stalling. This type of orchestration came directly out of the 1920s, derived from the orchestras that played in nightclubs or in Broadway shows of the day. This fun-time sound, which was very popular on the radio and on phonograph records, included these 1920s hits which influenced the music used in early Disney cartoons: "I'm Just Wild about Animal Crackers," as recorded by Irving Aaronson and his Commanders; "The Japanese Sandman," as recorded by Paul Whiteman; "Sax-O-Phun" (a study in laugh and slap tongue) and "Horses," both recorded by George Olson. These records have been reissued on 33 rpms and can be found in the nostalgia bins of your local record shop. There's nothing like listening to one of these songs to capture the feel of Mickey Mouse cartoons and Mickey Mouse music.

A bright orange Mickey-Minnie party horn. Litho on cardboard with Mickey and Minnie wearing the green. Marks Brothers Company, Boston, 1934.

College jazz babies of the 1920s loved this type of "flaming youth" rhythmic sound, but in the 1930s the new hotel orchestras were featuring strings and a more sophisticated music to go along with the repeal of prohibition. Subsequently the snobs of the 1930s frowned on some of the best music of the 1920s, calling it Mickey Mouse music—meant to be a derogatory term, which eventually worked its way into some dictionaries and came to mean trite, slick, and commercial. In fact, the *Random House Dictionary of the English Language* (unabridged version) has this definition for Mickey Mouse: "(often caps) slang. Trite and commercially slick in character: Mickey Mouse music. (After a cartoon character created by Walt Disney.)"

However, some of the better composers of the 1930s did not forget to include Mickey Mouse himself in the lyrics of their songs. In 1934, when Ethel Merman first sang the renowned "You're the Top" from Cole Porter's Broadway show *Anything Goes*, the audience broke into wild applause when they heard:

You're a melody from a
    symphony by Strauss,
You're a Bendel bonnet—
A Shakespeare sonnet—
You're—*Mickey Mouse!*

Miss Merman continued her song tribute to Mickey Mouse in the movies when she sang the Mack Gordon-Harry Revel song "It's the Animal in Me" from Paramount's film *The Big Broadcast of 1936*. This lyric contained the musical observation:

Look at Mickey Mouse,
Look at Minnie Mouse,
They just live on love and
    cheese.

Two lithographed metal toy drums manufactured by the Ohio Art Company, Bryan, Ohio, 1933.

THE THREE LITTLE PIGS (& A BIG BAD DEPRESSION)

By 1933 America was in the grip of a depression that had hit deeply, and Walt Disney responded to these hard times by making a color cartoon based on a Grimms' fairy tale about three little pigs and a menacing big bad wolf. The cartoon film called *The Three Little Pigs* is the most famous of all the Silly Symphonies, many of which had been developed from fairy tales, and it captivated Depression audiences, adults and children alike.

For many Americans in 1933 the wolf at the door, huffing, puffing and threatening to "blow the house in" was a euphemism for the landlord demanding monthly rent money that the tenants simply did not have. The public identified with the three fearful Disney pigs and their frantic search for security, trying house after house until one is finally found that is safe from the big bad wolf. When the wolf discovers he cannot blow down a brick house, he climbs into the chimney and, to the delight of everyone watching the film, falls into a big pot of boiling water. Thus the audience, who had paid no more than a quarter to get into the Ritz or Rialto Theaters across the country to see, perhaps two features, a newsreel, and *The Three*

Sheet music "Who's Afraid of the Big Bad Wolf," by Frank Churchill, with additional lyric by Ann Ronell, from the Silly Symphony cartoon Three Little Pigs, Bourne Company, New York, 1933.

"The Three Little Pigs" paint-on-reverse-glass framed wall picture, 8" x 12", for the living room. Practical Pig builds a secure house of brick while the Fifer Pig and Fiddler Pig with houses of straw and twigs dance a jig. Ca. 1934.

A 78 rpm Victor record of *"Who's Afraid of the Big Bad Wolf,"* which was the theme song of the Great Depression. R.C.A. Victor Company, Inc., Camden, N.J., 1934.

Little Pigs in color, took vicarious pleasure at getting back at the enemy, who was actually, in their minds, the big bad Depression.

R. D. Feild, in his notable and scholarly book *The Art of Walt Disney* (Macmillan, 1942), now itself a rare Disney collectible, says of this film: "No one will ever know to what extent *The Three Little Pigs* may be held responsible for pulling us out of the Depression, but certainly the lyrical jeer at the Big Bad Wolf contributed not a little to the raising of people's spirits and to their defiance of circumstance."

Much of the great success of *The Three Little Pigs* Silly Symphony had to do with the song written for it by Frank E. Churchill called "Who's Afraid of the Big Bad Wolf," which the three pigs merrily and defiantly sing. One of the most popular songs of the era, it became the theme song for the Depression, with many noted singers and orchestras, like Ben Bernie's in America or Henry Hall's of the BBC in England, incorporating it into their repertoires.

Many middle-class families of the Depression era lived in their own fairy-tale bungalow houses, the architecture of which usually consisted of a high slanted slate roof that peaked over the front door, with a tall "Big Bad Wolf" brick chimney brought directly into the frontal design. These happy-cartoon Humpty-Dumpty early suburban homes, often set up in rows, were the only security some folks had in the Depression, and they fought for them, just like the pigs, with a *Grimm* determination.

The Three Little Pigs, which the Disney Studios had worked on in 1932, opened at the Roxy Theatre in New York in 1933 and was brought back for three separate bookings, grossing $64,000—a good amount for a short subject in those days. The public was so enthralled by the three Disney pigs and the voracious Big Bad Wolf that merchandisers were enlisted to put these characters immediately to work. The first pig was Fifer, who played the flute and built his house of straw; the second pig, called Fiddler, built his house of sticks and twigs; the third little pig, who was called Drummer or Practical Pig, built his house of bricks and sang the merry tune: "Who's afraid of the Big Bad Wolf," as he pounded away on the ivories of a piano made of bricks just like his brick house.

The menacing Big Bad Wolf on a lithographed tin plate from a children's tea set, Ohio Art Company, Bryan, Ohio, 1934.

Three Little Pigs playing card in orange and green from Whitman Publishing Company, Racine, Wisc., 1934.

Three Little Pigs beer-parlor tray celebrating the repeal of Prohibition, color litho on metal, 1933.

Pinback button made by Walt Disney Enterprises as a give-away at screenings of Three Little Pigs, 1933.

A stuffed Disney character doll of one little pig, from Three Little Pigs. Looking like a teddy-bear pig, this Silly Symphony doll from the Knickerbocker Toy Company of New York has a wind-up music box built into its back which plays "Who's Afraid of the Big Bad Wolf," 1934.

Of the thousands of pig and wolf (and Little Red Riding Hood, who appeared in the 1934 Silly Symphony *The Big Bad Wolf*) items that were on the market in the 1930s and into the 1940s, these are some that Disney collectors look for, listed under their manufacturers:

George Borgfeldt Company, New York

- Borgfeldt distributed two different bisque toothbrush holders of the Three Little Pigs, many individual hand-painted bisque pieces of the pigs with and without musical instruments, all different sizes of the Big Bad Wolf, all made in Japan.
- They also distributed celluloid Three Little Pigs on a metal swing, made in Japan. From Germany, they distributed the Schuco Company felt and metal wind-ups of the Three Little Pigs, which are very desirable collectible pieces. Borgfeldt also manufactured a large plush Little Red Riding Hood doll.

Richard G. Krueger, Inc., New York

- Soft, stuffed Three Little Pigs dolls;
- Red Riding Hood dolls;
- Stuffed Big Bad Wolf shark-skin grain and cloth dolls;
- Nursery articles: Three Little Pigs lamp with shade, which played the musical tune "Who's Afraid of the Big Bad Wolf"; a Three Little Pigs feeding set for infants (decorated porcelain), including a drinking cup, creamer and sugar bowl, teapot, egg cup, bowl, plate, and serving tray. They also produced wooden coat hangers and a Baby Snapshot Book with moiré covers.

Knickerbocker Toy Company, New York

- Stuffed dolls of the Three Little Pigs (resembling pig Teddy bears), the Big Bad Wolf, and Little Red Riding Hood. Some of these plush dolls had musical-box wind-ups inside them which played "Who's Afraid of the Big Bad Wolf."

Sieberling Latex Products Company, Akron, Ohio

- Three Little Pigs rubber figurines, 6 inches;
- Big Bad Wolf rubber figurine, 10 inches (these brightly painted, molded rubber figures originally sold for 39 cents each and were packaged in beautifully lithographed boxed sets).

Emerson Radio and Phonograph Corporation, New York

- A Three Little Pigs table-model baby radio, made of wood Syroco.

Powers Paper Company, Springfield, Massachusetts

- Three Little Pigs writing tablets and stationery.

Joseph Dixon Crucible Company, Jersey City, New Jersey

- Pencil boxes of the Three Little Pigs, Red Riding Hood and the Big Bad Wolf.

The Ohio Art Company, Bryan, Ohio

- Three Little Pigs and Big Bad Wolf toy teaset, in colorful tin-litho;
- A Three Little Pigs laundry set with a washbasin, a tin washboard, clothesline, and clothespins;
- Metal-litho Three Little Pigs drum;
- Metal-litho Three Little Pigs seashore pails.

Kay Kamen
- Three pigs (all individual) plus Wolf paper masks—a movie-theater giveaway premium from Walt Disney Enterprises.

A. S. Fishback, Inc., New York
- Three Little Pigs and Big Bad Wolf children's Halloween costumes.

Parker Brothers, Inc., Salem, Massachusetts
- "Who's Afraid of the Big Bad Wolf" game;
- Red Riding Hood and the Big Bad Wolf game.

Herrmann Handkerchief Company, Inc., New York
- Three Little Pigs and Big Bad Wolf handkerchiefs.

William Rogers, International Silver Company, Meriden, Connecticut
- Little Red Riding Hood, Three Little Pigs, and Big Bad Wolf forks, knives, spoons, and cups.

Salem China Company, Salem, Ohio
- Juvenile chinaware of the Three Little Pigs, including plates, cereal bowls, and mugs.

Sheffield Farms, distributor
- All-Star Parade Sealtest Cottage Cheese packaged in Three Little Pigs and Big Bad Wolf drinking glasses.

Einson-Freeman Company, Long Island City, New York
- Three Little Pigs game.

Fulton Specialty Company
- "Who's Afraid of the Big Bad Wolf" toy printing set.

U.S. Electric Manufacturing Company, New York
- Big Bad Wolf and Three Little Pigs flashlights.

A fine porcelain figurine of Disney's Fiddler Pig, after Three Little Pigs. Made in Germany in 1934.

A black furry big-toothed Big Bad Wolf stuffed doll from the Knickerbocker Toy Company, New York. This magnificent wolf-doll was produced in 1934.

The Fiddler Pig and the Big Bad Wolf, color litho action toy wind-up jumpers from Linemar Company, Inc., made in Japan in the late 1940s.

General Foods

■ Post Toasties back-of-the-box "Mickey Mouse presents: Silly Symphony Three Little Pigs" cut-outs.

Bates Art Industries, Chicago

■ Full-color pictures of the Three Little Pigs and the Big Bad Wolf.

Blue Ribbon Publishers, Jersey City, New Jersey

■ *The Three Little Pigs* book in hardback.

David McKay Publishers, Philadelphia

■ *The Three Little Pigs* book in softcover and *Little Red Riding Hood and the Big Bad Wolf* in hardback and softcover.

Whitman Publishers, Racine, Wisconsin

■ Set of Silly Symphony cut-out figures of the Three Little Pigs and the Wolf, with cut-out clothes, a house of hay, a house of twigs, and a house of bricks.

Ingersoll–Waterbury Clock Company, Waterbury, Connecticut

■ Wristwatches, pocket watches, and wind-up alarm clocks featuring the Big Bad Wolf in the center, with a red background, animated jaws, and a winking eye; Three Little Pigs featured on clock and watch faces.

A 1934 advertisement from the Sunday comic section of the Philadelphia Inquirer for Post Toasties Corn Flakes with Big Bad Wolf and Three Little Pigs toy cut-outs on the back of the box.

OTHER "SILLY" CHARACTERS

The Silly Symphonies of the 1930s, as presented by Mickey Mouse, are thought of by critics and cartoon buffs as among the best and most creative cartoons produced by Disney Studios in those years. Most Silly Symphony merchandise is prewar, and there are other Silly Symphony cartoon characters (besides the Three Little Pigs and Mickey Mouse and Donald Duck) that turn up as character merchandising items in the form of stuffed dolls, children's books, soap figurines, wind-ups, coloring and paintbooks, games, etc. These items are desirable pieces to collect, as the characters had less of a run than the stars, and consequently the manufacturers produced fewer. Primary among the characters are: Elmer the Elephant, the Funny Bunnies (Miss Cottontail), the Robber Kitten, Bucky Bug, the Three Orphan Kittens, Toby Tortoise, Clara Cluck, the Wise Little Hen, Peter Pig, the Ugly Duckling, the Peculiar Penguins, the Country Cousin, and Hiawatha. One of the most popular later thirties characters was Ferdinand the Bull from the cartoon of the same name (1938). The bull merchandise featuring Ferdinand includes books, song sheets, records, wind-up toys, bisque figurines, dolls, games, and coloring books. The following list of Silly Symphonies may help in collecting and identifying the many characters and products identified with them.

Clara Cluck, the operatic hen who was introduced in 1934 in the Disney short, The Orphan's Benefit, celebrates a fiftieth birthday in 1984. Shown here on a paper litho on wood nursery pull-toy produced in 1936 by Fisher-Price Toys, Inc. of East Aurora, N. Y.

Mickey Mouse presents a Walt Disney Silly Symphony in the form of a Big Little Book featuring Bucky Bug on the cover. Whitman Publishing Company, Racine, Wisc., 1934.

A color lithographed metal Silly Symphony paint box made in Great Britain featuring Donald Duck, Elmer Elephant holding a picture of Mickey, and a jubilant pig, ca. 1938.

An Elmer Elephant drinking tumbler from Libbey Glass Company and Owens-Illinois Glass Company, 1939. Disney comic-character glasses often came in sets (there were twelve different glasses for Pinocchio and eight for Snow White).

Elmer, Le Petit Eléphant, the story of Elmer the Elephant, published in France by Hachette, 1937.

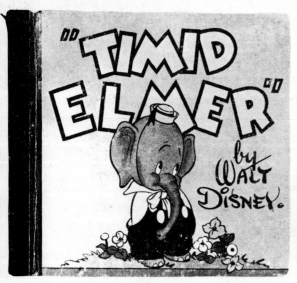

Timid Elmer, a 5" x 5½" cardboard cover book with black and white illustrations featuring the Silly Symphony characters Elmer Elephant, Tillie Tiger, and Tuffy Tiger; from Whitman Publishing Company, Racine, Wisc., 1939.

Mickey Mouse presents Walt Disney's Three Little Kittens, also known as the Orphan Kittens, as cardboard cut-out toys on the back of a Post Toasties cereal box from General Foods Corp., 1936.

The Three Orphan Kittens in storybook form "written and illustrated by the staff of the Walt Disney Studios" and published by Whitman Publishing Company, Racine, Wisc., 1935.

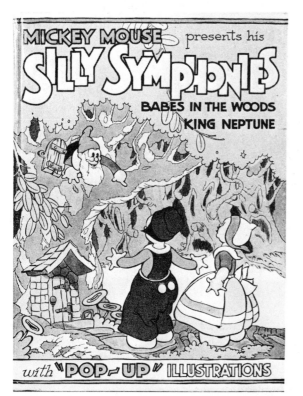

Mickey Mouse presents his Silly Symphonies, "Babes in the Woods" and "King Neptune," in a story book with pop-up illustrations, Blue Ribbon Books, New York, 1933.

Another popular Silly Symphony cat is The Robber Kitten, here featured in a colorful large-format story book from Whitman Publishing Company, Racine, Wisc., 1935.

A COMPLETE LIST OF SILLY SYMPHONY FILMS

A small painted bisque figurine of Disney's Ferdinand the Bull, which was made in Japan for distribution in the U.S. in 1938.

1929
- The Skeleton Dance
- El Terrible Toreador
- Springtime
- Hell's Bells
- The Merry Dwarfs

1930
- Summer
- Autumn
- Cannibal Capers
- Night
- Frolicking Fish
- Arctic Antics
- Midnight in a Toy Shop
- Monkey Melodies
- Winter
- Playful Pan

1931
- Birds of a Feather
- Mother Goose Melodies
- The China Plate
- The Busy Beavers
- The Cat's Out
- Egyptian Melodies
- The Clock Store
- The Spider and the Fly
- The Fox Hunt
- The Ugly Duckling

1932
- The Bird Store
- The Bears and the Bees
- Just Dogs
- Flowers and Trees (Academy Award winner)
- King Neptune
- Bugs in Love
- Babes in the Woods
- Santa's Workshop

1933
- Birds in the Spring
- Father Noah's Ark
- Three Little Pigs (Academy Award winner)
- Old King Cole
- Lullaby Land
- The Pied Piper
- The Night Before Christmas

1934
- The China Shop
- The Grasshopper and the Ants
- Funny Little Bunnies
- The Big Bad Wolf
- The Wise Little Hen
- The Flying Mouse
- Peculiar Penguins
- The Goddess of Spring

1935

- *The Tortoise and the Hare* (Academy Award winner)
- *The Golden Touch*
- *The Robber Kitten*
- *Water Babies*
- *The Cookie Carnival*
- *Who Killed Cock Robin?*
- *Music Land*
- *Three Orphan Kittens* (Academy Award winner)
- *Cock o' the Walk*
- *Broken Toys*

1936

- *Elmer Elephant*
- *Three Little Wolves*
- *Toby Tortoise Returns*
- *Three Blind Mouseketeers*
- *The Country Cousin* (Academy Award winner)
- *Mother Pluto*
- *More Kittens*

1937

- *Woodland Café*
- *Little Hiawatha*
- *The Old Mill* (Academy Award winner)

1938

- *Farmyard Symphony*
- *Merbabies*
- *The Moth and the Flame*
- *Wynken, Blynken and Nod*
- *Mother Goose Goes Hollywood*
- *Ferdinand the Bull* (released as a "special short")

1939

- *The Practical Pig*
- *The Ugly Duckling* (remake, Academy Award winner)

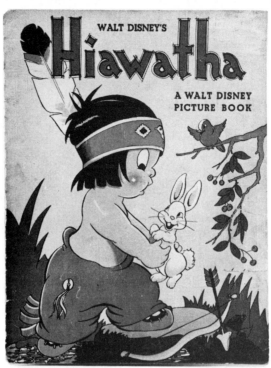

Hiawatha, a Walt Disney Silly Symphony character in a large-size picture book that was "linen-like and sewed" from Whitman Publishing Company, Racine, Wisc., 1938.

A colorful 1940s record jacket of Ferdinand the Bull, told by Don Wilson. From Capitol Records, Hollywood, Cal.

Painted bisque band set figurines of Snow White and the Seven Dwarfs. Left to right: Bashful, Happy, Grumpy, Snow White, Sleepy, Doc, Dopey, and Sneezy. These 1939 made in Japan figurines sold by the millions in dime stores across America and were used as prizes in amusement parks.

Child's leatherette purse manufactured by King Innovations, Inc., New York, in 1938. Collection of Lady Hope Stansbury, New York.

SNOW WHITE AND THE SEVEN DWARFS

Snow White and the Seven Dwarfs is the magnum opus full-length animated film retelling of the old Grimms' fairy tale that is regarded by critics and Disney scholars as his masterpiece. This 1938 movie in multiplane Technicolor never loses its appeal whenever it is reissued by the studio, and it has been shown in at least forty-one countries in ten different languages.

The film actually premiered on December 21, 1937, but was released on February 4, 1938. It initially ran for five weeks at Radio City Music Hall, and for a record-breaking thirty-one weeks in Paris. Wherever it played throughout the world, new records were set at the box office. In the first year of release, *Snow White* earned $4.2 million in the United States and Canada alone. In reissues in 1943, 1952, 1958, and 1967, it made close to $16 million in domestic grosses and an estimated $30 million worldwide.

Critic Howard Barnes of the *New York Herald Tribune* wrote: "After seeing *Snow White* for the third time, I am more certain than ever that it belongs with the few great masterpieces of the screen." The cartoon character Snow White, whose on-screen

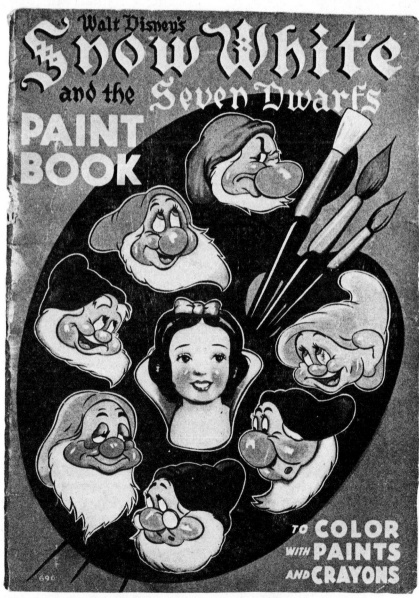

Snow White and the Seven Dwarfs, 11" x 15" paint book from Whitman Publishing Company, Racine, Wisc., 1938.

A 1939 Snow White premium give-away pinback membership button made for the Snow White Jingle Club. An inserted paper on the back of the button reads, "Walt Disney Enterprises, Kay Kamen Ltd., Sole Representative, 1270 Sixth Ave., New York."

Snow White and the Seven Dwarfs as a Big Little Book with the Wicked Queen on the spine (the Wicked Witch is on the back cover). Whitman Publishing Company, 1938.

voice was that of Adrianna Caselotti, captured audiences almost as if she were a new flesh-and-blood 1930s star coming forth out of the Hollywood dream factory like Hedy Lamarr, Jeannette MacDonald, Sonja Henie, or Shirley Temple. Indeed, in 1938 child star Shirley Temple presented seven miniature Academy Awards to Walt Disney for each of the seven dwarfs, and one regulation-size Oscar for Snow White. Marjorie Belcher, the wife of animator Art Babbitt, posed for Snow White, and Louis Hightower for the Prince. The public adored the seven dwarfs, Doc, Grumpy, Sleepy, Bashful, Happy, Sneezy, and Dopey. Dopey was probably the most beloved. The Wicked Queen, with her blood-red lips, white skin, and heavy black arched eyebrows, is said by members of the original *Snow White* animation team to have been modeled after Joan Crawford, and was feared by children when the film was first shown almost as much as the ferocious Big Bad Wolf. When the Queen drank her secret magic potion and turned into a cackling old witch, children of the thirties and forties were frightened and flabbergasted, many hiding under their movie-theater seats in tears.

Snow White and Doc, Grumpy, Sleepy, Bashful, Happy, Sneezy, and especially Dopey flooded the merchandise marketplace. They were a sensation, and reported sales by manufacturers were voluminous. During this prewar period, the Depression was easing up, and people were buying more. For Disney, *Snow White* hit the jackpot as a movie as well as in the wonderful world of magical merchandise supervised by the ever-watchful Kay Kamen.

Products on which Snow White and the Seven Dwarfs appeared included Snow White ice cream and a Dopey drink, both from National Dairy Products; Snow White soda; Snow White candy from P. H. Wunderle, Inc.; Indianhead sheets from Nashua Manufacturing Company; a Snow White dress pattern offered by William Wrigley, Jr., Company; flower seeds featuring Snow White, the Dwarfs and the Wicked Queen (in conjunction as a premium for Allsweet Margarine, from Swift and Company); Snow White–Seven Dwarfs cut-outs on the back of Post Toasties cereal boxes from General Foods; advertising tie-ins (posters, puzzles, games, color pictures, etc.) with Tek Toothbrushes from Johnson and Johnson; Royal Typewriter Company typewriter ribbons; Super Suds featuring Snow White from Colgate-Palmolive Peet Company; Armour's Star Ham featuring Snow White from Armour and Company; Procter and Gamble giveaway paper masks; and even a ladies' foundation garment from Miller Corsets, Inc., of Canandaigua, New York, which featured Snow White woven or printed on the corsets. Kay Kamen giveaways included color-litho paper masks of the Dwarfs, Snow White, and the Witch.

Collectible song sheets from the hit songs of the movie include: "I'm Wishing," "One Song," "With a Smile and a Song," "Whistle While You Work," "Heigh Ho," "Bluddle-uddle-um-Dum," (the dwarfs' yodel song), and "Some Day My Prince Will Come." Other *Snow White and the Seven Dwarfs* memorabilia collectible today are listed below under the manufacturer.

Alexander Doll Company, New York

- Snow White and the Seven Dwarfs marionettes and dolls.

Ideal Novelty and Toy Company, New York

- Snow White and the Seven Dwarfs stuffed and composition dolls in a complete range of sizes. Each dwarf-doll actually whistles when squeezed.

Knickerbocker Toy Company, New York

- Stuffed cloth dolls of Snow White and the Seven Dwarfs in three different sizes, packaged in a display house and in doll suitcases. A set of Seven Dwarfs also came with built-in music boxes.

Richard G. Krueger, Inc., of New York and San Francisco

- Snow White and all seven Dwarfs as individual dolls.

Sieberling Latex Products Company, Akron, Ohio

- Hand-colored, molded rubber figures of Snow White and the Seven Dwarfs, packaged individually or sold in boxed sets.

Cartier of New York, Paris, London

- Charm necklaces with all seven Dwarfs and Snow White; pins; tie clasps.

Brier Manufacturing Company, Providence, Rhode Island

- Snow White jewelry, rings, pins.

Lapin-Kurley Kew, Inc., New York

- Snow White barrettes.

American Toy Works, New York

- Snow White and the Seven Dwarfs target game, beautifully lithographed in full color, with handgun and darts.

Parker Brothers, Inc., Salem, Massachusetts

- Snow White and the Seven Dwarfs game;
- Dopey bean bag game.

Standard Toy Kraft Products, Inc., Brooklyn, New York

- Snow White embroidery set.

Marks Brothers Company, Boston, Massachusetts

- Pyrography set—burnt-wood etching outfit with electric pencil;
- Miniature Snow White toy piano.

Amloid Company, Lodi, New Jersey

- Celluloid Snow White baby rattles.

Bryant Electric Company, Bridgeport, Connecticut

- Snow White beetleware, including a "Meal Time Set," with a Snow White cup, a Sneezy dish, and a Dopey bowl.

Joseph Dixon Crucible Company, Jersey City, New Jersey

- Snow White pencil boxes, single-level or with two- and three-drawer compartments.

Emerson Radio and Phonograph Corporation, New York

- Wood Syroco baby table-model Snow White and the Seven Dwarfs radio (originally sold for $14.95).

A. S. Fishback, Inc., New York

- Costumes and masks for Halloween, including Snow White and all the Dwarfs, the Witch, and the Wicked Queen.

One of the most popular films shown in Soviet Russia is Snow White and the Seven Dwarfs, *and the painted Grumpy (left) and Dopey (right) are frosted-glass perfume decanter bottles made in the U.S.S.R., ca. 1952.*

Sheet music for "Heigh-Ho" ("It's off to work we go!"), from Snow White and the Seven Dwarfs, *Bourne Company, New York, dated 1939.*

A porcelain Dopey creamer from a Snow White child's tea set, made in Japan for George Borgfeldt Corp. of New York, marked "© 1937 W.D. Ent." on the bottom.

William Rogers, Meriden, Connecticut
- Snow White baby spoons and baby fork-and-knife sets.

La Mode Studios, Inc., New York
- Painted plaster hang-up lamps, radio lamps, and nightlights with shades manufactured by Doris Lamp Shades Inc., New York;
- Snow White and Dopey bookends.

Micro-Lite Company, Inc., New York
- Dopey Kiddie Lite, battery-run.

Lightfoot Schultz Company, New York
- Molded soap figurines of Snow White and the Seven Dwarfs.

Storkline Furniture Corporation of Chicago
- Juvenile furniture, complete set for nursery, made of wood with Snow White and the Seven Dwarfs lithography, including a table, two chairs, a high-chair, crib, chest of drawers, and a coat rack.

Owens-Illinois Glass Company of Toledo, Ohio
- Snow White beverage glass bottle;
- Set of eight glass character tumblers with Snow White and the Seven Dwarfs and one tumbler with Snow White and all the Dwarfs together;
- Snow White metal-litho lunchpail and a Snow White sandwich tray.

Fisher–Price Toys, Inc., East Aurora, New York
- Dopey and Doc action pull-toys, Snow White pull-toys.

N. N. Hill Brass Company, East Hampton, Connecticut
- Snow White telephone;
- Pull-action-toys featuring Snow White and the Seven Dwarfs.

Louis Marx & Company, New York
- Dopey wind-up tin-litho mechanical figure.

Odoro Company, Inc., New York
- Snow White and Seven Dwarfs toy treasure chest, litho on cardboard.

The Ohio Art Company, Bryan, Ohio
- Tin-litho toy teasets featuring Snow White and the Seven Dwarfs, drums, sandpails, shovels, watering cans.

Plastic Novelties, Inc., New York
- Pencil sharpeners and napkin rings of Snow White and the Seven Dwarfs in brightly colored Catalin with decals.

Crown Toy Manufacturing Company, Brooklyn, New York
- Figurine coin bank of Dopey.

George Borgfeldt & Company, New York
- Porcelain toy teaset in boxed set including four cups and saucers, four dishes, a teapot, creamer and sugar bowl, and a bowl;
- Borgfeldt imported from Japan many large-sized, medium, and miniature sets of Snow White and the Seven Dwarfs hand-painted bisque figurines. The dwarfs played musical instruments in some of these beautiful figurine sets.

J. L. Wright, Inc., Chicago
- Snow White and all Seven Dwarfs single figurine sets and cast sets of salt and pepper shakers made of painted unbreakable metal.

Evan K. Shaw Pottery Company
- Snow White glazed ceramic figurines, and all Seven Dwarfs.

American Pottery Company, Los Angeles, California
- Ceramic figures of Snow White and the Seven Dwarfs.

Leeds Pottery Company
- A Snow White figurine planter, a Dopey planter, a Dopey bank, and a Snow White bank.

Capitol Cravat Company, New York
- Boys' neckties featuring just the Seven Dwarfs.

D. H. Neumann Company, New York
- Seven Dwarfs ties and a tie rack.

Ira G. Katz, New York
- Girls' hats and bonnets.

Converse Rubber Company, Malden, Massachusetts
- Snow White children's canvas oxfords and rubber boots.

H. Jacob & Sons, Brooklyn, New York
- Girls' slippers and shoes featuring Snow White.

Hughes-Autograf Company, Inc., New York
- Hairbrush-and-comb sets;
- Toothbrushes featuring Snow White and Grumpy and Doc.

Louis Weiss, New York
- Snow White umbrella;
- Dopey umbrella;
- Snow White printed oil-silk raincapes for little girls, including a matching purse and umbrella, as a set.

Rubber 5½" doll of Dopey painted yellow (the suit) and purple (the hat), manufactured in 1938 by the Seiberling Latex Products Company of Akron, Ohio. A boxed set of Snow White and all seven dwarfs was available, or they were sold separately.

Whitman Publishing Company, Racine, Wisconsin

- Snow White cut-out dolls and dresses;
- Paint books, storybooks of the animals from the movie, a Snow White and the Seven Dwarfs Big Little Book, linen books, etc.

Ingersoll–Waterbury Clock Company, Waterbury, Connecticut

- Snow White (U.S. Time Division), 1940 wristwatch packaged in box with imitation cel from movie-scene);
- Dopey wristwatch, 1948.

Bayard Company, France

- *Blanche Neige* animated alarm clock, 1969.

New York Graphic Society, New York

- Beautiful lithographed prints with Freplex frames without glass in three different sizes: 20 by 24 inches, 15 by 18 inches, 10 by 12 inches.

Tin plate from a children's Snow White tea set. Ohio Art Company, Bryan, Ohio, dated 1937.

PINOCCHIO

Pinocchio, Walt Disney's second full-length animated Technicolor feature was released on February 23, 1940, and has been referred to by many critics as one of the studio's most innovative and beautifully animated films. Christopher Finch, in his book *The Art of Walt Disney* (Abrams, 1973), said that *Snow White* may have provided Disney with his finest moment, but *Pinocchio* is probably his greatest film, adding that *Pinocchio* possesses a technical brilliance that has never been surpassed. With a gripping story line and a memorable musical score, it is the top favorite of many Disney fans.

On Christmas Day 1939, just prior to its release, Disney's version of *Pinocchio*, the story of the wooden marionette who becomes a real boy, was introduced in an on-the-air preview by Hollywood director Cecil B. De Mille on the famous Lux Radio Theatre, to the delight of children and their parents. The adventures of Pinocchio begin at Gepetto's workshop, where the wooden marionette meets the Blue Fairy, who introduces him to his conscience, tiny Jiminy Cricket. Figaro the Cat and Cleo the Goldfish are on hand for Pinocchio to play with, but Gepetto longs for his creation to be a real live boy. This wish is practically granted; the next day his marionette has been transformed into a talking, walking wooden boy, free of strings.

Pinocchio, who always seems to have an intense curiosity as well as a long nose for finding trouble, meets a sly fox named J.

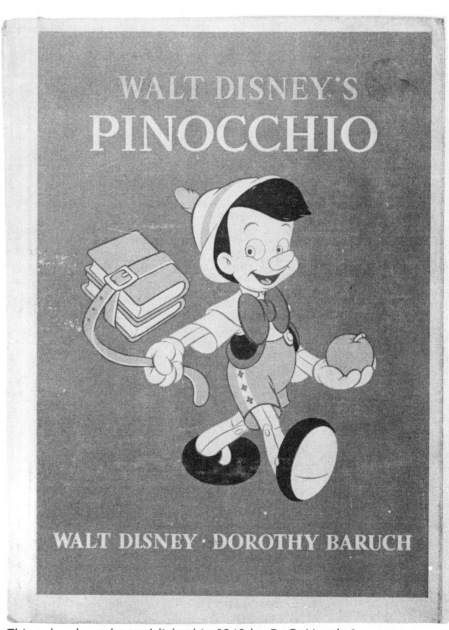

This school reader, published in 1940 by D. C. Heath & Company of Boston, has a linen-like cover and contains full-color illustrations with a vocabulary-building text after Disney's feature film Pinocchio.

Pinocchio pinback button used as a promotional give-away at movie houses in 1940 and 1941, from Kay Kamen Ltd., "representing Walt Disney Productions."

Worthington Foulfellow (Honest John) and his dour pussycat pal Gideon (Giddy) on his way to school. Promising Pinocchio a glamorous life in the theater as an actor, the two kidnappers lure him to the traveling caravan of Stromboli, the cruel fat puppeteer, who keeps him imprisoned in a cage, allowing him out only to perform the song "I've Got No Strings" onstage. Jiminy Cricket warned Pinocchio that he was heading for trouble, and calls out for the Blue Fairy to come to the rescue. When the beautiful, glowing Blue Fairy appears to ask Pinocchio how he got into his awful predicament, he invents a tall tale, only to find his nose growing longer with each new twist of his fabricated story. Although Pinocchio does get a second chance and is released from Stromboli's locks and chains, he succumbs once again to the manipulative charms of sly Foulfellow and Gideon. They convince him to join a band of boys going to Pleasure Island, a place where these ruffians are given to ex-

cessive good times, only to be turned into work donkeys.

Pinocchio, not realizing what the consequences will be, decides to go, opting for a life of fun and pleasure. Soon after arriving on the island, he sees his new friend Lampwick, who brazenly smokes, drinks beer, and plays pool, turn into a braying donkey right before his eyes. When Pinocchio notices that he too is growing a tail and two donkey ears, he runs to a cliff at the edge of Pleasure Island and, with Jiminy hanging on tightly, jumps into the sea. Once in the ocean, these two are swallowed by Monstro the Whale and live for some time on a raft inside the huge whale's belly, eating the fish swallowed by Monstro. Lonely old Gepetto, the cat Figaro, and Cleo the goldfish come to rescue Pinocchio out of the whale's belly. In the end, after being thought dead by Gepetto, Pinocchio is brought back to life by the Blue Fairy and her magic wand. She gives him real flesh and blood, and he becomes a

Pinocchio (center) is a made in Japan painted chinaware figurine. Others (left to right) are Figaro the Cat, Jiminy Cricket, Honest John, and Giddy the Cat, in a green glaze from the National Porcelain Company, Inc. of Trenton, N. J. In 1940 these knick-knacks sold for 10 cents each at the dime store.

good and honest fellow, having learned some hard lessons about the real world.

Pinocchio is now considered a Disney masterpiece but, unlike *Snow White*, was not a financial success when it was released. But "When You Wish Upon a Star," sung by Cliff Edwards (also known as the popular recording artist "Ukulele Ike") as Jiminy Cricket, and written by Leigh Harline and Ned Washington, received an Academy Award in 1941 as the best song. Mr. Harline and Mr. Washington shared another award from the Academy, with Paul J. Smith, for best original musical score. Besides Cliff "Ukulele Ike" Edwards, participating in the making of *Pinocchio* were two other

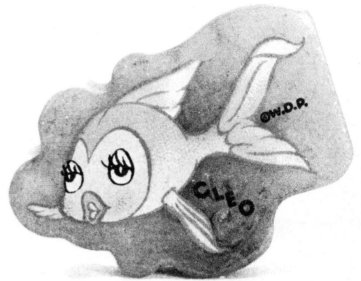

School pencil sharpener in Catalin featuring a glamorous Cleo the Goldfish from Pinocchio. Plastic Novelties Inc. of New York sold this school novelty item for 10 cents in the early 1940s.

Original release 1940 photo still from Pinocchio showing a sad little puppet with bad-boy donkey ears and tail accompanied by his conscience Jiminy Cricket, just after their escape from Pleasure Island.

Pinocchio soap figurine with the original box from the Lightfoot Schultz Company of New York, 1940. Soap sculpture is especially desirable as a collectible because it is very perishable.

An R.K.O. newsette program dated April 4, 1940 for Pinocchio, "direct from seven weeks at Radio City Center Theatre."

stars, child actors Dickie Jones, the voice of Pinocchio, and Frankie Darro as the voice of Lampwick. Marge Champion, the dancer, posed as model for the beautiful Blue Fairy.

All the characters in *Pinocchio* were used on every kind of merchandise, with the same impact on the marketplace as that of *Snow White and the Seven Dwarfs*. The character of Pinocchio was an instant merchandising success as a stuffed doll and wooden marionette, and following his decided little wooden boy lead were Jiminy Cricket, Figaro the Cat, Cleo the Goldfish, Gepetto, the Blue Fairy, Stromboli, J. Worthington Foulfellow (Honest John) the Sly Fox, Gideon the Cat, Monstro the Whale, the Donkey, and Lampwick, the Pleasure Island bad boy. The image of Pinocchio was lent to advertisers to sell Royal gelatin desserts; Cocomalt, Du Pont Duco enamel paints; Sunlight Butter (which offered Pinocchio hats as a premium); Pinocchio ice cream in a cup from National Dairy Products; Jiminy Cricket bubble gum; Pinocchio lollipops with his likeness on the candy; Pinocchio wrapped-stick chewing gum and other "gay wrapped character candies," all from Overland Candy Corporation; Pinocchio Diamond Crystal Shaker salt; General Foods Corporation Post Toasties (Pinocchio cutouts on the back of the box); Gillette Safety Razor Company blue-blade safety razors and shaving blades; Calox antiseptic mouthwash from McKesson & Robbins, Inc.; and giveaway glasses, posters, and stamps distributed through Independent Grocers' Alliance. There were a Monstro soda, a Pinocchio milkshake (National Dairy Products), and Pinocchio Bread (a

wax-paper bread-wrapper with Pinocchio's image on it was used by hundreds of different bakers). The following is a list of *Pinocchio* collectibles, listed by manufacturer, that are considered very desirable by Disneyphiles:

George Borgfeldt & Company, New York
- A wind-up Pinocchio mechanical doll, 10½ inches, with key;
- Pinocchio wood puppet;
- Pinocchio and Jiminy Cricket bisque figurines.

Crown Toy Manufacturing Company, Inc., Brooklyn, New York
- Pinocchio doll, 12 inches, fully clothed with movable wooden arms and head;
- Painted wood composition bank with lock and key;
- Hand puppet of Pinocchio.

Ideal Novelty and Toy Company, New York
- Pinocchio 12-inch flexible doll;
- Pinocchio 12-inch jointed doll;
- Pinocchio 10-inch wood-composition doll with jointed legs and arms.

Knickerbocker Toy Company, New York
- Pinocchio dolls of composition with jointed legs and arms;
- Stuffed Pinocchio dolls;
- Donkey doll made of long pile;
- Figaro doll made with mohair;
- Figaro doll of composition, fully jointed;
- Jiminy Cricket doll, composition, fully jointed;
- Cleo doll, stuffed.

Richard G. Krueger, Inc., New York
- Pinocchio dolls made of wood with jointed legs and arms, stuffed bodies, fully clothed, with lifelike wool hair.

Louis Marx & Company, New York
- Tin-litho action toys of Pinocchio walking, and Pinocchio the Acrobat.

Sieberling Latex Products Company, Akron, Ohio
- Molded rubber figures of Pinocchio, Donkey, Jiminy Cricket, Cleo, and Figaro.

Bryant Electric Company, Bridgeport, Connecticut
- Beetleware set, colored plastic with two-color character imprint.

Relaxon Products, Chicago
- Teeny-tot line of washable imitation-leather furniture in red, green, and two-tone brown.

De-Ward Novelty Company, Inc., Angola, New York
- Ring-toss game, lithographed on wood in bright colors— "You Toss a Ring on Pinocchio's nose."

Joseph Dixon Crucible Company, Jersey City, New Jersey
- Pencil boxes of Pinocchio and Jiminy Cricket.

Fisher-Price Toys, Inc., East Aurora, New York
- Pinocchio and Jiminy Cricket pull-toys.

N. N. Hill Brass Company, East Hampton, Connecticut
- Pinocchio and Jiminy Cricket pull-toys.

Flexo Products Corporation, Chicago
- Pinocchio and Jiminy Cricket lamps of thermo-plastic wood fiber simulating hand-carved wood, finished by air-brush and by hand, with beautiful decorated parchment shades.

A. S. Fishback, Inc., New York
- Halloween costumes and masks of Pinocchio, Jiminy Cricket, and the Blue Fairy.

Hughes—Autograf Brush Company, New York
- Pinocchio metal-litho brushes and plastic combs.

Lightfoot Schultz Company, New York
- Cleo, Pinocchio, and the other characters in soap.

Multi-Products, Chicago
- Molded wood-fiber figures of all the characters from Pinocchio, brush sets, pen sets, bookends, figurines, and wall plaques.

William Rogers, Meriden, Connecticut
- Sets of knives, forks, and spoons for young adults with Pinocchio, Jiminy Cricket, and the Donkey featured.

The Ohio Art Company, Bryan, Ohio
- Tin-lithographed toy teaset with metal tray.

Libbey Glass Company, Toledo, Ohio
- Set of twelve Pinocchio-character safedge tumblers.

Plastic Novelties, Inc., New York
- Catalin pencil sharpeners and thermometers, decals of Cleo, Figaro, the Blue Fairy, and the other characters on bright plastic.

National Dairy Products offered free Pinocchio merchandise prizes including belts, hats, toss toys, rubber stamp sets, paper masks, hand puppets, pencil tablets, and handkerchiefs to children who saved and sent in their 1940 ice cream Dixie-cup lids.

Sheet music for "When You Wish Upon a Star," from Walt Disney's Pinocchio. This song, with lyrics by Ned Washington and music by Leigh Harline, won the Academy Award as best song in 1941. Another Oscar went to the musical score.

Transogram Company, Inc., New York

- Tin lithographed crayon box with crayons, featuring Pinocchio, Jiminy Cricket, and others.

Western Table and Stationery Corporation, St. Joseph, Missouri

- Pinocchio school and writing tablets.

Brier Manufacturing Company, Providence, Rhode Island

- Charm jewelry of Pinocchio, Jiminy Cricket, and Cleo.

L. Lewis & Son, New York

- Girls' Pinocchio hats;
- Boys' Pinocchio caps.

Newark Felt Novelty Company, Newark, New Jersey

- Children's felt Pinocchio hats with feather quills.

D. H. Neumann Company, New York

- Boys' Pinocchio ties and suspenders and a tie rack.

Philbert Hat Company, New York

- Gay sports fuzzies for women in twenty-three brand-new 1940s colors.

Milton Bradley Company, Springfield, Massachusetts

- Pinocchio game set.

Amloid Company, Rochelle Park, New Jersey

- Celluloid baby rattles featuring Pinocchio.

Brayton's Laguna Pottery, Laguna Beach, California

- Pinocchio figurines in pastel pottery.

National Porcelain Company, Trenton, New Jersey

- Highly glazed, one-color china figurines, 2½ and 3½ inches, featuring all the *Pinocchio* characters.

Evan K. Shaw Pottery Company

- Ceramic figurines of all *Pinocchio* characters.

American Pottery Company, Los Angeles, California

- Pottery figurines of the *Pinocchio* characters.

Ingersoll-Waterbury Clock Company, Waterbury, Connecticut

- Pinocchio watch, produced in 1948;
- Jiminy Cricket watch, produced in 1948.

Bayard Company, France

- Pinocchio wind-up alarm clock, 1960.

Photo still from Pinocchio *shows the little wooden boy locked in Stromboli's cage. Re-release photo dated 1961.*

MICKEY MOUSE GOES TO WAR

Disney's war cartoons included *Der Fuehrer's Face*, which was a film originally designed to sell war bonds to movie audiences. It starred an angry Donald Duck in Nutziland. The film received an Academy Award for Walt Disney in 1943 as the best of the 1942–1943 war period. The song "Der Fuehrer's Face" was a top hit on jukeboxes and with servicemen in those years, as recorded by Spike Jones and His City Slickers.

The most important Disney wartime short is *Victory Through Air Power*, which was based on a best-selling book by Major Alexander de Seversky in which the major outlined his ideas about strategic long-range bombing. Though de Seversky's ideas were opposed by American military planners, Disney felt so strongly about them that he produced the film version himself, releasing it into movie theaters in the belief that it would help America win World War II. As it turned out de Seversky was correct in his thinking. During the war years, Disney Studios had engaged in making Army and Navy training films for the U.S. government, which Disney himself estimated in 1948 had used up over three hundred thousand feet of film.

Mickey Mouse and Donald Duck did their part in morale-building for all branches of the armed services through appearing as mascots on all sorts of mil-

© WALT DISNEY PRODUCTIONS

Two-dimensional cardboard wall picture, "Mickey marches to War," ca. 1943.

An angry Donald Duck throws an apple in the swastika eye of Adolf Hitler on the cover of this 1942 sheet music from the cartoon short, "Der Fuehrer's Face," which won an Academy Award as best cartoon short subject for 1942–43. Southern Music Publishing Company, Inc., New York.

itary insignia, patches, emblems, and special flags. The first insignia emblem, created by Disney in 1940, pictured a venomous mosquito riding the Mosquito Fleet PT boat torpedoes. Thousands of requests poured into Disney Studios, and they did their patriotic duty for the war effort, designing each and every insignia for each outfit that asked for it. All this effort took a tremendous amount of time, but there was never a charge for the work.

Donald Duck was more frequently used than Mickey Mouse on insignia, as he could really express the necessary rage and anger the boyish, smiling Mickey could never quite muster up for the enemy. It is astonishing today to see a picture of Mickey Mouse with a childlike grin watching a Japanese ship sink, but he was used in just this way during the war effort.

A wartime postcard from Great Britain showing Mickey Mouse on his way to Scotland Yard in a police helmet, 1940s.

Three match books produced for the war effort by the Pepsi Cola Company. left to right: a flying squirrel for the Aviation Cadets (U.S. Naval Aviation Station), a Fantasia character for the P40 45th Air Base Squadron, and an alligator from Fantasia for the Jackson Air Base. All Disney designed war insignia from the early 1940s.

World War II insignia designed by Walt Disney Studios on service matchbooks. Left: an angry Donald Duck marching to war for the U.S. Naval Reserve. Right: A young centaurette from Fantasia in a Wac's uniform and carrying a box of first aid for the Women's Ambulance and Defense Corps of America.

Disney Studios designed a special World War II war bond featuring a grouping of popular Disney characters. Baby Weems, bottom center, was introduced in 1941 in The Reluctant Dragon. U.S. Government Printing Office, 1944.

Liberty magazine, dedicated to "The American Way of Life," sold for 5 cents in October 1940. Walt Disney cover art depicts Donald Duck driving a U.S. 1776 car. Note the hawk-like duck that serves as a hood ornament ready to fly off to war once it breaks free of its ropes.

Pluto was second to Donald in insignia-land, and other characters like Snow White and all the Dwarfs, Ferdinand the Bull, Thumper, Dumbo, Jiminy Cricket, Peg Leg Pete, the Three Little Pigs, and the Big Bad Wolf were all seen on special Disney insignia, either sitting on top of whizzing bombs, nursing the wounded, or blowing up submarines. Disney studio characters that previously did not exist also turn up on insignia, making it difficult for collectors to ferret out these memorabilia, which are found on embroidered patches, tumblers, match sets, pinback buttons, wall plaques, and somewhere—God help us—on a bomb. Among the best known military groups to use Disney insignia were the Sea-Bees, the Alaskan Command, and the Flying Tigers.

Mickey Mouse certainly appeared on his share of Marine, Navy, and Army military unit insignia, and, as fired up at the enemy as Donald could get, the beatific Mickey may have had the last word. The secret password for the D-Day landing was M-I-C-K-E-Y M-O-U-S-E!

V-for Victory symbol—on target—with Mickey, Donald, the Three Little Pigs and Pluto the Pup from the reverse side of sheet music of "Der Fuehrer's Face," 1942.

THE FORTIES FEATURE FILMS

Disney was concerned that Donald Duck seemed to be gaining in popularity over his pet favorite, Mickey Mouse, and in 1938 decided to create an artful short feature especially for Mickey, called *The Sorcerer's Apprentice*—a story based on a Goethe poem and set to music in 1897 by Paul Dukas. At a party, Disney met Leopold Stokowski, who agreed to conduct the score for this proposed cartoon, with the proviso that Disney expand his ideas and the film itself to feature length. Disney immediately saw this as a great opportunity to develop new ideas and concepts centered around live action and animated film. Throughout the 1930s, he had encouraged his staff of animators and artists to improve their skills and techniques by sending them to special art classes, always demanding high-quality work from them, if not perfection. Here was a situation where music, animation, and visual fantasy were to make the greatest demand of all on the Disney staff. Creating a new popular animation form that could become high art had always been a goal of Walt Disney, and with *Fantasia* he finally fully achieved it.

Fantasia, in Technicolor and Fantasound, was released on November 13, 1940, running two full hours, with narrative by Deems Taylor and with Leopold Stokowski conducting the Phila-

"*Dance of the Hours*" child's book from Fantasia, Harper & Brothers, Publishers, New York, London, 1940.

Pinback promotional give-away button from the 1941 feature-length Disney film Dumbo. On reverse: "Kay Kamen Ltd., representing Walt Disney Productions."

Dumbo, the flying elephant; glazed midnight-blue ceramic figurine from Vernon Kiln, 8½" high, 1942.

delphia Orchestra in Tchaikovsky's *Nutcracker Suite*, *The Rite of Spring* by Stravinsky, *Pastoral Symphony* by Beethoven, *Dance of the Hours* by Ponchielli, *Night on Bald Mountain* by Mussorgsky, and *Toccata and Fugue in D Minor* by Bach—all to cartoon configurations. Mickey Mouse was an instant success in the "Sorcerer's Apprentice" segment, but the film, like *Pinocchio*, was not successful at the box office. However, it did well in its subsequent rereleases in 1944, 1946, 1953, 1956, 1963, 1969 and on into the 1970s and 1980s, when it enjoyed a "perpetual" run. Sometime in the late 1960s the film was seen both as a visual acid trip and a high-on-pot scene for tuned-in dropouts, who would see *Fantasia* over and over again.

By 1970 *Fantasia* had become an early "cult film," and Disney Studio's character-merchandise division issued a statement in the company's annual report that Mickey Mouse merchandise featuring the early Mickey rodent image was also enjoying a new wave of popularity among these hip young people. This report coincides with the beginnings of the incredible road to revival for Mickey Mouse memorabilia, which began in the psychedelic period and continues unabated to this day.

The comic cartoon characters from *Fantasia*, the dancing hippos, ostriches, alligators, Chinese mushrooms with faces, unicorns, centaurs, mythological gods, cupids, dinosaurs and pterodactyls, did not inspire a great deal of merchandise—though there is some, such as *Fantasia* paint books, story-

books, Art Deco style pottery vases, plates, and figurines. A particularly beautiful art book called simply *Walt Disney's "Fantasia"* by Deems Taylor (published in 1940 by Simon and Schuster) is 158 pages long (measuring 13 by 9¾ inches), with excellent color reproductions from the film tipped in. Posters, cels, stills, and original programs from *Fantasia* are especially collectible, and many lithos abound of Mickey in his wizard's cap—reproduced by now into the millions.

The Reluctant Dragon, released on June 20, 1941, followed on the heels of *Fantasia*, and it was meant to tell the inside story of how cartoons are made. Robert Benchley narrated the film, and it was successful in showing the inside of the Disney studio. In black-and-white and also in color, this film had two notable characters—the Reluctant Dragon (an inspiration for a later Disney animated film, *Pete's Dragon*) and a little baby boy with a giant IQ called Baby Weems.

While the critics were cool to *The Reluctant Dragon* and *Fantasia*, they were very enthusiastic about *Dumbo*, released by RKO Radio Pictures on October 23, 1941, and produced for a then still low figure for an animated feature of $800,000. The film was a resounding success, the type of warm story expressing universal truths in animal guise—this time an elephant that could fly. Dumbo resembled the earlier Elmer Elephant but with much bigger ears. The musical score for *Dumbo* included the songs "Baby Mine," "All Aboard," "Look Out for Mrs.

Mickey Mouse child's wooden pull-toy from Fisher-Price Toys, Inc., New York, ca. 1940s.

Walking Pinocchio wind-up action toy with rolling eyes, color litho on tin, Louis Marx & Company, New York; marked "1939 Walt Disney Enterprises." Shown with the original box. Collection of Robert Lesser.

Metal sparkler toy, 5½", litho on metal. Press lever and sparks shoot out of eyes and mouth. A Nifty Toy, sold by George Borgfeldt Corp., New York, 1931. Hake's Americana and Collectibles, York, Pa.

Mickey Mouse paint set, Marks Brothers Company of Boston, 1934.

Mickey and Minnie "Helpmate" child's tea set, color lithograph on tin, Ohio Art Company, 1934.

Child's spinning top, color litho on metal, featuring a Mickey Mouse band, produced by George Borgfeldt Corp., New York, 1934.

Mickey Mouse safety blocks, painted wooden Disney character alphabet blocks by Halsam Products Company of Chicago, 1935. Hake's Americana and Collectibles, York, Pa.

Mickey Mouse 'Vera' puzzle, cardboard puzzle and box, made in Paris, France, ca. 1933.

Mickey Mouse scatter ball game, color litho on cardboard, manufactured by Marks Brothers Company, of Boston, 1934.

Mickey Mouse bagatelle game, litho on paper, wood, and metal, manufactured by Marks Brothers Company of Boston, 1934.

dream segment has the best and most imaginative animation art to be seen in a Disney film.

Bambi, a Technicolor feature cartoon, opened on August 21, 1942, at Radio City Music Hall. Based on a story by Felix Salten, the film and the array of wonderful woodland animal characters, notably Bambi the young deer, Thumper the rabbit, Flower the skunk, and the Wise Old Owl delighted audiences and remain today one of Disney's most endearing creations. The sequences when Bambi's mother is shot by man-the-enemy, and the blazing forest fire—started by man's carelessness—are among the film's most startling moments. *Bambi* continues to be enchanting on each rerelease.

The Better Little Book of Walt Disney's Bambi, based on the famous story by Felix Salten. Whitman Publishing Company, Racine, Wisc., 1942.

Catalin Bambi pencil sharpener with decal applique from Plastic Novelties, Inc. of New York, ca. 1942.

One of the most beloved Disney characters to emerge out of the feature film Bambi is Thumper the Rabbit, illustrated on the cover of a book published by Grosset & Dunlap, Inc., New York, 1942.

Glazed ceramic figurines, left to right: Thumper the Rabbit's girlfriend who "twitterpated" the boy bunnies in the forest, Flower the Skunk and Thumper, all made by the Evan K. Shaw Company in 1946 after cartoon characters from the 1942 feature film, Bambi.

Glazed ceramic figurines of Donald Duck, made in 1940 by Brayton's Laguna Pottery of Laguna Beach, Cal., and José Carioca, made in 1946 by the Evan K. Shaw Company.

Decca Records produced this album of songs on 78 rpm records from Walt Disney's The Three Caballeros, a South American good-neighbor policy feature-length film, 1944.

Stork," "When I See an Elephant Fly," and "Pink Elephants on Parade." The "Pink Elephants"

During the early years of World War II the United States government asked Disney and his staff to travel south of the border to help establish and maintain friendly relations with South America. These visits resulted in two films of neighborly goodwill, *Saludos Amigos* (1943) and *The Three Caballeros* (1945). *Saludos Amigos* features Donald Duck, Goofy, a plane called *Little Pedro*, and Walt Disney himself; and introduces the famous cartoon star parrot José Carioca. The song "Brazil" was incorporated into this film, which was actually just a format for the much better *The Three Caballeros*. The three good pals in this almost psychedelic live-action-combined-with-animation movie were José (Joe) Carioca, Panchito (a pistol-packing chicken), and Donald Duck. Carmen Miranda's (the original 1940s chica-boom-chic Brazilian bombshell) sister Aurora Miranda, dancing with Donald Duck, contributed to the South American fun and box-office success of this movie, which had two 1940s song hits, "Baia" and "You Belong to My Heart" ("*Solamente Una Vez*"). This film is seldom seen in rerelease, but when it is, it's shamefully cut. Seen in its entirety, it is one of Disney's most attractive features.

The Song of the South, featuring the wonderful stories of Uncle Remus and Br'er Rabbit in live action with animation, and starring a live Luana Patten, Bobby Driscoll, and an especially wonderful James Baskett as Uncle Remus singing "Zip-a-Dee Doo-Dah," is one of Disney's all-time greats. This movie was a major moneymaker for Disney in 1946 and in the 1956 rerelease, but was withheld during the angry civil-rights period of the 1960s. When it was finally shown once again in 1972, it was the most successful rerelease in Disney's history, proving that an Uncle Remus story is still the best in the whole wide world and breaks all barriers of racial conflict. The role of old Uncle Remus as played by James Baskett is one that comes from the heart.

Make Mine Music, also in 1946, with Willie the Whale, features the sounds of Benny Goodman's Orchestra, Dinah Shore, Jerry Colonna, Nelson Eddy, the Pied Pipers, and the Andrews Sisters.

Fun and Fancy Free (1947), featuring ventriloquist Edgar Bergen with his pals Charlie McCarthy and Mortimer Snerd; Cliff Edwards; the Dinning Sisters; Dinah Shore; and Luana Patten—with special guest appearances from Mickey Mouse, Donald Duck, and Goofy in an exciting cartoon segment entitled *Mickey and the Beanstalk*—is a lightweight Disney feature with live action and animation combined.

Melody Time (1948), had a cast that included movie cowboy Roy Rogers, Luana Patten, Bobby Driscoll, the Sons of the Pioneers, and Ethel Smith, using also the voices of Buddy Clark, the Andrews Sisters, Frances Langford, and Dennis Day as "Johnny Appleseed." One no-

Caballero Panchito, the gun-totin' South American bandito chicken from the feature film, The Three Caballeros. Glazed ceramic figurine made by the Evan K. Shaw Company in 1946.

José Carioca, painted ceramic turnabout cookie jar made by the Leeds China Company of Chicago, 1947. On the reverse side is caballero Donald Duck.

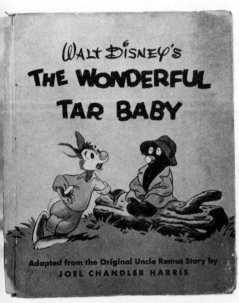

Walt Disney's The Wonderful Tar Baby *as told by Marion Palmer and adapted from the original Uncle Remus story by Joel Chandler Harris. From the Disney film Song of the South, this children's book was published by Grosset & Dunlap, New York, in 1946.*

Mickey and the Beanstalk, *based on the story in the Walt Disney motion picture,* Fun and Fancy Free. *The book, featuring Mickey, Goofy, and Donald on the cover and with picture illustrations by Campbell Grant, was published in 1947 by Grosset & Dunlap, New York.*

table sequence features Ethel Smith, the organist, dancing to "Blame It on the Samba" with Donald Duck and his South American sidekicks Panchito and José Carioca.

So Dear to my Heart (1948), featuring Bobby Driscoll and Luana Patten again, Burl Ives, Harry Carey, and Beulah Bondi, is live action with a minimum of animation. A nostalgic film in the manner of other 1940s turn-of-the-century films like *Meet Me in St. Louis* or *Centennial Summer*, it received commendable reviews but was not a money-maker. Disney himself loved this particular film because it reminded him of his early boyhood on the farm.

Ichabod and Mr. Toad (1949), the last of the 1940s features, has the Ichabod character narrated by Bing Crosby and the *Willows* segment narrated by Basil Rathbone. This film proved once again to doubting critics that Disney could still produce an entertaining first-rate all-animated feature, and it is among the perennials of single reissues, as well as having had a good deal of exposure on Disney's television shows.

This even dozen of films produced very little in the way of collectible character merchandise, but each film generated memorabilia in the form of theater programs, posters, lobby cards, stills, storybooks, and other related ephemera. *Fantasia, Dumbo,* and *Bambi* especially inspired manufacturers of ceramic and pottery pieces, like the American Pottery and Laguna Pottery Companies of Los Angeles, to produce vases, planters, and figurines—including a beautiful José Carioca figure from *The Three Caballeros.*

THE TELEVISION 1950S — MICKEY, DAVY, & ZORRO

Disney memorabilia from the 1950s are often referred to by collectors as "latter-day Disney-ana" from "the silver age in collectibles." The feature films from which latter-day Disneyana exist include *Cinderella* (1950), *Alice in Wonderland* (1951), *Peter Pan* (1953), *20,000 Leagues under the Sea* (a non-cartoon live-action color film based on Jules Verne's novel, released in 1954), *Davy Crockett, King of the Wild Frontier* (live-action color, 1955), *Lady and the Tramp* (1955), and *Sleeping Beauty* (1959). Collectibles include watches (Cinderella, Alice, and Sleeping Beauty), figurines in china and bisque, Golden Books, Big Little Books, paint books, dolls, records, paper-doll cut-outs, movie posters, lobby cards, stills, jewelry, savings banks, and other items. For many collectors the products from the 1950s as well as the design concept and graphics on them represent the end of the golden age of Disney collectibles. However, the nostalgia market for items from the 1950s is a burgeoning one, and many new collectors of 1950s memorabilia are now seeking out collectibles associated with the aforementioned feature films, which promoted character merchandise in stores along with the opening of each film. Memora-

A club member pinback button in red, white, and black with a pink-faced Mickey Mouse from the television *Mickey Mouse Club,* which premiered on October 3, 1955 on the American Broadcasting Company network.

Quick magazine, a pocketsize
newsweekly that sold for 10 cents, calls
Cinderella Walt Disney's greatest star.
Walt himself with Cinderella on the
cover, April 24, 1950.

bilia from *Cinderella*, *Alice in Wonderland*, *Peter Pan*, *Lady and the Tramp*, and *Sleeping Beauty* are now plentiful and represent a solid future investment to a beginning collector of Disneyana.

Much of the best of the 1950s Disney memorabilia comes out of or was inspired by the second Mickey Mouse Club. The television Mickey Mouse Club had its premier network telecast on October 3, 1955, on American Broadcasting Company. During the first two years the Monday-to-Friday one-hour black-and-white program was shown to kids after school from 5 to 6 p.m. Following this two-year period, the show used a half-hour format through 1958, when the popular series came to an end. The show also had great success when it was reissued (from 1962 to 1965) throughout America and in Spain, Italy, France, Japan, Germany, Australia, Finland, Mexico, Switzerland, and Canada, as well as many South American countries, although in these countries sometimes only portions were shown. In 1975 *The New Mickey Mouse Club*, a half-hour program strongly reminiscent of the 1950s program, was videotaped and distributed in fifty-four markets.

Nonbreakable 78 rpm record set album from R.C.A. Victor, with a
storybook included. Note Cinderella's mouse friends Jacques and
Gus-Gus in lower-right corner.

Jacket for 45 rpm record, endorsed by the official 1950s
Mickey Mouse Club, and with all the Mouseketeers singing
"We're the Mouseketeers", led by handsome blonde
Jimmie Dodd.

Mickey Mouse Club Newsreel ushers in the television era.
Toy projector came with sound and slides and is shown
with the original box from Mattel, Inc. Toymakers of Los
Angeles, 1956.

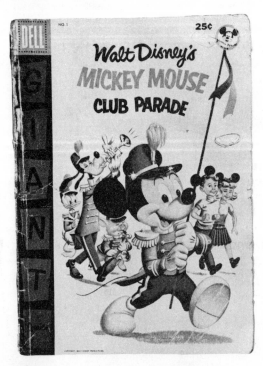

Mickey Mouse carries the Mickey Mouse Club banner on the cover of a giant comic, Dell Publishing Company, New York, (no. 1) dated 1955. This comic book is listed in the Comic Book Price Guide for $56 in mint condition.

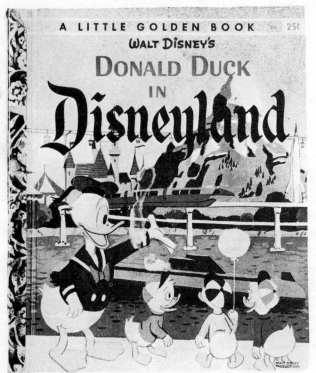

Donald Duck in Disneyland, with his nephews Huey, Dewey, and Louie, a Little Golden Book published by Golden Press, New York, in 1960.

Disney issued a quarterly periodical associated with this 1950s television show, called *Walt Disney's Mickey Mouse Club Magazine*, in which many of the feature articles focused on the young Mouseketeers stars—Annette Funicello, Doreen Tracy, Jay Solari, Dennis Day, Sherry Allen, Bobby Burgess, Margene Storey, Lonnie Burr, Eileen Diamond, Larry Larsen, Tommy Cole, Cheryl Holdridge, Darlene Gillespie, Sharon Baird, Karen Pendleton, Cubby O'Brien, and, as chief Mouseketeer, Jimmie Dodd. This magazine had a peak circulation of four hundred thousand the first two years, and in 1957 changed its title to *Walt Disney's Magazine* when it became bimonthly. Circulation held to three hundred thousand in the third year, but when it dropped to one hundred thousand in the fourth year it was deemed advisable by studio heads to discontinue publication. This magazine is a bona fide magazine collectible today, as many were discarded at a time when people did not think to save them as they might in today's collectibles-conscious age.

Mickey Mouse went from becoming a movie-star mouse to a full-fledged television star on the Mouseketeer TV show. It was as if this second career gave Mickey and his creator, Walt Disney, a further push into cartoonland immortality. The club show ended with the Mouseketeers leading the kids at home with the cheer: "M-I-C-K-E-Y M-O-U-S-E!" spelling Mickey's name out over and over again for millions upon millions of viewers. Mickey Mouse Club merchandise abounded in the five-and-dimes, department stores, and gift shops, including T-shirts, Mickey Mouse hats with ears, records, balloons, banners, pin-back Mouseketeer buttons, and a number of Little Golden Books dedicated to the Mickey Mouse Club and the Mouseketeers.

The Mickey Mouse Editions of Little Golden Books included:

- *Donald Duck and the Mouseketeers*
- *Donald Duck in Disneyland*
- *Donald Duck, Prize Driver*
- *Donald Duck's Safety Book*
- *Goofy, Movie Star*
- *Jiminy Cricket*
- *Mickey Mouse and the Missing Mouseketeers*
- *Mickey Mouse Flies the Christmas Mail*

There were also several Mickey Mouse Club coloring books, a *Mickey Mouse Club Giant Funtime Coloring Book*, a *Mickey Mouse Club Scrap Book*, a *Mickey Mouse Dot-to-Dot Coloring Book*, a *Mickey Mouse Stamp Book*, a *Mousekartoon Coloring Book*, *Walt Disney's Mickey Mouse Club Annual*, *Walt Disney's Mickey Mouse Club Box of 12 Books to Color*, and *Walt Disney's Big Book*. Recordings included *Songs for all the Holidays by the Mouseketeers*, *Songs from the Mickey Mouse Club Serials*, *27 New Songs from the Mickey Mouse Club TV Show*, *Walt Disney's Song Fest*, *Mickey's Big Show*, starring Donald Duck and Clara Cluck, and *We're the Mouseketeers*.

Annette Funicello was the most popular Mouseketeer, receiving as many as 6,000 fan letters a month, and a number of books featured her alone on the cover. These included Annette coloring books, cut-out doll portfolios, comics, and boxed paper dolls, all promoted between 1956 and 1967. Mystery stories like *Annette and the Mystery at Smug-gler's Cove*, *Annette: Desert Mystery Inn*, *Annette: Mystery at Moonstone Bay* had a great success with schoolchildren viewers.

Some of the multitudinous items that featured the jovial 1950s-style Mickey Mouse included the Mousegetar (23 inches) and the Mousegetar Jr. (14 inches) from Mattel, Inc.; Mickey Mouse Club white plastic dinner sets, cups, plates, and bowls from Molded Plastics Inc. of Cleveland, Ohio; a Mouseketeer Western outfit by L. M. Eddy Manufacturing Company, Inc., of Framingham, Massachusetts, which included a hat, tie, badge, belt, two guns, and two holsters; a Mickey Mouse Club Explorer's Club outfit; and a Mickey Mouse bandleader outfit. An attractive Mickey Mouse Club tool chest was manufactured with a variety of tools by the American Toy and Furniture Company of Chicago. The famous black mouse ears in hard-cotton felt were set on a plastic earmuff-type band, called "Mouseketeer Ears," and stamped on each ear "Walt Disney Prod. Mouseketeers." These ears were made by the Empire Plastic Corporation of Tarboro, North Carolina. Hats with ears and ears with plastic bands continue to be manufactured and sold as new collectibles to this day. Many of these Mickey Mouse Club items were offered at and promoted by Disneyland in the 1950s. Toys from Disneyland included a Disneyland Ferris Wheel made by J. Chien & Company of Newark, New Jersey, which features a mechanical bell, six gondolas, and an image of Mickey dead-center. A Disneyland Melody Player Music Box with musical wheels is a fine Disneyland collectible. Strombecker Company wooden toys sold at Disneyland include a

Mousegetar-Jr. with turning musical attachment which plays the official Mouseketeer song, made of black plastic. Selling for $2 in 1955, this instrument measures 14" x 5". Manufactured by Mattel, Inc., which also offered a larger 23" red plastic Mousegetar for $4.

Casey Jr. train set and a Mickey Mouse bus with Donald Duck.

In the early 1930s Roy and Walt Disney had already become aware of the future potential of television. Mickey Mouse cartoons were used in early tests of transmitting equipment, and Disney held all television rights to his films. This was to his advantage when ABC expressed interest in producing a series called *Disneyland*. Part of the understanding that was reached called for ABC to invest in Disney's theme-park dream, which took the name from the series—Disneyland.

The *Disneyland* TV series began in 1954, and the phenomonally popular *Davy Crockett Show*, starring the handsome Fess Parker as Davy, emerged a winner. Originally Walt Disney had thought of developing Daniel Boone or Johnny Appleseed as popular American folk heroes on this show; but when Davy Crockett was chosen, he became an immediate wildlife hero for children of the Eisenhower era. During the run of *Davy Crockett*, a veritable avalanche of Davy Crockett—Indian fighter character merchandise was produced, including fur hats with raccoon tails, suede-fringed frontier jackets and pants, schoolbags, watches, clocks, lunchboxes and vacuum bottles, a Davy Crockett guitar, cookie jars, cups, plates, penknives, toy guns, pinback buttons, storybooks, tents, wagons—all labeled "Walt Disney's Official . . ."

Another popular character to emerge out of this *Disneyland* series was Zorro, the Masked Avenger, who also inspired a great deal of collectible merchandise. Zorro on TV was played by Guy Williams, a dashing figure in an all-black outfit—

Mickey Mouse school lunch box, color litho on metal, ca. 1958.

hat, mask, and cape—and carrying a long whip. This character and Davy Crockett were meant to compete with the immense popularity on TV of the Lone Ranger (also a ''masked avenger'' of justice), Hopalong Cassidy—who dressed all in black—Roy Rogers, and Gene Autry, all of whom achieved great comebacks on black-and-white television. Lash La Rue was the only other 1950s cowboy star to crack a mean whip, and he too preferred all-black attire—hats, shirts, pants, and boots. Zorro, who had originally been played in the movies by both Douglas Fairbanks, Sr., and Tyrone Power, reached a zenith on television when it was reported that *Zorro*, starring Guy Williams, was seen each week during its two-year run by 35 million viewers.

There were hundreds of Zorro items that are among today's early-TV and Disney collectibles. The most popular items are a black hat with a mask attachment from Bailey Company of Los Angeles, California; a Zorro target game and water pistol from Knickerbocker Plastic Company of North Hollywood, California; and a Zorro whip set, including a whip, mask, lariat, and Zorro ring, from M. Shimmel Sons of New York. Boys of the 1950s liked to dress up as Zorro, so capes and outfits—with whip and mask—were also available.

With television, Davy Crockett, Zorro, the Mickey Mouse Club and the Mouseketeers, and all the merchandising in full swing—and Disneyland opening to resounding success in Anaheim, California—the Disney Studios were on the way to becoming an empire. There was to be no stop put on them, and it was all due to M-I-C-K-E-Y M-O-U-S-E!

Reverse side of lunchbox, featuring Donald Duck and his nephews.

Box for the official Disneyland tea set, ca. 1955.

Serving tray from 1955 Disneyland tea set, color litho on metal.

Color litho on metal Disneyland tea set has a bright yellow border, four cups and saucers, four cookie plates, a teapot, and the serving tray. Made by J. Chein Company, Burlington, N.J., ca. 1955.

THAT'S NOT ALL, FOLKS!

In the 1960s, 1970s, and 1980s, new Mickey Mouse memorabilia and new merchandise produced in conjunction with the release of a film became what are regarded today in the nostalgia marketplace as instant collectibles. Many Mickey Mouse items found in the five-and-dime store, department store, specialty gift store, or toy store at present are produced on a limited run. Still others are manufactured in a limited quantity, with the intention that they increase in value each year. These include annual plates and cups or Christmas ornaments with Disney characters—and the date of issue—on them.

Some very beautiful investibles in a limited-run collectors' series are being manufactured by Pride Lines Ltd., 620 N. Queens Avenue, Lindenhurst, New York—including a Mickey Mouse coin bank, a Minnie Mouse coin bank, a Mickey and Minnie streetcar, a Maestro Mickey symphony bandleader, a Santa's Little Helper standard-gauge motorized handcar featuring Mickey and Santa Claus, and a fantastic reproduction of the Mickey–Minnie handcar in the original box. On the assembly line are reproductions of the Donald Duck-and-Pluto-in-the-doghouse handcar, the Easter Bunny handcar, and a reproduction of the Mickey Mouse Circus Train including Mickey, the barker figurine, and the Mickey coal-stoker car. A Horace Horse-

"Avon calling!" The 7" novelty plastic figurine bottle of Mickey with an unscrewable head contains 4.5 fluid ounces of liquid bubble bath from Avon Products, Inc., New York. Shown with the original box, 1960s.

collar—Clarabelle Cow handcar and others are in this special line of heavy-metal, high quality products, licensed and made with the approval of the Disney Studios. These items are not mass marketed or mass produced, and are usually available only through mail-order toy catalogues or at antique toy shows. Attention is paid to creating a likeness of Mickey Mouse based on the 1930s design concept of the mouse character, and the pieces are all reasonably priced for those collectors who can't afford (or find) an original.

An exact replica of the 1930s Lionel Corporation Mickey Mouse handcar manufactured by Pride Lines Ltd. of Lindenhurst, New York. Tracks are included with this toy just as in the original. This new handcar, however, has a standard gauge motor. The box is also a Pride Lines reproduction of the original. A 1983–84 "investibles" product.

Many of the most desirable new items sought after by collectors today feature the look of the early Mickey Mouse. The Color-forms Company of Ramsey, New Jersey, has produced a very good line of Mickey games or play pieces in colorful boxes, the graphics often drawn by Mel Birnkrant, an accomplished Mickey artist and a famous Mickey memorabilia collector. Mr. Birnkrant has brought his finely attuned aesthetic as a Disney collector and his artistic awareness of the early Mickey, which he cherishes, to these instantly collectible boxed products. Many of these can be found at the five-and-dime or the toy section of large department stores today. Some of these Colorform games include: Mickey Mouse Run 'n' Play Magic Transfer Set, which features die-cut blank cardboard standing outlines of various Disney characters such as Peg Leg Pete; a Mickey Mouse Magic Glow Fun House, featuring a truly stunning box approximately 12 by 18 inches, as well as a magnificent interior cardboard meant to stand in front of a lamp, showing Minnie kissing Mickey, ghosts appearing, lights lighting, and various other festive things happening—almost a Disney Disco; a Mickey Mouse Sewing Card set; a Mickey Mouse Play House; and many others. Originally issued in 1978, they sold for $2.49 each and vary in price today. When a set is discontinued, it enters the collectibles marketplace at a much higher price.

Mickey Mouse pop-up play set designed for Colorforms
Company of Ramsey, N.J. by collector-designer Mel
Birnkrant, 1970s.

Mickey Mouse pop-up play set opened. The band includes the
original barnyard group, Mickey, Minnie, Clarabelle, Horace,
Pluto, and Ferdy Mouse on the top. This activity toy contains
"colorforms magic plastic stick-ons" of hats, refreshments, and
other "trimmings" for children and adults. Colorforms Company,
1970s.

Mickey collectibles from special events are always sought after by collectors. Items manufactured in conjunction with Mickey Mouse's fiftieth birthday, or museum birthday celebrations such as the one at the Museum of Modern Art, which offered booklet programs, a striking black, white, yellow, and red poster of the event, featuring Mickey, and a pinback Mickey button are already hard-to-find collectibles today. Some very good collectors' pieces produced for Lincoln Center's film retrospective celebrating Disney Studios' fiftieth anniversary in 1973 include, with original prices:

- Mickey Mouse canvas shoulder bag $5.50
- Mickey Mouse wallet $1.50
- Mickey Mouse puzzle (adult) $4.25
- Bambi & Thumper puzzle (children) $3.25
- Mickey Mouse poster $3.25
- Mickey and Minnie cut-outs $3.25
- Mickey Mouse T-shirt for children $2.00
- Mickey Mouse T-shirt for adults $3.25
- Walt Disney 50 Happy Years Double Album $4.25
- Mickey Mouse wristwatch $15.00
- Mickey Mouse bubble wristwatch $16.00
- Mickey Mouse bubble pendant watch $16.00
- Mickey Mouse travel alarm $10.75
- Mickey Mouse, Donald Duck, and Pinocchio radio $10.75
- Mickey Mouse and Minnie pendant radio $10.50
- Bookends $8.50
- Dumbo china set $5.00
- Dumbo mug $2.00

The Mickey Mouse sing-a-long portable radio is battery-operated and has an electric plug-in attachment. Microphone allows the singer to join in on the radio. This bright yellow plastic radio is made in Hong Kong by Concept 2000, model #459, 1970s and 1980s.

- Mickey Mouse milk cup $1.50
- Snow White figurine $16.00
- Mickey Mouse cufflinks $3.00
- Minnie Mouse earrings $2.25
- Goofy pin $2.25
- Mickey Mouse pin $2.25
- *Walt Disney Favorite Songbook* $3.25
- *Walt Disney Storyland Book* $5.50

- Golden Books of: Cinderella, Dumbo, Bambi, Peter Pan, Mary Poppins, Winnie the Pooh $1.25

Various 8- and 16-mm films are also included.

David McKay Company, Inc., of New York, the original Mickey Mouse publisher, reprinted in hardback, for $7.95, fiftieth-birthday editions (1978) of:

- *The Adventures of Mickey Mouse Book I*
- *The Adventures of Mickey Mouse Book II*
- *Mickey Mouse and His Horse Tanglefoot*

McKay also produced an original reprint of the 1930s *Mickey Mouse Story Book Album*, which includes the stories:

- "The Birthday Party"
- "Mickey Mouse in Giantland"
- "Pioneer Days"
- "Traffic Troubles"

and other originals with illustrations in color and black-and-white.

An *Elmer the Elephant*—plus *Peculiar Penguins* reprint of original stories from 1930s vintage Disney Silly Symphonies is handsomely produced by David McKay Company, Inc., of New York also. Many reproductions of early Mickey comics are being reissued as specials by Golden Books or Abbeville Press—instantly collectible. A nostalgia series of Whitman paintbooks was reissued in the 1970s; these are hard-to-find items today.

Lionel Trains produced a Disney train for Mickey's fiftieth birthday, with an engine, three boxcars, and a caboose, selling originally for $139. Today this set will sell for $300 at a toy-train convention, and the set of twelve plastic cars that was issued will be $600 or more—testimony to the increase in value of recently produced collectibles. A Mickey Mouse Sing-a-Long radio, which includes a microphone so you can join your favorite recording star right on the radio to create your own broadcast, is a handsome piece of plastic produced in the late 1970s in Hong Kong by Concept 2000—"Where the Future Starts."

In 1978 Bradley issued limited-edition Mickey Mouse watches for Mickey's birthday in three different sizes—a child's small size, a rounded adult size, and a square adult medium size. At any five-and-dime, jewelry, or variety store, a Bradley Mickey watch can still be purchased for about $20, but they are by no means as attractive as timepieces as originals from the 1930s.

Timex Mickey watches from the 1970s are collectibles today and are more attractive than the Bradley line; but again, do not compare with an original. However, an original might cost $300 in good working order.

There were hundreds of specialty items produced just for Mickey's fiftieth birthday, and some of them are already sought after as investibles, including tin-litho wastepaper baskets, tin litho tops, metal boxes, posters, and figurines.

Mickey Mouse color litho wastepaper basket from the oil and gas crisis period of the 1970s. Mickey seems perturbed by the state of affairs while Minnie sits forlorn in the car, which also has a flat tire. J. Chein Company, Burlington, N.J.

Reverse side of the wastebasket. Mickey offers Minnie hot soup on a snowy night. Since oil is scarce, they are using an old-fashioned coal burner stove. Color litho metal baskets came with either yellow or chartreuse backgrounds. J. Chein Company, Burlington, N.J., 1970s.

What many collectors look for in the new Mickey Mouse marketplace on collectibles from today for tomorrow is the iconography of the old Mickey Mouse image of the 1930s. It bears repeating here that even though an item from today may resemble the early Mickey Mouse, the inscription stamped on a new piece will read "Walt Disney Productions," while a prewar item is *always marked* "Walt Disney Enterprises." The change occurred after September 29, 1938, when Walt Disney Productions Ltd., Walt Disney Enterprises, and Liled Realty & Investment Company, Ltd., were consolidated to form Walt Disney Enterprises, and three months later the name was changed to Walt Disney Productions. Collectibles from the 1940s and 1950s are, naturally, also marked "Walt Disney Productions." Often an excited dealer will put the same price on a 1930s, 1940s, or 1950s piece of Mickey memorabilia without making a necessary distinction between prewar and postwar. "Walt Disney Enterprises," to a bona fide Mickeyite, is always preferable to "Walt Disney Productions." Early European items, however, do not always have an inscription.

Currently Walt Disney Productions licenses manufacturers to produce 165 different items with its characters. The character-merchandise department now grosses approximately $30 million per year. Tom De Staso, the Disney manager of licensing for Eastern United States, says that most manufacturers usually apply to Disney Productions for a one-year license to produce trademark items. Disney continues to conduct a thorough investigation of an applicant company and the proposed product, before granting a go-ahead on production rights. Today Walt Disney–inspired toys are everywhere—not just in the dime stores, department stores, toy or gift shops, but in motel lobbies, drugstores, novelty shops, shopping malls, variety stores, supermarkets, airline terminals, Howard Johnson Restaurant chains—and, of course, vast quantities arrive at Florida's Disney World or California's Disneyland, including every variety of souvenir and carnival paraphernalia.

Donald Duck car (with his nephews in the rumble seat) was made by Paperino-Politoys in Italy in the 1960s and 1970s.

Spinning tops from the 1970s nostalgia revival period, color litho on metal. Top on the left is from Straco Company, made in U.S.A. and dated 1978. The smaller top is from J. Chein Company of Newark, N. J. and is dated 1975.

Walt Disney Distributing Company, with offices at Lake Buena Vista, Florida, and at Anaheim, California, currently offers some very attractive items manufactured by various different companies in conjunction with its distribution company, for today's market. One series includes Mickey, Minnie, and Pluto decoratives, painted earthenware figurines. Also available in this series are Snow White and all Seven Dwarfs in individual pieces, Alice in Wonderland, the Mad Hatter, the March Hare, the White Rabbit, and an especially wonderful red-striped, grinning Cheshire Cat. Many people collect these knickknacks as sets. Other earthenware figurines include Lady, Tramp, Trusty, and Jock from *Lady and the Tramp*, as well as a set of Pongo and Perdita with six smaller Dalmatian pups from the movie *101 Dalmatians*. There is also the Donald Duck family, with Donald, Daisy, Scrooge McDuck, and all three nephews; as well as Dumbo, Mary Poppins, Pinocchio, Tinkerbell, Jiminy Cricket, and Bambi.

Some very impressive large-sized character bisque figurines, beautifully painted in special scenes with more than one character, are being produced and distributed by Walt Disney Distributing Company, some with a music-box attachment. The larger pieces include:

1. A Big Bad Wolf with the Three Little Pigs (all together—and in four separate pieces).
2. Alice in Wonderland with the Rabbit and the Cheshire Cat.
3. Lady and the Tramp.
4. A Marching Band with Mickey, Donald, and Goofy beating a drum.
5. Br'er Bear, Br'er Fox, and Br'er Rabbit, from Uncle Remus.

6. Mickey with Pluto the Pup.
7. Mickey and Minnie.
8. Snow White kissing Dopey on the forehead.

The execution of these new bisque figurines is excellent, and some of the many smaller pieces include: Mickey Mouse on a sled, skiing, with a kite, riding a bike, hunting, skin diving, playing at football, at golf; Minnie Mouse golfing, skiing, with a Valentine, in her garden, with a picnic basket, as an archer; Donald Duck golfing, swimming, bird-watching, playing football, skating; and Daisy Duck in the rain, playing croquet, skating, and at the beach.

Other notable recent new collectibles include colorful mugs in porcelain featuring Mickey, Goofy, Dumbo, Donald Duck, Pinocchio, Snow White and characters from *The Jungle Book*, *Lady and the Tramp*, and *Aristocats*. Boutique porcelain vases, perfumers, powder or pin boxes with Mickey, Minnie, Cinderella, Bambi, Daisy Duck, or Snow White are also extremely

Plastic back scratcher which is a current souvenir from Disney World, Florida. It measures 15¾" and features the old impish 1930s image of Mickey Mouse.

Two new painted bisque figurines showing Mickey Mouse on a sled and Donald Duck on ice.

attractive new pieces. A remarkable set of Disney porcelain large-sized coffee mugs and plates features the early impish white-faced Mickey Mouse against a bright yellow circle.

Handpainted papier-mâché banks and "nodders" (moving heads) of Mickey, Minnie, Pluto, and Donald are available, as well as finger and hand puppets, rag dolls (Mickey and Minnie), and inflatable toys (Mickey, Dumbo, Donald, Pluto, and a Dalmatian).

Plush stuffed dolls include Mickey Mouse (16, 20, 25, and 42 inches), Minnie Mouse (16, 25, and 34 inches), Pluto (12, 15, and 27 inches), Goofy (21 and 31 inches), and Dumbo (13, 20, and 28 inches). Other plush dolls include Donald Duck, the Aristocats, Lady Pup, Tramp Pup, Robin Hood, Thumper, Flower, Bambi, the Owl, Chip 'n' Dale (the chipmunks)—all in various sizes.

Soft-wear items always include the Mickey Mouse T-shirt, which after the 1970s revival has become an American standard, and sweatshirts, many with the early Mickey or Minnie embla-

zoned on them. All of the aforementioned are to be found in stores everywhere, from Walt Disney Distributing Company.

A great variety of character-merchandise items exists from *Mary Poppins* and *101 Dalmatians*, in the nature of figurines, mugs, jewelry, wallets, games, toys, and the like that are sought after as items expressly from the 1960s. The films of the 1960s and after from which collectibles exist include:

■ *101 Dalmatians* (1961), the first film to use the Xerox camera for backgrounds, which featured the best and meanest villainess in postwar Disney movies, Cruella de Vil.

■ *The Sword and the Stone* (1963)—King Arthur as a boy.

■ *Mary Poppins* (1964), starring Julie Andrews, Academy Award winner.

■ *The Jungle Book* (1967), from Rudyard Kipling's stories; considered by critics to have the best animation of the postwar period, with the voices of George Sanders, Phil Harris, Louis Prima, Sterling Holloway, and Sebastian Cabot featured.

■ *Winnie the Pooh and the Honey Tree* (1966 featurette).

■ *Winnie the Pooh and the Blustering Day* (1968 featurette), with its predecessor, from the A. A. Milne stories featuring Tigger, Eeyore, and Pooh Bear (Disney Pooh Bears continue to be a vastly popular item).

■ *The Aristocats* (1970)—the voice of the Duchess was Eva Gabor, and O'Malley the Alley Cat featured the voice of Phil Harris.

Five seed packets featuring early Mickey, Minnie, the Three Little Pigs, and the Wolf (center), with all-weather vinyl row markers from Colorforms Inc., Norwood, N. J., and packed by the Vaughn Jacklin Corp., 1970s.

Whether the new collectibles of your heart's desire are from the latter-day *Mary Poppins* era or present-day Disney World era, or from the 1980s *Fox and the Hound, Tron,* or *Tex* period, the main thing in collecting Disney— or Mickey in particular—is to have fun. But be sure, when you plant those Minnie Mouse zinnia seeds or Mickey Mouse radish seeds (from Colorforms Inc. of Norwood, New Jersey) in your garden, please to save the seed packages featuring the early Mickey and Minnie. They are beautiful new—old-style graphics to be collected now for fun and pleasure—and perhaps as future rarities, the Mickey Mouse ephemera of tomorrow.

It is also important to remember—lest we forget—that all of this fun in Memorabilialand, and in Disney collecting, was inspired by just one mouse named Mickey.

And what does the future hold in store for the famous, merry M-I-C-K-E-Y M-O-U-S-E? Some who have gazed into the crystal ball world of tomorrow say that by the year 2003, when Mickey will be celebrating his seventy-fifth birthday, he will be called upon to become the first computerized president of the United States. Seen over a giant television screen at his inauguration, which will probably take place at Epcot Center—if not a new Disney space-satellite city—a smiling President Mickey will address the world in his best falsetto voice with a hearty:

"Gee! Thanks, folks!"

Donald Duck crayons, showing Mickey and Donald heading for outer space in a crayon-rocketship. Color litho on metal "approved product" made by Transogram Company, Inc., New York, ca. 1950.

PIN THE TAIL ON 'MICKEY'

Pin-the-Tail-on-Mickey, from the Mickey Mouse party game, produced in 1934 by the Marks Brothers Company of Boston. The oilcloth linen-like fabric to be hung on the wall for fun, games, or for art's sake, measures 22" x 18".

ABOUT THE AUTHORS

Robert Heide grew up in New Jersey, was educated at Northwestern University and later studied theater with Stella Adler and Uta Hagen. He is the author of many plays, including the two off-Broadway classics *Moon* and *The Bed*. His theater work has been published in a number of anthologies and in acting editions. His scenarios, *The Bed* and *The Death of Lupe Velez* (written for Edie Sedgwick) were filmed by Andy Warhol. He has also written articles for *The Village Voice, Soho Weekly News* and *Other Stages*.

John Gilman was born in Honolulu and has been a journalist, stage manager, actor, producer, businessman, antique store dealer and interior design and antiques consultant. He also worked with autistic children and was executive director of the American Society of Magazine Photographers.

Heide and Gilman are co-authors of *Dime Store Dream Parade—Popular Culture 1925–1955* (E.P. Dutton, 1979) and *Cowboy Collectibles* (Harper & Row, 1982). They are acknowledged experts on American popular culture and have jointly lectured at the Cooper Hewitt Museum, the Delaware Art Museum, The National Antiques Show, the Park Avenue Armory Antiques Show and the National Arts Club for the Art Deco Society. They have also contributed to and created a number of pop art exhibitions and have appeared often on radio and television.

Bob Heide (left) and John Gilman.

Stanley Stellar

BIBLIOGRAPHY

Abrams, Robert and Canemaker, John. *Treasures of Disney Animation Art*. New York: Abbeville Press, 1982.

Bailey, Adrian. *Walt Disney's World of Fantasy*. New York: Everest House, 1982.

Bain, David and Harris, Bruce, editors. *Mickey Mouse, Fifty Happy Years*. New York: Harmony Books, 1978.

Blitz, Marcia, *Donald Duck*. New York: Harmony Books, 1979.

Feild, Robert D. *The Art of Walt Disney*. English edition, London & Glasgow: Collins, 1947.

Finch, Christopher. *The Art of Walt Disney: From Mickey Mouse to the Magic Kingdoms*. New York: Harry N. Abrams, 1973.

Geis, Darlene, editor. *Walt Disney's Treasury of Silly Symphonies*. New York: Harry N. Abrams, 1981.

Lesser, Robert. *A Celebration of Comic Art and Memorabilia*. New York: Hawthorn Books, 1975.

Maltin, Leonard. *The Disney Films*. New York: Crown Publishers, 1973.

Munsey, Cecil. *Disneyana*. New York: Hawthorn Books, 1974.

Overstreet, Robert M. *The Comic Book Price Guide #13*. Cleveland, Tn.: Overstreet Publications, 1983.

Peary, Gerald and Peary, Danny, editors. *The American Animated Cartoon: A Critical Anthology*. New York: E.P. Dutton, 1980.

Rublowsky, John and Heyman, Kenneth. *Pop Art*. New York: Basic Books, 1965.

Taylor, Deems, Foreword by Stokowski, Leopold. *Walt Disney's Fantasia*. New York: Simon and Schuster, 1940.

Thomas, Frank and Johnston, Ollie. *Disney Animation, the Illusion of Life*. New York: Abbeville Press, 1981.

Waugh, Coulton. *The Comics*. New York: Macmillan, 1947.

Articles

Skolsky, Sidney. "Mickey Mouse." *Cosmopolitan* Magazine, February 1934.

Johnston, Alva. "Mickey Mouse." *Woman's Home Companion*, July 1934.

Miller, Diane Disney. "My Dad, Walt Disney." *Saturday Evening Post*, November 17, 1956.

Disney, Walt. "Merry Christmas, Mickey and Minnie Mouse." *Delineator*, December 1932.

"Walt Disney, A Biography"; "Animated Cartoon World of Walt Disney"; "Animated Feature Length World of Walt Disney"; "The Art of Animation"; "Live Action Movie-World of Walt Disney"; "Disneyland"; "Wisdom of Walt Disney"; *Wisdom* magazine, vol. 32, December 1959.

Carr, Harry. "The Only Unpaid Movie-Star." *American* Magazine, March 1931.

Syring, Richard H. "One of the Greats." *Silver Screen* Magazine, November 1932.

"Mickey Mouse, the First Fifty Years." *Catalogue*, Department of Film of the Museum of Modern Art, New York, 1978.

Hake's Americana and Collectibles. Auction catalogue, Ted Hake, P.O. Box 1444, York, Pa., 17405.

INDEX

Aaronson, Irving, 189
Academy Awards, 58, 204, 212, 215
Accordionist, *101*
Adventure (comic strip), 96
The Adventures of Donald Duck, 63
The Adventures of Mickey Mouse, 75, 76
Alexander Doll Co., 205
Alice in Cartoonland (film), 51
Alice in Wonderland (film), 22, 48, 229
"All Aboard" (song), 220
Allen, Sherry, 232
Allen, S. L. and Co., 57
Alphabet block, *121*
Aluminum Specialty Co., 141
American Broadcasting Co., 230
American Hard Rubber Co., 124
American Latex Corp., 122
American Pottery, 178, 207, 214, 228
American Toy, 144, 205, 233
Amloid Co., 205, 214
Andrews, Julie, 244
Andrews Sisters, 227
Anything Goes (Porter), 190
The Aristocrats (film), 244
Armour and Co., 204
The Art of Walt Disney (Finch), 22, 209
The Art of Walt Disney (Feild), 192
Ashtrays, *180*
Astaire, Fred, 32
Athletic Shoe Co., 126
Auctions, 19-20, 27, 41-44
Automatic Recording Safe Co., 141
Autry, Gene, 235

Babbitt, Art, 204
Babes in the Woods (book), 76
"Baby Mine" (song), 220
Back scratcher, 243
"Baia" (song), 226
Bailey Co., 235
Bain, David, 122
Baird, Sharon, 232
Balls, 101, 170
Bambi, 48, 95,225
Bambi's Children (comic book), 96
The Band Concert (film), 42, 65
Band sets, *108, 202*
Banks, *12, 23, 28, 35, 156, 179,* 244
Barks, Carl, 41, 42, 94, 96
Barnes, Howard, 203-204
Barricks Manufacturing Co., 130
Barrier, Michael, 38
Baskett, James, 227
Bayard Co., 163, 208, 214
Beery, Wallace, 62
Behind the Scenes of Disney Studio, 32

Belcher, Marjorie, 204
Ben and Me (film), 40
Benchley, Robert, 220
Bergen, Edgar, 227
Berkeley, Busby, 15
Berlin, Irving, 183
Bernie, Ben, 192
Bestor, Don, 184
Bibo, Bobette, 73
Bibo and Lange, 73
Big Bad Wolf, 34, *186,* 193
The Big Bad Wolf and Little Red Riding Hood (book), 185
Big Little Books, 64, 79-80, 82-85, 197
Birnkrant, Mel, 17, 18, 23-25, 26, 238
Birthday card, *30, 37, 121*
The Birthday Party (film), 75
Birthplace, Mickey Mouse, 44
Blackboards, 130
Blankets, *125*
Blocks, *121, 223*
"Blue Shadows on the Trail" (song), 182
Boardman, Thelma, 176
Bondi, Beulah, 228
Bookends, *65, 86*
Borgfeldt, George & Co., 100-101, 102, 121, 153, 178, 194, 206, 212
Bottles, 205, 237
Bourne Music Publishers, 183
Bow, Clara, 73
Bradley Co., 165, 214, 241
Brayton-Laguna Pottery, 153, 214
"Brazil" (song), *182,* 226
Bread, advertising, *114,150, 151*
Br'er Rabbit, 227; (book), 83
Brier Co., 126, 144, 205, 214
Broadsides, *98, 114, 115, 117*
Bryant Electric Co., 121, 205, 213
Buchanan, Stuart, 176
Bucky Bug, 197
Building a Building (film), 76
Burgess, Bobby, 232
Burnett, Carol, 17
Burr, Lonnie, 232
Buttons, pinback, *13, 21, 176, 181, 194, 204, 210, 220,* 229

Cabot, Sebastian, 244
The Cactus Kid (film), 20
Caesar, Irving, 181, 183
Calendar, *136, 150*
Camera, 29, 68
Can Can (film), 48
Candy, *114, 150*
Cantor, Eddie, 11
Capitol Cravat Co., 126, 207
Car, *155, 242*
Cards, *30, 37, 121, 136, 154, 177*

Carey, Harry, 228
Carson, Johnny, 17
Cartier, 205
Caselotti, Adrianna, 204
Cassidy, Hopalong, 235
A Celebration of Comic Art and Memorabilia (Lesser), 94
Champion, Marge, 212
Chaplin, Charlie, 49-50
Charlie McCarthy, 227
Chien, J. & Co., 233
"Chim Chim Cher-ee" (song), 182
Chinaware, *121-123*
Christie's, 43
Christmas, 22-25, 135-156
Christmas Carolers (painting), 42
Christmas Parade (comic book), *142*
Churchill, Frank E., 192
Cinderella, 22, 182, 229, 230
Cinderella and the Magic Wand (book), 83
Clampett, Bob, 99
Clarabelle Cow, 10, 13, 65
Clara Cluck, 65, 197
Clark, Buddy, 227
Clark, Charlotte, 99, 102-103
Clock. *See* Watches and clocks
Clock Cleaners (book), *88*
Clothes, *125-127*
Coca-Cola (Japan), 46
Cohn & Rosenberg, 126
Cole, Tommy, 232
Colgate-Palmolive-Peet Co., 204
The Collector's Guide to Big Little Books and Similar Books (Lowery), 81
Collier's magazine, *89*
Colonna, Jerry, 227
Colorforms Co., 26, 238
Comet Candy Co., 114
The Comic Book Price Guide, 93
Comic books, 17, 93-96
Cone Export and Commission Co., *126*
Converse Rubber Co., 126, 207
Cookies, 114; jars, *145, 179, 180,* 227; poster, *152;* tin, *29*
Costumes, Halloween, *134*
Cover art, *38, 89, 149, 218, 225,* 230
Crandell Co., 179
Crayons, *131,* 245
Crosby, Bing, 228
Crown Overall Manufacturing Co., 126
Crown Toy Co., 144, 206, 212
Culhane, John, 18
Cup, *123*
Cut-outs, *23, 118, 167, 187*

Dancer, toy, *109*

Darro, Frankie, 212
Darrow, Chick, 26
Davis, Sammy Jr., 20
Davy Crockett, 40, 48, 229, 234
Day, Dennis, 227, 232
Dean's Rag Book Co. Ltd., 29, 102
De Gaulle, Charles, 58
De Marco Girls, 184
Demarest, William, 61
De Mille, Cecil, 209
Desk-tabletop, *130*
De Staso, Tom, 242
De-Ward Novelty Co., 213
Diamond, Eileen, 232
Dinning Sisters, 227
Dionne quintuplets, 122
Disney, Lillian, 51, 52
Disney, Roy, 21, 45, 51, 53, 59, 102
Disney, Walt, 14, 15, 21, 31, 45, 50, 51-53, 59, 98, 99, 102, 176
Disney Cable, TV channel, 48
Disney Channel Magazine, 48
Disney Collection, 12
Disney Distributing Co., 243-244
Disney Enterprises, 88, 89, 100, 242
Disneyland, 14, 21, 22, 30, 46, 58, 233-234, 235, 242
The Disney Poster Book, 21
Disney Productions, 46, 88, 242
Disney Song Folios, 181
Disney Studios, 21-22, 27, 240
Disney World, 14, 21, 22, 30, 46, 58, 242
A Dispatch from Disney (magazine), 92
Dixon Crucible Co., 128, 194, 205, 213
Dodd, Jimmie, 232
Dolls, 23, 65, 69, 99, 100, *101-104, 106-108*, 170, 194, 195, 207, 244
Donald Duck, 10, 13-14, 34-35, 41-43, 63-68, 96, *147*, 150, 215-218, 242, 245
Donald Duck and the Mystery of the Double X (book), 83
Donald Duck Finds Pirate Gold, 41, 95
Donald Duck in Disneyland (book), 232
"Donald Duck's Biggest Moments" (Sharpe), 64
Donald Duck's Swing Band, 176
Donald's Ostrich (film), 66
"A Dream Is a Wish Your Heart Makes" (song), 182
Driscoll, Bobby, 227, 228
Drum, 100, *190*
Drummer, 100, *101, 109,*
Dukas, Paul, 219
Dumbo, 32, 48, 95, 184, *220*
The Dumbo Weekly, 92
Dunham, David, 41

Eagle Rubber Co., 170
Eddy, Nelson, 227
Eddy, L. M. Mfg. Co., 233

Edwards, Cliff (Ukulele Ike), 211, 227
Einson-Freeman Co., 195
Elfego Baca (film), 40
Elmer Elephant, 34, *198*, 241
Emerson, Caroline D., *85*
Emerson Radio Corp., 194, 205
Empire Plastic Corp., 233
Empire Product Corp., 170
Ensign Ltd., 29
Epcot Center, 46, 245
Etting, Ruth, 15

Fairbanks, Douglas Sr., 235
Fandango, 27
Fantasia (film), 22, 38, 48, 219-220
Faulkner, William, 62
Fawcett, John, 17-18
Feild, R. D., 192
Felix the Cat, 51
Ferdinand the Bull, 34, 197, *200, 201;* song, 182
Fiddler Pig, *195*
Fifty Happy Years of Disney (film), 22
Figurines, 34-35, 41, 65, 69, *105, 178, 179,* 195, *200, 210,* 220, 226, 227, 237, 243
Finch, Christopher, 22, 209
Fishback, A. S., 195, 205, 213
Fisher-Price Toys, 141, 206, 213
Fishin' Around (film), 75
Fishing kit, *170*
Five Mile Creek (TV series), 48
Flexo Products Corp., 213
Flip the Frog, 98
Flivver, *155*
Flowers and Trees (film), 58
The Flying Mouse (film), 182
Folio of Songs, 182
Foods, 114-115
Fork, *123*
Forster, E. M., 13
The Fox and the Hound (film), 39
Der Fuehrer's Face: film, 215; song, 182, 215; sheet music, *216, 218*
Fuji Photo Film Co., 46
Fulton Electric Mfg. Co., 195
Fulton Specialty Co., 141
Fun Antiques, 26
Fun and Fancy Free (film), 32, 227
Funicello, Annette, 40, 232, 233

Gabor, Eva, 244
Gallopin' Gaucho (film), 53
Games, 8, 100, *153, 158,* 224, *246*
Garner, Lee, 131
General Foods Corp., 115, 204, 212
Geuder, Paeschke and Frey Co., 131
Gill, Florence, 176
Gillespie, Darlene, 232
Gillett, Burton, 100, 106
Gillette Safety Razor Co., 212
"Give a Little Whistle" (song), 182
Gladstone Gander, 95
Glaser Crandell Co., 114
Glasses, *120, 179, 180, 198*

Globetrotter's Club, *151*
Gold Key Comics, 95
Goodman, Benny, 227
Goofy, 47, 65
Gottfredson, Floyd, 31, 94, 96
Gould, Stephen Jay, 14
Great Songs from Disney Movies, 184
Gulliver Mickey (film), 32, 76
Gum cards, 10, 19, 52, 62, 97, 158, 184
Gund Manufacturing Co., 102-103

Hall, Henry, 192
Halloween, 133-134
Halsam Products Co., 141
Hamilton Galleries, 43
Hamilton Metal Products Co., 170
Handcar, *139, 140, 146,* 238
Hans Brinker (film), 40
Harline, Leigh, 211
Harris, Phil, 181, 244
Harris (O. K.) Gallery, 17
Hassenfeld Bros., 128-129
Hat, *114*
"Heigh Ho" (song), 182
Heinz, H. J. Soup Co., 115
Herrmann Handkerchief Co., 126, 195
Hiawatha (book), *201*
Hickok, 126
"Hi Diddle Dee Dee" (song), 182
Hightower, Louis, 204
Hill, N. N. Brass Co., 141, 206, 213
Holdridge, Cheryl, 232
Holloway, Sterling, 244
Hollywood Heritage, 44
Horace Horsecollar, 10, 13, 65
Horen, Al, 165
Horne, Hal, 90, 92
"Horses" (song), 189
Hughes-Autograf Co., 207, 213
Hughes, Henry L. Co., 124
Hughes, Robert, 22
Hurter, Albert, 22

Ice-cream cones and cups, 114
Ice skates, 157
Ichabod and Mr. Toad (film), 228
Ideal Novelty and Toy Co., 205, 212
Independent Grocers' Alliance, 212
Ingersoll, 13, 17, 159-160, 208, 214
InkoGraph Co., *130*
International Silver Co., 121
It's Tough to Be a Bird (film), 32
Ives, Burl, 228
Iwerks, Ub, 21, 31, 32, 45, 50, 51, 53, 96, 98

Jacob, H. & Sons, 207
"The Japanese Sandman" (song), 189
The Jazz Singer (film), 53
Jewelry, *126*
Jigsaw puzzle, *173*
Jiminy Cricket, 32
Johnson, Ray, 10

Johnsons of Hendon Ltd., 29
Johnston, Alva, 49
Jolson, Al, 53
Jones, Dickie, 212
Jones, Spike, and His City Slickers, 215
José Carioca, 84
The Jungle Book (film), 45, 244

Kamen, Kate, 45
Kamen, Kay, 19, 31, 45, 89, 90, 92, 113-
　118, 125, 134, 195, 204
Kamen Publications, 95
Katz, Ira, G., 207
Keeler, Ruby, 15
Kent Dental Laboratories, 119
Kerk Guild, 174
Keystone Manufacturing Co., 49, 178
Kid Millions (film), 11
Kidnapped (film), 40
Kikkoman Corp., 46
Kilgore Manufacturing Co., 143
Kimball, Ward, 31, 32
King Features, 13, 96
King Innovations, 126
King Neptune (book), 76
Klondike Kid (film), 44, 76
Kneitel, Kenny, 27
Knickerbocker Plastic Co., 235
Knickerbocker Co., 102, 194, 205, 212
Krueger, Richard G., 194, 205, 213

Lady and the Tramp (film), 48, 229
Laguna Pottery Co., 178, 228
Lake, Veronica, 61
La Mode Studios, 144, 206
L'Amour, Louis, 48
Langer Knitting Mills, 126
Langford, Frances, 227
Lantz, Walter, 51
Lapin-Kurley Kew, Inc., 205
Larsen, Larry, 232
La Rue, Lash, 235
Laugh-O-Gram Studios, 51
Laundry set, 187
Leeds China Co., 179
Leeds Lottery Co., 207
Lesser, Robert, 17, 20, 94, 160
Levin, Ed, 39
Levy, William Banks, 28-29, 71, 92
Lewis, L. & Sons, 214
Lewis Knight Ltd., 29
Libbey Glass Co., 179, 213
Librizzi, Nemo, 65
Lichtenstein, Roy, 10
Lightfoot Shultz Co., 124, 206, 213
Lights, for Christmas, *137*, *188*
Lionel Corp., 14, 139, 241
Lipton, Betty (Bascha), 27
London, Gene, 26, 27
"Look Out for Mrs. Stork" (song), 220
Lorenz, Konrad, 14
Lowery, Larry, 81
Lucas, George, 44
"Lullaby of Nowhere" (song), 182
Lunchboxes, 130-131, 234-235

Luther, Frank, 184
Lux Radio Theatre, 209

Macy, R. H. & Co., 13, 30, 136-137
Madame Tussaud's, London, 13
The Mad Doctor (film), 76
Magazines, 89-92, *113*
Mahler, Paul, 44
The Mail Pilot (film), 76
Make Mine Music (film), 227
Malce, Michael, 27
"A March for Mickey Mouse," 183
Marks Brothers Co., 143, 205
Marx, Louis & Co., 206, 213
Marx, Samuel, 62
Mary Poppins (film), 48, 244
Masks, *33*, *133-134*
Match book covers, 217
Matchbox container, *170*
Matsushita Co., 46-47
Mattel, Inc., 233
Mayer and Thalberg (Marx), 62
Mayfair Togs, 157
Mazzeo, Henry Jr., 31
McCall Co., 102
McKay, David Co., 74, 240, 241
McKesson & Robbins, 212
Melody Time (film), 182, 227-228
Merchandising, 113-118
Merman, Ethel, 190
Messmer, Otto, 51
Metro Goldwin Mayer (MGM), 62
Michener, James A., 22
Mickey and Minnie Cut-Out Doll, *23*
Mickey and the Beanstalk: book, 228;
　film, 32, 227
Mickey Detective (book), 86
Mickey Mouse, at auctions, 19-20, 27,
　41-44; birthdays, 15, 17, 21-22, 30-
　32, 240; at Christmas, 22-25, 135-
　156; first dolls, 99-112; merchandis-
　ing, 113-118; music, 181-190; as
　1920s movie star, 49-54; and World
　War II, 215-218
Mickey Mouse (book), 74
"Mickey Mouse" (Johnston), 49-50
Mickey Mouse (painting, Oldenburg),
　19
Mickey Mouse Alphabet Book, 132
*Mickey Mouse and Minnie at Ma-
　cy's*, 137
*Mickey Mouse and Minnie March to
　Macy's* (book, 136-*137*
"Mickey Mouse and Minnie's in Town"
　(recording), *184*
Mickey Mouse and Pluto (book), 78
*Mickey Mouse and the Magic Car-
　pet*, 153
Mickey Mouse Book, 70
Mickey Mouse Book for Coloring,
　157
Mickey Mouse Club, 39, 59-60, 229,
　230; magazine, 232; TV show, 46
Mickey Mouse Comics, 74-75, 78

*The Mickey Mouse–Donald Duck
　Gag Book*, 78
Mickey Mouse—Fifty Happy Years
　(Bain), 122
*The Mickey Mouse Globe Trotter
　Weekly*, 92
Mickey Mouse Goes to Macy's
　(book), 70
Mickey Mouse Has a Party (book),
　132
*Mickey Mouse Illustrated Movie-Sto-
　ries*, 76, 77
Mickey Mouse in Giantland (Book),
　87
Mickey Mouse in King Arthur's Court,
　76
Mickey Mouse Magazine, 60, 72, 90-
　91, 92, 135, 159, 161, 232
"Mickey Mouse Meets Konrad Lor-
　enz" (Gould), 14
The Mickey Mouse Melodeon (mag-
　azine), 92
Mickey Mouse Movie Stories, 76, 77
*Mickey Mouse on the Haunted Is-
　land*, 83
Mickey Mouse on the Home Front, 92
The Mickey Mouse Paint Book, 78
*Mickey Mouse Presents His Silly Sym-
　phonies* (book), 76
*Mickey Mouse Sails for Treasure Is-
　land* (book), 9, 90
"Mickey Mouse's Birthday Party," 36
Mickey Mouse Ski Jumping game, *158*
Mickey Mouse Stories, 76
Mickey Mouse Story Book, 73, 75,
　240
Mickey Mouse Theater of the Air, 175
Mickey Mouse vs. the Phantom Blot,
　95
Mickey Mouse Waddle Book, 70, 76
Mickey Mouse Weekly, 29, 71, 92
"Mickey-nazi-coke" (drawing, Faw-
　cett), *18*
Mickey Never Fails (book), 84
Mickey sans Culotte, 58
Mickey's Birthday Party (film), 27, 32
Mickey's Christmas Carol (film), 47
Mickey's Dog Pluto (book), 83
Mickey's 50th, 39
Mickey's Follies (film), 32, 181
Mickey's Good Deed (film), 76
Mickey's Mechanical Man (film), 76
Mickey's Pal Pluto (film), 76
Mickey's Rival (book), 96
Mickey's Service Station (film), *32*
Mickey's Steamroller (film), 76
Mickey Steps Out (film), 75
Micro-Lite Co., 144, 206
Miller, Ron, 45
Miller Corsets, Inc., 204
Mills Orchestra, Felix, 176
Milne, A. A., 48, 244
Minnie Mouse, 10, 13, 33, 34, 35, 65
Minnie Mouse Book, 76
Minnie Mouse Woodland Choir, 176

"Minnie's Yoo Hoo" (song), 32, 181
Miranda, Aurora, 226
Molded Plastics, 233
Money, 20, 45, 97
Monroe, Marilyn, 49
Moore, Fred, 22, 31
Mortimer Mouse, 96
Mortimer Snerd, 227
Mother Goose Goes Hollywood
    (film), 41
Motion Picture Herald, 19
Motorcycle, 110
The Mouse Factory (film), 32
Mousegetar-Jr., 233
The Mouse Group Newsletter, 39
The Mouseketeer Reunion, 39-40
Mouseketeers, 14, 40, 231, 232-233
Mousterpiece Theater (TV series), 48
Movie Jector, Inc., 178
Movies, 49-54; posters, 43; projectors,
    49, 149, 178, 231
Movies for the Millions (Seldes), 50
Mug, 123
Multi-Products, 213
Music, 181-190, 182-183
Musical decal appliqué, 138
Music box, 194

Napkin rings, 180
Nashua Manufacturing Co., 204
Nash, Clarence, 176
National Biscuit Co., 114
National Dairy Co., 114, 204
National Dairy Products, 212
National Porcelain Co., 178, 214
Necklace, 126
Nelson, Victor, 26
Neuman, Alfred E., 47
Neumann, D. H. Co., 207, 214
The New Adventures of Dumbo, 92
Newark Felt Novelty Co., 214
New Better Little Books, 83
The New Mickey Mouse Club (TV
    show), 230
New York Graphic Society, 208
The Night Before Christmas (film), 136
Nodder, 42
Noisemaker, 100
Noma Electric Corp., 137
Norwich Knitting Co., 126
Nostalgia, 18

O'Brien, Cubby, 232
Odoro Co., 175, 206
Official Bulletin of the Mickey Mouse
    Clubs, 59, 92
Official Mickey Mouse store card, 60
Ohio Art Co., 143, 169, 194, 206, 213
The Old Castle's Secret (comic book),
    96
Oldenburg, Claes, 10, 19
Old Friends, 26
Old King Cole Display Co., 23
Olson, George, 189
101 Dalmatians (film), 244

On Ice (film), 157
The Orphan's Benefit (film), 197
Oswald the Lucky Rabbit, 42, 51, 98
Overland Candy Corp., 212
Owens-Illinois Glass Co., 179, 206

Paileontologist's Report, 131
Pails, sand, 171, 187
Paint book, 203
Paint box, 198
Painting, 173
Paint set, 222
Paris-Match, 14
Parker, Fess, 234
Parker Brothers, 144, 195, 205
Party horn, 189
Patten, Luana, 227, 228
Pattern, 102
Peg Leg Pete, 65, 76
Pen, 130
Pencil box, 36, 128-129, 130, 131
Pencil sharpener, 221, 225
Pendleton, Karen, 232
"The Penguin Is a Very Funny Crea-
    ture" (song), 182
Penny Arcade, 26
Perfume bottles, 205
Peter and the Wolf (film), 40
Peter Pan (film), 229
Peter Pig, 65
Pete's Dragon (film), 220
Phelan, Russ, 26
Philadelphia Orchestra, 219-220
Philbert Hat Co., 214
Phillips Son & Neale, 41-43
Pickford, Mary, 58, 73
Picture-Story Book Series, 84
Pied Piper (film), 182
Pied Pipers, 227
Pillowcase, 148
Pinball game, 158
"Pink Elephants on Parade" (song),
    220, 225
Pinocchio, 209-214; book, 209; comic
    book, 96; film, 34, 41, 182, 184
Pin-the-tail party game, 153, 246
Plane Crazy (film), 32, 53
Planters, 179
Plastic Novelties, Inc., 130, 206, 213
Plate, 29, 123, 193, 208
Playing cards, 154, 177, 193
Pluto the Pup, 10, 13, 47, 76, 83, 95
The Pointer (film), 32
Pop art, 10, 17, 22
Popcorn popper, 170
Popeye (film), 48
Pop-up Mickey Mouse, 76, 77
Porter, Cole, 190
Postcard, 30, 168, 216
Posters, 43, 152
Power, Tyrone, 235
Powers, Pat, 98
Powers Paper Co., 194
Prensky, Bill, 19
Pride Lines, 237

Prima, Louis, 244
Print shop set, 141
Procter & Gamble, 204
Projectors, 49, 149, 178, 231
Purse, 202
Puzzle, 153, 173, 223

Quick magazine, 230

Radiator caps, 105
Radio, 149, 174, 176-177, 240
Radio Mirror, 176
Railcar, Donald Duck, 147
Ramsaye, Terry, 19
Rathbone, Basil, 228
"Rats" (song), 182
RCA Victor Co., 184
Reagan, Ronald, 65
Recordings, 184, 201, 226, 230, 231,
    233
Reif, Rita, 27
Relaxon Products, 213
The Reluctant Dragon: comic book,
    95; film, 32, 220, 225
Richmond School Furniture Co., 130
The Robber Kitten (book), 199
Roger Rabbit, 47
Rogers, Buddy, 73
Rogers, Roy, 227, 235
Rogers & Son, 121, 179, 195, 206, 213
Ronell, Ann, 184, 191
Royal Typewriter Co., 204

Sackin, Les, 27
Salem China Co., 121-122, 179, 195
Salten, Felix, 225
Saludos Amigos (film), 182, 184
Sanders, George, 244
Sand pails, 171, 187
Sand sifters, 169
Santa's Workshop (film), 136
"Sax-O-Phun" (song), 189
Scatter ball game, 224
Schneider, Joseph, 153
School Days in Disneyville (Emerson),
    85
School necessities, 128-132
Sears, Roebuck & Co., 138, 139, 143,
    144, 156, 162, 166, 178, 179
Second Childhood, 26
Seed packets, 244
Seiberling Latex Products, 103-104, 121
Seldes, Gilbert, 13, 50
Sendak, Maurice, 21
Seversky, Alexander de, 215
Shanghai'd (film), 76
Sharpe, Howard, 64
Shaw Pottery Co., 153, 207, 214
Sheet music, 182, 183, 205, 216, 218
Sheets, 125
Sheffield Farms, 120, 195
Sheppard, Eugenia, 11
Sherry, Frank, 184
Shimmel, M. Sons, 235
Shore, Dinah, 227

Shovel, *171, 172*
Sieberling Latex Products Co., 170, 194, 205, 213
Silly Symphony, 44, 50, *58*, 136, *150*, 188, *197-199*, 200-201
Silverware, 121, *122-123*
The Simple Things (film), 14, 32
Skates, 157
The Skeleton Dance (film), 58
Sled, *145*, 157
Sleeping Beauty (film), 229
Smith, Ethel, 227, 228
Smith, Paul J., 211
Smith, Pete, 18
Smith and Peters, 114
Smith Carpet Co., 174
Smith, Hogg & Co., 122
Snow suits, 157
Snow White and the Seven Dwarfs, 34, 41, 96, 202, 203-208; film, 27, 44, 48, *133, 134*, 182, 184
Snow White Jingle Club, 204
Society Dog Show (film), 57
So Dear to My Heart (film), 228
Solaris, Jay, 232
"Some Day My Prince Will Come," 182
Song of the South (film), 182, 184, 227
Sons of the Pioneers, 227
Sorcerer's Apprentice (film), 32, 219
Soreng-Manegold Co., 153, 175
Soup, *116*
Southern Dairies, 114
Sparkler, 100, 222
Spielberg, Steven (E. T.), 44
Spoon, *122, 123*
Stalling, Carl, 189
Stamp pad box, *130*
Standard Toy Kraft Products, 144, 205
Stark Bros. Ribbon Corp., 126
Steamboat Willie, 30-31, *53-54*, 74, 98
Steiff, Margarete & Co., Inc., 102
Stokowski, Leopold, 22, 32, 219-220
Storey, Margene, 232
Storkline Furniture Corp., 206
Story of Clarabelle Cow (book), 80
Story of Mickey Mouse, 71, 73, 81
Story of Pluto the Pup (book), *81*
Strombecker Co., 233
Sturges, Preston, 61
Sullivan's Travels (film), 61
Sun Rubber Co., 153
Sweatshirts, 18
The Sword and the Stone (film), 244

Taliaferro, Al, 41, 42
Tall Comics, 83
Target game, 8
Tatum, Donn, 45
Taylor, Deems, 219, 220
Tea sets, 28, 29, 100, 180, 206, 222, 236
Television, 14, 30, 48, 229-236
Temple, Shirley, 58
"This Is Your Life, Mickey Mouse," 30

The Three Caballeros, 32, 41, 96, 182, 184, 226
Three Little Kittens, 199
Three Little Pigs, 34, 42, *185-187*, 191-196
The Three Orphan Kittens (book), 199
Thru the Mirror (film), 32
Thumper (comic book), 96
Tie, *127*
Timex, 17, 165, 241
Timid Elmer (book), *198*
Tiny Tim, 15
Tobias, Charles Bros., 126
Tokyo Disneyland, 46-47
Tomy Kogyo Co., Inc., 47
Tool chest, 154
Toothbrushes, 204
Toothbrush holder, *11, 34-35, 69, 101, 105*, 186
Tooth paste, *119*
Toot, Whistle, Plunk and Boom (film), 32
Top, 101, 223, 242
Topolino, 58; magazine, 92
Topolino Pompiere (book), 71
Touchdown Mickey (film), 76
Towels, *124*
Toy(s), 11, 13, *107, 109, 110, 111*, 121-122, *181, 197*, 221
Toy chests, *175*
Toy Craft Co., 122
Tracy, Doreen, 232
Traeger, Norman, 18
Traffic Troubles (film), 75
Train, 30, *138-139, 147*
Transfers, *151*, 174
Transogram, 214
"Travel Tykes Weekly," 92
Tray, *108, 193, 236*
Treasure Island (film), 40
Trova, Ernest, 17, 49
T-shirts, *40*
"Turkey in the Straw" (song), 65
20,000 Leagues Under the Sea (film), 229
Tytla, Bill, 22

Uncle Remus, 227
Uncle Scrooge, 95, 96
Utensil set, *123*
United Artists Pictures Corp., 113
U.S. Electric, 153, 195
United Wall Paper Factories, 174
Universal Pictures, 51

Van Dexter, Grover, 26
Vanguard Corp., 170
Vase, *148*
Victory Through Air Power (film), 215
Village Voice, 26-27
Villa Morét, 183

Walker, E. Cardon, 45
Wallpaper, *174, 175*
Wall picture, *192, 215*

Walt Disney's Christmas Parade, 95
Walt Disney's Comics and Stories, 41, 94
Walt Disney's "Fantasia" (Taylor), 220
Walt Disney's Magazine, 232
Walt Disney's Showcase (comic book), 95
War bond, 217
Warhol, Andy, 10, 65
Washington, Ned, 211
Wastebasket, *241*
Watches and clocks, 13, 17, 18, *34, 112, 159-166*, 186
Watering can, *169*
Wee Little Books, 41, 80, *81*
Weiss, Louis, 126, 207
Welcome to Pooh Corner (TV series), 48
"We're the Mouseketeers" (song), *231*
Western Table and Stationery Corp., 214
Weutweiler, Charles, 165
"What! No Mickey Mouse?", 183
"When I See an Elephant Fly" (song), 220
"When My Ship Comes In" (song), 11
"When You Wish upon a Star," 182, 211
"Whistle While You Work" (song), 182
Whiteman, Paul, 189
Who Censored Roger Rabbit? (film), 47
"Who's Afraid of the Big Bad Wolf" (song), 182, *191, 192*
Wilkinson Designs, 104
Williams, Guy, 234, 235
Willie the Whale, 227
Willits, Malcolm, 20
Wind-up toys, 27, 65, 69, 110, 155, 156, 186, 195, 221
Winnie the Pooh (film), 244
The Wise Little Hen, 42, 65, 66, 182
Wish Upon a Star (TV show), 48
Withers, Jane, 58
The Wonderful Tar Baby (book), 228
Woo, Willie, 11
Woodin, Harry W., 59
Wornova Manufacturing Co., 134
Wright, J. L., 206
Wrigley, William Co., 204
Writing tablet, 98
Wunderle, P. H., 204

Ye Olden Days (film), 76
You and Me Kid (TV show), 48
"You Belong to My Heart," 182, 226
"You're the Top" (song), 190
"You'r Nothin' but a Nothin'," *182*

Zell Products Corp., 153
"Zip-a-Dee-Doo-Dah" (song), 182, 227
Zorro, 48, 234-235